BRITISH NARRATIVES OF EXPLORATION: CASE STUDIES OF THE SELF AND OTHER

Empires in Perspective

Series Editors: Tony Ballantyne
Duncan Bell
Francisco Bethencourt
Caroline Elkins
Durba Ghosh

Advisory Editor: Masaie Matsumura

Titles in this Series

www.pickeringchatto.com/empires

BRITISH NARRATIVES OF EXPLORATION: CASE STUDIES OF THE SELF AND OTHER

EDITED BY

Frederic Regard

LONDON
PICKERING & CHATTO
2009

Published by Pickering & Chatto (Publishers) Limited
21 Bloomsbury Way, London WC1A 2TH

2252 Ridge Road, Brookfield, Vermont 05036-9704, USA

www.pickeringchatto.com

British narratives of exploration : case studies on the self and other. – (Empires
in perspective)
1. Travelers' writings, English – History and criticism 2. Geographical discoveries
in literature 3. Identity (Psychology) in literature 4. Intercultural communication in literature 5. Other (Philosophy) in literature 6. English prose literature
– 17th century – History and criticism 7. English prose literature – 18th century
– History and criticism 8. English prose literature – 19th century – History and
criticism
I. Regard, Frederic
820.9'32'0903

ISBN-13: 9781851966202
e: 9781851965953

This publication is printed on acid-free paper that conforms to the American
National Standard for the Permanence of Paper for Printed Library Materials.

Typeset by Pickering & Chatto (Publishers) Limited
Printed in the UK by the MPG Books Group

CONTENTS

INTRODUCTION: ARTICULATING EMPIRE'S UNSTABLE ZONES

Frederic Regard

The idea of this collection first arose in the course of a research seminar I conducted at the École Normale Supérieure, Lyon, France, between the spring of 2003 and that of 2006, a seminar which ENS-Éditions very rapidly chose to publish as a book.[1] It then took its final, international form during the conference on 'Unstable Zones: Self and Other in British Narratives of Exploration' which I convened at the ENS in March 2007. The carefully selected, heavily revised essays presented here are not focused on 'travel narratives' as a literary genre or as emblems of a 'tourist' culture, two fields of research which have been substantially dealt with in recent years. Nor do we attempt to define the characteristic features of a genre in relation to other genres – such as the pilgrimage narrative[2] – or to employ the historian's method of examining the great projects of territorial expansion and the effects of a continued relationship with the foreign. This is a book on *exploration*, and more precisely on exploration *narratives* written by British explorers on their return from 'contact zones', understood here not as predetermined spaces where Self and Other come to meet on fixed grounds, but as 'social spaces where cultures meet, clash, and grapple with each other'.[3]

As a consequence, the essays collected in this volume deal mainly with accounts of *first encounters*, focusing on the *pragmatic* aspects of communication between Self and Other, from the medieval and Renaissance period to the late nineteenth century, in North or South America, in Asia as well as in Africa, from the South Pacific to the Antarctic; from Mandeville, Drake and Ralegh to Franklin, Stanley and Burton. The main objective is to scrutinize what has hitherto been ignored; namely, the precise moment of mutual discovery experienced in the field, as recorded by the Western observer, the one participant to the scene supposed to have known how to *write about* this shared experience – a practice traditionally assumed to signal the 'Great Divide' between oral and literate cultures, pre-logical and logical systems of thought, pre-capitalist and capitalist economies, non-ethical and ethical social organizations.[4] The volume should thus be of particular significance to all those interested in the history of travel, piracy and exploration, but also to those interested in anthropology, in the sociology of communication, in the production of knowledge systems, and finally those interested in the issues of national or personal identity in the context of the British Empire(s).

Until now, scholarly attention on exploration narratives has been somewhat erratic. Such narratives have been used as a store for collections of 'adventure narratives', as in Benedict Allen's *Faber Book of Exploration,* or Fleming and Merullo's *The Explorer's Eye.* Symptomatically, those two works offer exploration narratives of the twentieth century, focusing either on interstellar space or on the great marine depths, where there can in fact be no surprise of a first encounter, where technology constitutes an obvious screen between Man and the realm he explores, and where a tradition of writing – journals, logs, diaries, travelogues, 'personal narratives', etc. – is lost. Exploration narratives will also often serve as anecdotal supporting evidence for historians[5] or geographers.[6] And of course it is certainly the case that we are becoming more and more interested in the history of maps, as is attested by a number of books published by the British Library.[7]

All in all, it seems such works make the issue of 'representation' the sole object of their curiosity. Without ever questioning the possibility that there might have existed other procedures of knowledge-production than the process which Michel Foucault called the 'tableau' – the Enlightenment 'table' as symbol of a reordering of reality performed by penetrating and sage clinical observation – such works take it for granted that the world can indeed not only exhaust itself in visibility and readability, but also divide itself between observer and observed.[8] Using Edward Saïd's work on 'Orientalism' as a major theoretical reference point, impressive work has been undertaken to analyse how discourse was employed by the West to ensure its superiority over the rest of the world, the representation of difference conceived in terms of 'a Western style for dominating, restructuring, and having authority over the Orient'.[9] Paradoxically enough, however, it is to be feared that the perspective common to all such approaches has ended up reaffirming the preeminence of one of the most potent myths of the West: the explorer's status as an avatar of progress, reason and civilization, a myth which in fact seems not to have gathered full momentum before the mid-nineteenth century.

To be sure, Stanley's late nineteenth-century narratives seem to be anxious to construct an *ethos* – an image of the self projected through discursive practice and personal scenography[10] – of the white explorer's supremacy. But such an *ethos* seems at variance with the more qualified, sometimes even disturbing, public image of themselves some of his nineteenth-century predecessors – Tod, Clapperton and Burton in his pre-African years – had sought to construct. These men belonged to the first half of the nineteenth century, or to the early Victorian period, when the belief in progress seems to have been tempered with a joy in discovery and a largeness in spirit. It is only as the century moved towards centralization and uniformity, that self-images started to rely more and more on practicality and steadiness, and that the humour, eccentricity and sometimes even theatricality of the early Victorians started to be less acceptable than the often arrogant postures of their followers. Of course – and Darwin's view of life not only as evolution from primitive to civilized state, but also as Godforsaken contextual placing and unpredictable conflict for survival, was no doubt a major source of secret terrors here – one should never overlook the possibility that violent polarization may have been the symptom of a desperate late-nineteenth-century struggle to maintain coherence, a battle against anxiety, division and self-doubt.

Still, we should keep in mind that the protocols of geographical observation and measurement which constitute what we consider to be the traditional tools of the West's scientific outlook were not in fact fully worked out before the second half of the nineteenth century. Highly popular books such as John Herschel's *Manual of Scientific Enquiry* (1849) and Francis Galton's *Art of Travel* (1855), alongside with equally popular tracts and lectures such as E. G. Wakefield's *A View of the Art of Colonization* (1849) and J. R. Seeley's *Expansion of England* (1883), undoubtedly conditioned Western explorers' perception of otherness, and therefore inevitably their conception of intersubjectivity.[11] The traveller was then transformed into a professional explorer by a specific rhetoric, which turned the adventurer into both a statutory national hero and an institutionally recognized scientist, a combination of postures which inevitably predetermined the outcome of any encounter by polarizing positions.

This unwilling perpetuation of an after all very recent myth of extreme polarization has had an unforeseen impact on our knowledge of first encounters. Not only is the current work on this topic still predominantly focused on the question of 'representation', but more surprisingly, it is still this question which continues to form the basis of the most recent studies emerging from 'postcolonial' approaches, or 'feminist' ones. Fundamentally, it is always a matter of identifying the secret or implicit 'motivations' *behind* the 'representations' elaborated by both the rhetoric of conquest and that of 'anti-conquest'.[12] And in aiming to unearth the secret behind the 'tableau', one that is always inevitably linked to colonialist violence even under the guise of innocent natural history, the uncertain event of the encounter itself is forgotten. What we propose to do here, on the contrary, is to articulate the links between the formation of multiple imperial narratives, at different historical moments, and the shifting politics of intersubjectivity with which they intersect, by focusing on the actual moment of this 'encounter', a term to be understood henceforth in its Goffmanian sense of an unpredictable 'social situation', a moment when individuals find themselves and the others accessible to the naked senses of one another, required to ratify one another as authorized focuses of attention, but without the guarantee – due to the unrehearsed nature of the event – that the expected, cultural structuring of conduct will work effectively.[13] The focus is thus made to bear on the dialectics of proximity and distance between Self and Other, a central concern of eighteenth-century British explorers, as will be established by studies of Wallis's, Cook's and Forster's logs.

If the initial expectations presiding over first encounters may have been constrained by a set of polarities – the colonizer and the colonized looking at each other from the two sides of an unbridgeable gulf, cultural, technological, racial, linguistic and so forth –, and reaffirmed through the production of the explorers' *narratives* addressed to a national community at home, our assumption here is that they must also have been challenged while on the terrain, causing each interlocutor to enter into a dialectics of self-images and status hierarchy, and therefore to experience uncertainty and trouble, on both sides, irrespective of time periods. Differentiating between the writings of first-hand eye-witnesses to Indian culture and the armchair writers of colonization, Karen Kupperman has convincingly argued that the earliest encounters between the English and the Indian societies were in fact characterized by ambivalence and complexity.[14] Indeed, the uncertainty and contingency experienced by those who participated in the early encounters should induce us to surmise that in context, with all the unpredictability of verbal or non-verbal interaction and communicational exchange, knowledge systems must have been challenged, frames of meaning-making disrupted, 'representations' shattered, postures undermined, positions reversed, and identities transformed. When Spivak writes that 'empire messes with identity', she means that empire distorts the identity of the colonized. Perhaps we should contemplate the possibility that the colonizing subject's identity, too, is distorted in the process of encounter.[15] Surely, what took place in first-encounter scenes was less transaction, or translation, than *negotiation*, a process by which 'sides' could no longer be secured: in any genuine process of communicative exchange, very little is in fact left immune, and much may be lost, or gained.

What happens in the field when the performance of self-identity does not function properly in the interactional ritual? The book concentrates on such moments, when the differences the ritual of encounter is supposed to establish or re-establish break down; when misrepresentations prevail over intended representations; when the 'stigmatized' Other manages to efface his or her 'virtual identity' in the eyes of the 'normal' self to assert his or her own 'actual identity';[16] or worse even, when the 'normal' Self's identity suddenly allows itself to be 'contaminated' by the Other's, engaging into mimicry and more or less furtive impersonations of 'barbarians' and 'savages' – as is indeed the case, although with varying amplitude, in the accounts brought back by Drake, Ralegh, Cook and Burton. Do we have traces of those unstable zones of interaction? Were such encounters recorded, and, most importantly, *how*?

Where, for example, were such scenes *staged*: on board a navigator's ship? On a beach? Inside a primitive hut? Along the road? Alongside a boat caught in ice? In the course of a trekking expedition though a jungle? Or, if one comes to think of Anna Jameson and Georg Forster, during 'rambling' excursions? How did context affect not only the explorers' conception of knowledge and self-identity, but also the very nature and structure of their reports? Were dialogues recorded? Using direct or reported speech? Through which procedures of accommodation or domestication – quoting, translating, naming, renaming – was the Other's speech allowed to be articulated? What were the perspectives adopted? Through whose eyes were shock, wonder, admiration, awe, recorded? How were such experiences dramatized, narrativized and even fictionalized in the explorers' subsequent accounts? For example, what happens to the myth of the 'noble savage' when Hawkesworth processes Cook's logbook to adapt it to the expectations of a British nationalist audience? What takes place between Wallis's first log and his second one? When on board the same ship one officer records his experience from the safety of his cabin while another feels free to go ashore and venture into unknown territory, both geographical and social? When one happens to be a *woman* explorer? A botanist? An artist? A Scotsman, a Welshman, an Irishman? A Catholic? A Protestant? A British exile hired by an American newspaper? And what does it tell us, not only about the varied processes of 'othering' the not-Self, but also about self-fashioning? Discovery narratives as anthropology, but also, most importantly, as autobiography: portrayals of a fantasized Other as much as narratives of an 'imagined' Self – personal, communal, national.[17]

It will come as no surprise that after Erving Goffman's redefinition of encounter as interaction and performance, Johannes Fabian's indictment of anthropology's denial of simultaneity – what Fabian calls the anthropologist's 'allochronism'[18] – became of central importance to the colleagues who attended the Lyon seminar and the ensuing international conference: had Western culture always been so successful in refusing to occupy the same temporal space as its observed object of knowledge? Had the explorer and the explored engaged in face-to-face encounter never managed to live 'in the same Time'? What use, then, had been indigenous guides, translators and interpreters? We began to perceive the relevance for our purpose of studies examining the perils of the translation of linguistic and cultural 'alterity',[19] and in fact the perils of any 'discourse of the other' – what Certeau calls 'heterology'.[20] But, precisely, had explorers' reports been necessarily and inevitably 'heterological'? Our central question became the following: if a social role requires validation by other social participants, did it really never happen that instead of presenting themselves unfavourably and fully cooperating in the expected manner, the non-Westerners refused their inferior status and articulated not necessarily violent claims to full-fledged humanity? Clapperton's anecdote of a pantomime parodying colonial practices, staged by the Africans to entertain their European visitors, should definitely alert us to this possibility. In Certeau's words, did it never happen, then, that the Other's 'inscribable' body did not fully comply with the heterologist's conquering written word? That the Other's reluctant body resisted the cultural patterns of the visitor, and even spoke out? Was the Other always bound to be the dead corpus of the ethnographer? Or did this muted Other's corpse manage to resist objectification, resurrect from the table, and become a haunting presence, preventing both the explorer and the explored from resting in peace? 'Who's there?', Shakespeare's Barnardo famously asks before Hamlet's story even begins to unravel. Who was there, at the exact moment of the first encounter, and even in the immediate aftermath of contact, when Self and Other had to be couched in writing?

This is not another book on British imperialism, on its ideological assumptions, its procedures and practices. What we deal with here is the history of the construction of a British identity 'in context', which is to say as an *intersubjective* linguistic event occurring on a specific terrain.[21] We examine this uncertain space where Self faces Other, where the two are wrenched from their alloted fixed places and thrown together on a stage to be shared as ego and alter ego. We argue by the same token that this staging is not necessarily based upon the traditional agonistic model of colonial combat or trauma, that foreign travel itself, from the Middle Ages to the late nineteenth century, may have come 'perilously close to subversiveness',[22] that, even before the eighteenth-century British rejection of the Catholic model of 'Conquest' in favour of the more democratic, Protestant model of peaceful transaction and negotiation[23] – of which Cook was indeed the emblem, 'an Orpheus-like hero exemplifying the highest British values of peaceful exploration and enlightened cultural contact'[24] – the Renaissance discourse of 'wonder' may have demonstrated the contextual relativity of difference.[25] What we suggest is that the great ethnologists of the twentieth century, Malinowski, Radcliffe-Brown or Evans-Pritchard, may have had very early timid predecessors, who certainly realized that there was no knowing the Other outside a *cultural dialectic*, and did not hesitate therefore to transform the monologic, 'allochronic' discourse of the Western outsider into a dialogic, polyphonic one. If the Protestant ethics of negotiation effectively prevailed, successful commercial relationships implied that exchange be beneficial to *both* sides, thus allowing for the possibility not only of a shared ground of mutual understanding, but also of a potentially unpredictable communicational dialectics.

Perhaps there was an even deeper specificity to British narratives in that they were all written . . . in English. As Anthony Burgess and Peter Ackroyd have claimed, the English language itself seems to have been an extraordinary vehicle for alterity, rich enough *in itself* to accommodate otherness, created in such a way that it originally presented all the attributes of a 'melting pot', on the model of Drake's ship, precisely: 'The language itself was a melting pot – not fixed and elegant and controlled by academics, but coarsely rich and ready for any adventures that would make it richer. English was a sort of Golden Hind'.[26] Was such linguistic disposition why Ralegh's tale easily fitted into an 'indigenous cultural praxis', recuperating myths of Indian origin and giving over to homophonic language play even in a foreign tongue?[27] Should we here perceive the first step towards a linguistic transformation of the British outsider into an *insider*, the secret of a profound cultural kinship between, say, Ralegh and Burton? As will often appear in the essays collected in this volume, alterity in British exploration narratives is effectively encountered, pragmatically experienced and linguistically tested, so that the representational crisis enacted is also a self-representational crisis.

Still, the stage of this crisis was brought to us by narratives, 'narrativization' being assumed to be integral to all cognitive procedures.[28] The essays thus focus on scenes of hesitation, disquiet, trouble, not as those scenes actually happened – a truth for ever irretrievable – but as they were *recorded* and *related* in writing, mediated through a particular rhetoric. David Amigoni's comments on Alfred Russel Wallace's *The Malay Archipelago* (1894) may be illuminating here. He notes that when Wallace entered a Dyak village in Borneo and was stared at as if he had been some strange animal, thus 'swap[ping] roles to become one of the creatures [an orang-utan] that in other circumstances he ha[d] hunted and observed', this post-Darwinian blurring of the frontier between Self and Other was made conspicuous through Wallace's *fictional* devices. Everything happens, Amigoni remarks, as if there were some kind of correlation between breaking down the species barrier and collapsing the partitioning between natural historical and fictional writing.[29] If scientific revolutions come about through a change of metaphor of the world,[30] how could the Westerner's frames of perception and patterns of meaning concerning his or her Other be redefined without similar rhetorical upheavals? But how, then, are we to reconcile this inescapability of metaphorical redescription with the traditional aspiration of the exploration narrative to an absence of style, to a form of writing anxious to present the bare facts in all their freshness, without the mediation of the perverted figures of metaphor and comparison?[31]

At the end of the eighteenth century, Mungo Park's aim was indeed to offer his reader 'a plain, unvarnished tale' of his African adventures.[32] But since we may feel entitled to suspect that Park was in fact quoting less from the dictates of the Royal Society than from Shakespeare's *Othello* ('I will a round unvarnish'd tale deliver / Of my whole course of love')[33], to what extent should we trust the tale's vow of transparency and believe in the explorer's presence to himself? Narratives may even be of a more intimate stuff and betray secret, personal fantasies. When he arrived at the entry to the long-sought Northwest Passage in 1818, John Ross really saw a wide range of mountains blocking the view across Lancaster Sound, which he described and even charted, while all his men, sailors and officers alike, assured him that in place of the 'Croker Mountains' there seemed indeed to be a passage.[34] Very often, the material conditions of exploration were enough in themselves to distort perception. Like Livingstone, most explorers 'returned to England emaciated shells of their former selves',[35] in a state of what Fabian has called 'ecstasis', having had to endure privation, exhaustion or fevers, and to consume alcohol or opiates to alleviate their sufferings, which, worked together, greatly undermined their sense of objectivity and rationality, while paradoxically furnishing a ground for cross-cultural understanding.[36]

Even if we admit the possibility that British explorers remained unaffected by illnesses or hallucinations and retained intact their ability to carry out the scientific tasks they had been assigned, does not the very vindication of 'scientific' or 'realist' objectivity betray an 'imperialist' rhetoric used to produce *effects* of scientificity, and therefore effects of authority or superiority? The very ideal of a transparent discourse, untarnished by the tropes of a given culture, paradoxically evokes the biblical myth of an original, pre-Babel form of communication. The most apparently neutral description by Cook of a trunk or of an unknown foliage observed on a Pacific island – 'some kind of leaves'[37] – implies a referent from which implicit comparisons can be made by the intended reader at home. When Mary Kingsley perceives the African mangrove as a metaphor for the origin of the world,[38] does she not also reactivate the myth of undifferentiated chaos before divine intervention – a topos Stanley would later merge with that of the providential arrival of the white colonizer? British explorers could never undo their own inherited rhetoric, for without their idiosyncratic vision of the world, the interpretative work would simply have been a sheer impossibility. There never was a 'new world'. The world the explorers discovered and described was always already constrained and therefore constructed by 'discourses', fantasies, knowledge systems, cultural structures of meaning-making, including the myths and other narratives which make up a national community and ensure that the message is effectively *received* by those who have stayed at home.

The articles in this volume strive to establish the way in which each explorer, in the historical and cultural context to which he or she belonged, strove to reconcile the shock of the unknown and the recognition of the familiar, the new gaze and the inherited discourse, the naked surprise and the cultural filter, in his or her own particular style. This may result in tensions, even internal dissensions; this may also produce disturbing effects. For example, although they shared the same Enlightenment culture and explored the same regions at approximately the same time, Hearne and Mackenzie had widely diverging interpretations of what empiricism induced them to do at a practical level. And when Darwin invites his contemporaries to understand the unknown through the known,[39] doesn't this porous interchange between the civilized and the primitive produce a rhetoric which is already accepting the necessity of a *hybridity* of scientific thought? If we accept this fundamental premise that all narratives of first encounters were written at this juncture between an inherited national 'culture' ('best seen ... as a set of control mechanisms ... for the governing of behavior')[40] and a revolutionary cognitive or hermeneutic event demanding *personal* adaptation to the new situation, several other questions emerge.

One may wonder whether the historically-determined metaphors of the interpretative schema which produced and guaranteed the effectiveness of knowledge in a specific cultural context were systematically inscribed in the exploration narratives of the same period. Did this 'ideological' structuring of knowledge differ fundamentally according to whether the exploration and encounter occurred in the sixteenth or in the nineteenth century? For instance, did commerce or profit, which motivated the expeditions of Drake and Ralegh supply the Protestant English, then British explorers with the first and most prevalent of metaphorical filters in everything relating to non-violent, peaceful exchange? This would indeed seem to be the case of Clapperton's and Stanley's nineteenth-century visions of Africa. But even so, were the *situations* of dialogue conceived in the same terms? Were the general procedures which determined the pragmatic effectiveness of such scenes identical? What were the various *signs* – verbal and non-verbal: gestures, rituals, dumb shows, pantomimes, even silences – which the individual explorers thought worth recording? Can we sketch a history of first exchanges, and of the way they were mediated in narrative? For example, can we safely claim that communication between Self and Other gradually transformed from misunderstanding or disdain, to comprehension, then to mutual enrichment and finally to postcolonial hybridity and postmodern disillusionment (one would think here of Bruce Chatwin's *In Patagonia*)? Or should we, rather, speak of individual postures, dictated to the explorers by specific contexts, through the circumstances these individuals sometimes unexpectedly found themselves in? Perhaps we should then also accept the possibility that we need to distinguish between several *successive* postures in the same historical context, and even within the same explorer. Should we not, for example, distinguish between the Franklin of the beginning of his mission and the Franklin who realizes that the hierarchical relation linking the civilized to the primitive is crumbling down and is even being inverted? Or between the Burton representing the East India Company, stationed in Sindh to supervise its annexation, and the same man mandated by the Royal Geographical Society, nomadizing through the Arabian sands?

And what about the postures dictated by the haunting ghost of a preceding explorer, and more crucially still, of a preceding exploration *text*? Like any other narrative, an explorer's account inevitably quotes from various other texts, thus gaining consistency through internal 'dialogism', or 'inter-textuality'.[41] We do need to wonder whether the intertextual postures inherent in *any* situation of enunciation were not equally overdetermining in the production of various Self–Other differential systems. Drake and Ralegh were keen to dissociate their accounts from earlier Spanish and Portuguese – and therefore Catholic – narratives; Cook's apprehension of the Polynesians' 'thievish' tendencies was informed by Wallis's log; Tod's understanding of Rajasthan's laws and customs was determined by his knowledge of the European feudal system of land ownership; Stanley's ideological recuperation of Africa's economic potential largely drew on biblical prophetic imagery. The Self's relation to the Other is always, so to speak, 'predicted' by a narrative mediation – etymology, prophecy, myth, logbook, journal, treatise, essay, novel, advertisement, etc. – whose relevance is either validated or invalidated by individual field experience and personal (re)inscription. To a certain extent, every explorer-writer may be said to produce him or herself as the effect of an 'anxiety of influence'.

'There is nothing outside the text', deconstructionists argue:[42] yes, indeed, texts there were, both *before* and *after* the experience of encounter, text upon text therefore, a hyper-intertextuality from which the unpredictability of face-to-face encounter was bound to emerge transfigured. The challenge therefore is to study how the destabilizing presence of otherness transpires all the same, more or less repressed, adulterated, domesticated, accommodated, glorified, in a textual unstable zone poised between the singularity of personal field experience, the individual desire to open unbeaten tracks in the art of description and the more or less limiting awareness of the existence of previous records. As a matter of fact, such tension may be the source of these exploration narratives' enduring power of fascination, perhaps even the source of their surprising *literary* quality. The eighteenth-century incestuous proximity of established writers and supposedly inarticulate explorers – John Hawkesworth's rewritings of several Commanders' logbooks, George Keate's re-elaboration of Captain Wilson's reports of his amicable relations with the Palauan inhabitants in the Western part of the Pacific Ocean – should not divert our attention from the obvious fact: all reports – log entries, journals, retrospective narratives, fictional reelaborations – were *narratives*, complex fabrics of lexicon, viewpoint, trope, quotation, elision, temporality, plot. Exploration accounts, as well as ethnographic descriptions or anthropological studies, were, and still are, *literary artefacts*.

The book was initially composed as a succession of 'case studies' arranged chronologically. It seemed this basic principle of consecutive chapters was perfectly adapted to the philosophy of a volume whose ambition was to demonstrate that field experience, whatever the historical period or geographical location, could only yield undetermined responses which therefore required specific case studies. But objection could be made that such a structuring device could prove an unreliable tool in colonial and postcolonial studies. The possibility of formatting the whole enterprise according to thematic units, which could be called 'chapters', uniting individual essays irrespective of historical context, was then seriously considered. Transhistorical affinities and similarities between the individual narratives of highly different personalities, in widely different contexts, could indeed be emphasized: instances of such affinities were to be perceived even between Mandeville and Stanley, whose narratives definitely seek to submit the not-Self to an ambivalent process of 'othering' and 'saming'; Lawson's 'prospective vision' of Carolina anticipates Stanley's capitalist gaze; Clapperton's universalizing perspective on the Africans could be placed alongside a number of eighteenth-century narratives, and his treatment of the theme of 'wonder' might even invite comparison with Drake's; cases of mimicry, linguistic or behavioural, may bring Ralegh and Burton into unexpected proximity, and so forth. Once ascertained, this continuity in discontinuity could easily delineate a number of recurrent modalities of encounter, entailing a limited number of chapters bearing alluring titles such as 'Inventing the Other', 'Domesticating the Other', 'Fictionalizing the Other', 'Destabilizing the Self', etc.

The major risk involved was of course decontextualization. There is indeed a cultural continuity between medieval and Renaissance narratives which ceases to exist in the course of the eighteenth century, when empiricism and nationalism radically redefine the coordinates of identities; and Darwin's revolutionary theories in the second half of the nineteenth century, together with the social, economic and political upheavals generated by a triumphant imperialist system, undisputably redefine the British explorer's conception of Self and Other. One is forced to admit, come to that, that more could have been achieved in articulating the formation of imperial narratives on Britain's shifting politics of intersubjectivity: for example, it is unquestionably the case that there were times when religious, political or commercial motivations were granted priority over genuine curiosity or cognitive ambitions, depending on the situation abroad or at home as well as on the intellectual climate of the day. Still, what case studies establish is the extreme variety of individual responses to specific situations: the official instructions – which most of the time accompanied the explorers to the ends of the earth – recommending 'intercourse' with the Other, could be interpreted with a certain degree of freedom once in context, as even eighteenth-century natural historians and anthropologists could adopt diverging postures regarding their objects of observation; and throughout the nineteenth century, the growing popularization of 'developmental' then 'evolutionary' theories helped reaffirm cultural hierarchies as much as it encouraged cultural relativism.

The structure of the book seeks therefore to steer a middle course between the purely successive and the purely thematic. By grouping various essays inside chapters dealing with historical periods, the book emphasizes the inevitability of historicization; by choosing general headings for such chapters, each offering a thematic thread to pursue through the case studies, it also underlines the profound unity linking the various exploration narratives within a specific cultural context.

In the first chapter, 'Fantasy, Wonder and Mimicry: Proto-Ethnography from the Middle Ages to the Renaissance', Kofi Campbell examines the most important Middle English travelogue, *The Book of John Mandeville* and focuses on two encounters in particular: Mandeville's meetings with a Muslim Sultan, and his observations on the cultures of Africa. In both cases, the author's descriptions were meant to function as enticements to colonization. Campbell argues this was accomplished through the confluence of two seemingly opposite rhetorical practices. By stressing the otherness of the Muslims and Africans, the author constructed them as dangerous people who needed to be contained. At the same time, by focusing on their fleeting similarities, he also suggested that they were similar enough, and that they therefore could be made more culturally like his audience. Indeed, he even calls for their conversion. The next essay broadens the perspective. Starting from a brief study of the process of naming in the medieval period, Nicholas Myers and Ladan Niayesh argue that during the Renaissance names corresponded to fantasmatic archetypes arising from the inner mental and cultural landscape of the West, a landscape which European explorers went in search of – and, inevitably, 'found'. Cannibalism was thus assumed to characterize the primitives, and the assumption became its own proof. Niayesh and Myers go on to argue that, as in John Nicholl's *Hourglasse of Indian Newes* (1607), the designation of the Other involved the use of book titles whose function was in fact to project fantasies of fascination and horror; in Richard Jobson's *Discovery of the River Gambra* (1623), which conceived of itself as a genuine attempt at proto-ethnography, naming became part of a trial-and-error hermeneutics of culture in which appellation, serving the purpose of ideological 'interpellation', supplanted or partly eclipsed ethnographic knowledge. All such approximations are recuperated within the providentialist framework, the naming of the Other turning out to be a (re)claiming of the territory of the Self.

Sophie Lemercier-Goddard then focuses on *The World Encompassed by Sir Francis Drake*, which rehearses the first English circumnavigation in history (1577–80), and shows how a Pirate's venture is transformed into a 'famous voyage' of discovery by emphasizing the importance of 'wonder', not so much before new lands or unknown passages as before other human beings. A close reading of the text shows that Drake's rhetoric of the body is an essential ingredient of the wonderful, as the English develop a form of discourse based on the use of visual signs, of objects and dumb shows, and as they participate in an Indian ceremony to change it and interpret it according to their own interests. Lemercier-Goddard analyses how it is in fact a pantomime which enables the Westerners to 'translate', that is to say to take possession of, the land. Line Cottegnies focuses her analysis on Sir Walter Ralegh's *Discovery of Guiana* (1595). Her study reveals that though Ralegh's account was inevitably informed by the topoi and myths elaborated through a tradition of 'fantastic ethnography', and though it reflected a detailed knowledge of previous travellers' accounts, it also evinced Ralegh's desire for a genuine dialogical encounter with native societies. But 'Waterali' seemed to be aware of the necessarily ambivalent nature of his enterprise. By focusing on the linguistic aspects of the encounter, on the question of communication and misinterpretation, Cottegnies manages to show that Ralegh's descriptions of scenes of first encounter involved in fact a mutual form of colonial 'mimicry'.

In the second chapter, 'Distance in Question: Translating the Other in the Eighteenth Century', Robert Sayre takes us to the east coast of North America at the dawn of the eighteenth century. In late December 1700, John Lawson and a group of nine Englishmen and Native Americans set off on a two-month trek into the Carolina backcountry. Lawson, who was in close contact with twenty Indian tribes, had then no other option but to rely on native translators to communicate with his hosts. Sayre places *A New Voyage to Carolina* (1709) within the tradition of accounts of travel in North American Indian territory, before he analyses the dynamics of domestication of the Indian 'Other' within the text. Lawson's narrative of encounter ultimately pictures a highly 'unstable zone', since a process of destabilization of certainties is enacted, leading ultimately to a partial and contradictory recognition of the specificity and value of the Other.

Of course the eighteenth century was the age of unprecedented systematic maritime exploration. Commander Samuel Wallis was the first Englishman to come across what is known today as the Polynesian archipelagos, specifically Tahiti (1767). His log has rarely been studied whereas his journal, written once back in England has attracted more critical attention (neither has been published). Considering the log to be the primordial written representation attesting to the very first encounter between the British and the Tahitians, Sandhya Patel proposes a comparison between the Wallis log and the Wallis journal which brings to light how the process of representation of Self and Other in the log cultivates ambivalence, while the journal seems to be intent on posting clearer markers for future colonization. Patel thus comes to the conclusion that the log's rendition of first encounters may be read as a site of uncertainty where the politics of encounter is shaped in a telegraphic but perhaps more accurate form. The journal of Cook's first voyage to Tahiti and New Zealand was published only a few years later by Hawkesworth (1773), containing not only Cook's description of new, as yet uncharted, territories but also his relation of the more or less successful attempts of the British at establishing links with indigenous populations – as were the Admiralty's explicit instructions. Anne Dromart shows how difficult it seems to have been for all actors in the field to know how close or how distant to each other the British and the islanders wanted, or needed, to be. Focusing her reading on aspects of communication and territoriality, but also on the metaphors and grammatical structures of Hawkesworth's narrative, Dromart perceives this trouble to have been generated by the Europeans' growing awareness of issues of *cultural* difference. Christian Moser then argues that in the late eighteenth century a shift had occurred in the European discourse of exploration. By comparing Cook's writings with those of the Anglo-German scientist Georg Forster, who accompanied Cook on his second voyage to the South Pacific and published his own account of the expedition, *A Voyage around the World* (1777), Moser relates Forster's mode of exploration to the emergent bourgeois practice of walking and analyses its implications for the negotiation between Self and Other in first-contact situations. Cook's descriptive labour depends on maintaining an outsider's position, using the ship as a mobile home that allows the explorer to extricate himself from his involvement in the foreign culture. Forster, for his part, attempts to integrate his observations of *how* he procured his information, thus opposing the off-shore practice of natural history and the inland practice of anthropology.

The close of the eighteenth century inaugurated the age of Empire. By the early 1800s several companies had established trading posts and forts across North America, where fur and copper were to be found in seemingly unlimited abundance. The mythical Northwest Passage – which could provide a water route to the trading markets of the Orient – became of crucial importance. Prominent among the explorers' narratives whose overt purpose was the expansion of the territory and trade interests of the British Empire were Samuel Hearne's *A Journey from Prince of Wales's Fort in Hudson's Bay to the Northern Ocean* (1795) and Alexander Mackenzie's *Voyages from Montreal on the River St. Laurence, through the Continent of North America, to the Frozen and Pacific Oceans* (1801). Cheryl Cundell's comparative study demonstrates that the two narratives reflected in fact opposite attitudes to empiricism, natural history and anthropology. She argues that these opposite interpretations of the same method entailed profoundly differing perceptual modes, which speak through the nature of the observations emphasized in each text, and inevitably shape the explorers' textual constructions of Self and Other.

In the third, final and longest chapter, 'Stereotypes Undermined: Shifting the Self in the Nineteenth Century', the authors focus on the growing unease which seems to have assailed a significant number of British explorers' narratives, even among the staunchest and most aggressive supporters of England's 'mission'. A perfect example of this is to be found in the continuation of Hearne's, Mackenzie's and Ross's vain efforts to find the Northwest Passage. In the 1820s, England sought to preserve the position of European leader which it had carved for itself during the war against Napoleon. Russia had to be beaten at its own game, and supremacy now urgently demanded that Britain should at long last discover the Passage. Hence the expedition led by John Franklin which he describes in his *Narrative of a Journey to the Shores of the Polar Sea* (1823). According to Catherine Lanone, the journal of the expedition questions the very concept of exploration, raising the problem of its ideological constructs, hermeneutic codes and ontological modes. As food becomes scarce and pain increases, Franklin's journal seems to relate an initiatory journey, complete with trials and hardships. Meeting the Other then becomes a twofold process: initially casting the Indians as inferior beings whose function is to serve and obey, Franklin is gradually forced to grant them a greater presence, notably when they come to the rescue of the starving survivors of the expedition. Lanone pinpoints various slips and gaps in Franklin's narrative, which she reads as symptoms of the collapse of stereotypes of Self and Other. The slave trade, gold and ivory, were other powerful lures for the Empire, whose arms reached therefore towards much warmer sub-Saharan latitudes. But even if British explorers were less in need of indigenous assistance than in the Arctic regions, it seems harsh polarization was not necessarily in order in their narratives. Anne-Pascale Bruneau argues that Hugh Clapperton's account of his second expedition into West Africa offers a surprisingly favourable portrait of Africans. Clapperton's *Journal of a Second Expedition into the Interior of Africa* (1829), a compilation of various documents that survived Clapperton's death by dysentery in 1827, is informed by a universalizing and broadly sympathetic outlook, which seems at times to be inherited from the eighteenth century. Through an analysis of the various forms of non-verbal exchanges reported by Clapperton, Bruneau brings to light the presence of codes underlying first encounters, and relates them to the existence of previous forms of commercial contact between Europeans and Africans, of which the journal itself provides evidence. More importantly still, her study focuses on how both the British and the Africans construct politically useful self-representations, and suggests that, in its textual representations of these encounters, Clapperton's journal tends rather to minimize than to emphasize the distinctions between Self and Other.

The crowning jewel of the British Empire, needless to say, was the Raj. James Tod was one of its major early architects. In 1799, he went to India as a cadet in the Bengal army of the East India Company, and in 1818 was appointed political agent for the states of western Rajputana. But Tod was also an extraordinary scholar, whose *Annals and Antiquities of Rajasthan* (1829–32) laid the foundation of the systematic study of Rajasthan's history and culture. Florence D'Souza shows how this formidable Orientalist accepted the help of Indian scholars, participated in local rituals and compared the nature of Rajput attachment to their ancestral lands with feudal or allodial systems of land ownership in medieval Europe. Tod also tried to render versions of Rajput history intelligible for his European readership, without failing to note Rajput moral, artistic and scientific advancement, to his superiors' great dismay and embarrassment. Another source of imperial 'trouble' from within was the presence of women explorers. Anna Jameson travelled to Upper Canada to join her estranged husband, and according to Jennifer Scott it is precisely through Jameson's liminal position in her marital status, her uncertain fate as a potential Upper-Canadian resident, and her wavering loyalty to the colonial project, that *Winter Studies and Summer Rambles in Canada* (1838) reveals fissures in the woman explorer's sense of national identity. Jameson describes moments of 'first contact' with the Native Canadians as well as the Upper-Canadian landscape using the already-politicized language of the picturesque with a view to domesticating otherness. But her portraits of individual Indians, the personal relationships that transpire through such 'sketches', together with the impetus to communicate cultural difference to her British readership, also demonstrate Jameson's willingness to acknowledge the complexity of Upper-Canadian oral culture. As a consequence, her journal seems to work towards an uneasy balance between national loyalty, feminism and a defence of racial equality.

At home a major cultural event reshuffled the cards of the game of differentiation. Those were the days of the gradual seeping in of evolutionary theories. Two decades before the official publication of *The Origin of Species* (1859), Charles Darwin had laid the foundations for his future theory during his circumnavigation of the globe (1831–6), not only by collecting specimens of exotic fauna and flora, but also by exposing his epistemological preconceptions to destabilizing contact with peoples on different 'rungs' of civilization. In particular the voyage to Patagonia (1832) proved a journey into the past, in which the inhabitants of Tierra del Fuego were cast as the fossilized remnants of an older, primitive stage of humanity. At the same time, the border between the civilized and the savage state of mankind proved to be precarious, as was demonstrated by the story of Jemmy Button and other 'Anglicized' Fuegians, returning on the *Beagle* to their native country and swiftly relapsing to their former 'savage' stage. Virginia Richter addresses two aspects of Darwin's encounter with the Patagonians: firstly, the concepts – such as ideas of scientific observation, discovery, civilization and racial difference – that have a bearing on his descriptions of the 'Other'; secondly, the textual strategies coming into play in the two versions of his travel report, the private diary and the public – and highly successful – narrative of his *Voyage on the Beagle* (1839). Another formidable figure of the mid-century was Richard Burton, explorer, soldier, Orientalist, ethnologist, linguist, diplomat and poet, one of the most fascinating characters ever produced by the East India Company, which had posted the young man to Sindh, one of the four provinces of today's Pakistan, where Burton lived with the Muslims and learned several Eastern languages and dialects. In 1853, Burton famously travelled incognito to the forbidden holy cities of Medina and Mecca disguised as a pilgrim. My contribution to the volume consists in putting Burton's *Personal Narrative of a Pilgrimage* (1855–6) into perspective by reading it alongside with his first book, *Sindh* (1851), and a short autobiographical sketch written at approximately the same time and appended as a postscript to *Falconry in the Valley of the Indus* (1852). I argue that what is fascinating about Burton's early, pre-African texts is that they never entirely manage to portray him as a fully reliable authority holding a statutory position and marking hierarchical differences between Self and Other. With Burton, the imperialist programme is in fact both implemented and undermined, as the explorer-ethnographer becomes aware of the linguistic postures implied by the situations of interlocution in which his adventures place him. Burton thus constructs a hybrid image of himself, blurring the demarcation line not only between the Westerner and the Oriental, but also between real and fantasized life, or between being and writing, breaking down the boundaries between ethnographic description and literary self-refashioning.

The volume closes on a notoriously controversial figure, Henry Morton Stanley, whose published work also closes the century. A major icon of American journalism as well as of British imperial heroism, muscular Christianity and late-Victorian masculinity, Stanley mapped large areas of Central and Eastern Africa and solved some of the continent's geographical enigmas, but was also involved in horrific crimes in the Congo. Focusing on the conspicuous textuality of Stanley's three major narratives of exploration, published between 1872 and 1890, Nicoletta Brazzelli argues that Stanley's reports in fact implicitly sought to construct Africa as a stage where he could refashion himself into a British national hero, which induced him to represent Africa as a place of darkness and savagery. The trope of the 'monarch-of-all-I-survey' then transforms the explorer into the God-like creator of an imaginary Africa turned into a utopian object of future exploitation and consumption. Simultaneously, however, the representation of African space provides Stanley's readers with a glimpse into the origins of civilization and the laws of evolution, which even in his case implies a redefinition of the borders between Self and Other.

1 ENCOUNTERING AFRICA: USES OF THE OTHER IN THE BOOK OF JOHN MANDEVILLE (1357)

Kofi Campbell

This essay discusses one of the most important travel documents from the medieval English period, *The Book of John Mandeville*.[1] *The Book* became the most popular travel narrative of the English Middle Ages, and describes the author's purported encounters with many different cultures. *The Book* first appeared in 1357, its author claiming to be an English knight born and bred in St Albans who left England in 1322 and travelled around the world for just over thirty-five years. The author's claims and descriptions of foreign lands were, for the most part, accepted without question, and the work came immediately to enjoy what Suzanne Akbari refers to as 'extraordinary popularity'.[2] Within a few short years it had been translated into almost every European vernacular. It was not until the late nineteenth century that comparisons with other contemporary texts proved 'beyond question for the most part, that the author had in fact 'done it at Home'.[3] No trace has ever been found of a real John Mandeville who might have written this book, and whoever wrote it never travelled to the places he describes. It is a compilation of several sources (both learned and anecdotal) whose author made several additions and changes to his sources, so that it forms a coherent narrative of his 'journeys' throughout the world. Iain Higgins reads *The Book* as multiple, as containing within the text several different genres:

> a piece of intermittent crusading propaganda; an occasional satire on the religious practices of Latin Christians; an implicit treatise on the right rule in both Christian and non-Christian worlds (a kind of mirror for Christian princes); a proof of the earth's sphericity, the existence of the inhabited antipodes, and the possibility of circumnavigation; a demonstration that most non-Christians have a 'natural' knowledge of the One, True God; a framed collection of tales and diversities, both exemplary and entertaining; and the desultory memoirs – the travel lies, in fact, of a 'verray parfit gentil' English Knight Errant.[4]

The text's 'typicality as a compilation,'[5] and the fact of its continual recopying, retransmission and re-editing, means that we must pay attention to the selection of materials the redactor of any particular version chooses to include, and the ideological shades with which he imbues them, as a means of tracing both that version's relationships with its foreign others, and the kinds of knowledge for which its audience hungered.

There are approximately 300 extant manuscripts, approximately forty-four in English, and some twenty-four known versions of *The Book*, six in English. The English versions are the Bodley, Cotton, Defective, Egerton, Metrical and Stanzaic Fragment. The version which will concern us most here is the Bodley text found in MS. Bodleian e Musaeo 116, a text which M. C. Seymour describes as 'an abridgement of a lost English translation of a Latin recension of the Insular Version, i.e. at five major removes from the original work';[6] in other words, it is a thoroughly Anglicized version of the text, translated and abridged for an English audience. Although the Bodley was not the most widely circulated version in the Middle Ages, it is the version with the second highest number of extant manuscripts. Furthermore, it is the version which is speculated to have been composed latest of all the English versions (as late as 1450), thereby suggesting that as the century progressed, interest in travellers' tales to Africa increased; unlike the other, earlier, English versions of *The Book*, the Bodley is positively obsessed with Africa.

The Metrical version has only this to say about Africa:

> In that land of Ethiopia there is a well, I swear, where during the day the water is so cold that no man may drink of it, and so hot at night that no man might touch it. The waters are hot, dirty and salty, because of the great heat that strikes them. And each person in that country has but one foot, and it is truly so broad that it covers his whole body when the sun is shining hotly, for they suffer greatly for the heat. And next to that land men shall find a land called Little India.[7]

The entire African area is covered in some fourteen lines. The narrator of the Defective version is equally brief:

> In the south of this land all the people are completely black. And in that place is a well in which the water that is so cold during the day that no man might drink it, and so hot at night that no man might suffer his hand in it. In this land the rivers and all the water are turbulent [lit. troubled] and somewhat salty because of the heat. And men of that land get drunk easily and have little appetite for food. And they commonly suffer from consumption and they do not live long. In Ethiopia are such people who have only one foot and they travel so fast that it is marvelous to see, and it is a large foot which makes a shadow and covers the whole body from the sun. And in Ethiopia is the city of Saba, of which one of the three lords who offered [gifts] to our lord was king. I have told you of Ethiopia, from where men go into India.[8]

This version can stand as well for the Cotton and Egerton versions which are very similar, which is explained by the fact that all three texts are descended, at least partly, from the Insular version. The Egerton text, though, is also descended from a lost text which is based on the Royal Latin version.

This is significant because the Bodley *Book* is also based on the Royal Latin version, making the Egerton text the English version to which the Bodley is most closely associated. This is relevant for two reasons. The first is that the Egerton version is the only English text of *The Book* to contain, in a section which deals with the diamond wealth of India, the following statement: 'And if ye will know the virtues of the diamond, I shall tell you as Isidore *libro* 16, *Ethicorum, capitulo de cristallo*, and Bartholomew *De Proprietatibus Rerum, libro* 16, *capitulo de adamante* say'.⁹ The Bodley redactor, in making his text, moves this entire discussion, originally focusing on India, into his description of Africa. The second reason has to do with the Bodley redactor's treatment of Africa. The Bodley version of *The Book*, unlike the other English versions, deals extensively with Africa. The redactor accomplished this by simply taking narratives from other sections of the book and placing them, often verbatim, into the sections of his *Book* which describe the lands of Africa. And, one of the sections he transposes is that which describes the diamond riches of India; this is the section which, in the Egerton (the only English version with which the Bodley shares a common ancestor), also contains a reference to Bartholomew's *De Proprietatibus Rerum*, a text which constructed Africans in rather negative ways, offering potential justifications for taking the wealth it also described. This connection is not sufficient to prove that that text's reading of blacks directly influenced the Bodley redactor's; what cannot be denied is that the Bodley redactor has read at least parts of Bartholomew, that he is fascinated with Africa in a way that none of the other English redactors is, and that the colonialist desire we can trace within many Middle English texts circulates within this text in many of the same ways that it does throughout that body of literature.

I will argue that, through his encounters with Africa and its peoples, the author asks his audience to reconsider their own cultural self-definitions in both positive and negative ways. I will also suggest that the author's descriptions are meant to function as enticements to colonialism. This is accomplished through the bringing together of two seemingly opposite rhetorical practices, namely the processes of 'othering' and 'saming'. By stressing the otherness of the Africans the author constructs them as dangerous people who need to be contained. At the same time, by focusing on their many similarities, he also suggests that they are similar enough to his audience that they could eventually be converted, and made more culturally like his audience, a conversion which he explicitly calls for at the end of his text. Of course, because this work is first and foremost a text which seeks to establish the inherent superiority of its own culture in relation to others, our narrator always begins by constructing his others as backward, uncivilized savages.

In the first place, he ensures that his audience encounters the Africans first as a manifestation of physical otherness, as almost completely other to his audience. There are some, for example, 'that have only one foot, and they can run so fast on that one foot that it is an amazing sight. And that foot is so big that it is an amazing sight; it will cover all his body against the heat of the sun'.[10] And, as the medieval body of writing dealing with Africa usually did, this text often associates these racial differences with heat. We are told soon after that 'that same island is so hot that because of the great heat in the air, men's private parts hang down to their knees'.[11] And although he has previously highlighted the unendurable heat of the place, the narrator also stresses its opposite: 'In that country of Ethiopia there is a country towards the west where the air is so cold that, because of the cold, there is a continual frost which freezes the water so that it turns to crystal'.[12] Thus, even the physical spaces of Africa are constructed as mercurial and unpredictable.

But the author of this text goes beyond mere physical difference, offering his audience a glimpse into the cultural realm of the Africans, and it is here that he ensures that his audience will encounter the Africans as not only other, but as uncivilized primitives.

We learn, for example, that 'In Ethiopia men and women, in the summertime, go together to streams and lie therein from morning till noon, all naked, because of the great heat of the sun'.[13] This imagery, and the hint of forbidden pleasure it offers, is part and parcel of the primitivizing process here, the suggestion that these people live in a world of unbridled sensuality. They are closer to animals than to reasoning humans. It is also somewhat of a commonplace in medieval travel literature. Geraldine Heng notes that the titillating nature of such images is 'a resonant example of the kind of narrative pleasure offered by European travel stories focusing on the exotic ... Audiences of travelogues are conditioned, from the proto-anthropology of Herodotus and Pliny on, to expect the exotic/erotic, the forbidden/taboo'.[14] In other words, savages in different parts of the world are expected to be erotic as well as exotic, for that is part of what makes them savages.

Indeed, the sense of decadence and the hint of sexuality deepen as we move into another part of Ethiopia, Lamore, where 'the heat is so great and burning that the custom there is that every man and woman goes about naked, and scorns those that are clothed. For they say that Adam was naked, and Eve also'.[15] This is a particularly inspired rhetorical strategy, in that the narrator has the Africans construct *themselves* as backward and primitive. Not only are they naked, but they excuse that nakedness themselves through an appeal to archaic times. In this way the text refutes John Friedman's assertion that 'cultural evolution' was simply not part of the 'conceptual vocabulary' of the medieval period, and that social differences were usually explained away as 'the result of degeneration', rather than as 'an earlier stage of cultural evolution'.[16] Here, the Lamorans are precisely constructed as being at an earlier stage of cultural/religious evolution, in a time prior to the more advanced audience of the text. The text's audience understands that humanity has moved beyond the age of the patriarchs, and that it is wrong to try and live in that way; the primitive Lamorans still live, culturally, in those earlier times. The redactor denies them 'coevalness', to use the terminology of Johannes Fabian. The 'denial of coevalness' is a concept he applies to early modern ethnography but, as is the case with many (post)colonial conventions, it has its origins in the Middle Ages. Fabian argues that early modern ethnographers denied 'coevalness', or contemporaneity, to the other cultures they encountered. The denial of coevalness describes the 'persistent and systematic tendency to place the referent(s) of anthropology in a Time other than the present of the producer of anthropological discourse'.[17] In other words, they subjected their others to a process of primitivism, constructing them as less culturally advanced than the ethnographers themselves. We can clearly see this process at work in *The Book*.

Even further, we learn that in Lamore 'there are no marriages between men and women, but rather all the women of that country are shared by every man'.[18] In this way the Africans of Lamore become not only primitive, decadent and uncivilized, but also specifically ungodly, for marriage was a sacred sacrament ordained by God, and such casual sexuality was perceived as being directly against the dictates of God. The text here again separates the Africans effectively from the Christian English audience encountering them, and lowers the Africans to the level almost of brute animals, wallowing naked in the water all day long and copulating at will with any woman they choose. There can be no doubt that this behaviour on the part of the Africans would have been read as offensive and blasphemous to the text's audience.

But Mandeville is not content to show the blasphemy of the Africans so indirectly. He tells us that 'in that same country of Ethiopia they honour the ox instead of god, because of his simpleness and goodness, and for the work that he does and the profit which comes because of him'.[19] Nor is it only the common people who act this way; even the king himself, we are told, 'has always an ox with him wherever he goes and honours it as his god ... and the king puts his hand into the dung and takes some, and rubs it on his teeth, his breast, his forehead and his face, so that he might be blessed through the virtue of that holy thing'.[20] Even as he discusses the blasphemous religion of the Africans Mandeville continues to emphasize their savagery: 'in the country of Ethiopia they slay their children before their gods as a sacrifice, and take the blood and sprinkle it on their idols'.[21]

As has often been observed, this story is reminiscent of the biblical narrative of Abraham, who was ordered by God to kill his son. But, in the civilized Christian paradigm, God steps in and stops the sacrifice, explaining that it was just a test. Here, a biblical exemplum is translated onto the African world, emphasizing the love and justice of Christianity over and against the bloody savagery of the Africans' religion. In this way *The Book* conflates racial otherness and religious difference, constructing the Africans as inferior in both categories. And we must always remember that religious difference was a particularly charged one during this time of Christian crusaderism; the expansion of the faith and conversion of unbelievers was still a fundamental part of Christian thinking, and therefore the construction of Africans as religiously different, indeed as heretics and blasphemers, was necessarily a politically charged one.

The fact that these ox-worshipping heretics are encountered in Africa brings us to the most important facet of the Mandeville-author's portrayal of the Africans and their culture, particularly as that culture relates to the English Christian culture which formed this text's audience. Andrew Fleck argues that Mandeville represents each culture he encounters based on a scale of similarity and difference in relation to his own: 'some cultures are very similar ... others are radically different, and in between are cultures of ambiguous difference'.[22] Heng echoes this idea, suggesting that Mandeville describes 'each far-off country on an implied or explicit scale of distance from Europe, and especially from England and France . . . [and] also constitutes the rest of the world as the periphery of Christian Europe.[23] Fleck argues further that the narrator tends to portray these foreign cultures as proto-Christian, claiming that, for the most part, they would embrace Christianity, and other Western cultural and social institutions, given the chance: an obvious gesture towards colonialism.

Fleck's schematic is useful, but flawed when applied to the Bodley version. He suggests that for Mandeville, the Greeks were the epitome of a similar-yet-different culture; the Africans are the epitome of a radically different culture; and the Muslim Saracens represent an ambiguously-different culture. He bases this division on the fact that the Africans are constructed purely as inhuman and indeed monstrous, such as the race of people who have only one foot; these 'monstrous races', he argues, are present 'to provide an aesthetic contrast, as a clearly sub-human other, to the reader's sense of self ... Their fantastically grotesque bodies serve to create 'absolute difference between reader and subject'.[24] These 'monstrous races' are then contrasted in Fleck's argument with the so-called 'human' races, with whom the audience would have more in common, such as the Saracens. As a result of closer contact, he argues, the Saracens occupy an ambivalent place in Mandeville's text, simultaneously attractive and repellant, while the still-distant Africans are completely inhuman and other.

But as we can see from some of the examples I gave above, Fleck's assessment of Mandeville's treatment of Africans does not apply to the Bodley version. While the Bodley redactor does indeed portray many Africans as monstrous, inhuman and utterly different, he also acknowledges *often* that there are lands in Ethiopia where the people are of the 'human' kind, to use Fleck's terminology. Thus, some Ethiopians may lie around naked in the water, but the shame in that is that they expose their *human* bodies, just as the women who have sex with many men make shameful use of their also human bodies.

But the Bodley redactor goes even further than this, at times identifying the Africans closely with his Christian audience, much more closely than one might expect. One of the tests of the ambivalence Fleck sees in Mandeville's portrayal of the Saracens, is that Mandeville often acknowledges many of the points of similarity between the two religions, creating an unstable space within which 'they' become both like and unlike 'us'. In fact, there are also several times when Mandeville creates such spaces of similarity between the African cultures and his own. The difference between the two spaces lies in Mandeville's differing reactions to the two cultures.

Immediately after describing the Lamorans' habit of walking around naked, for example, Mandeville tells us that they explain their actions by noting that Adam and Eve did the same. As I argued before, this explanation serves a primitivizing function, but at the same time it serves as a common reference point between these people and the text's English audience. This moment works to soften the absolute difference of the Africans and make them a touch more familiar. Likewise, the Lamorans excuse their lack of monogamous marriages through an appeal to the biblical injunction 'Crescite et multiplicamini', that is to say, 'Grow and multiply [and replenish the earth]': here too the narrator creates another moment of congruence and familiarity, however transitory, while at the same time re-identifying them as heretical.[25] In these moments, the Africans become startlingly similar for a brief instant.

Now, when the Muslim Saracens blur the lines between cultures, Mandeville responds, in the words of Andrew Fleck, by summarizing 'the points of faith not in contention between Christians and Saracens, and concludes that they believe in most of the essential tenets necessary to become Christian ... They are not irredeemably different and could ... be brought to accept Christian beliefs'.[26] But when the Africans blur those same lines, Mandeville is absolutely silent, letting their own explanations stand as the final word. His silence is not surprising. Mandeville's England was still quite concerned with the Saracens, not only as a religious, political and social other, but also commercially. Exchanges between Muslims and the Western world were important enough that his audience would have been deeply interested in such points of similarity, and so he speaks to them directly. I suggest that Mandeville's willingness to silently allow African similarity as well as difference, indeed to *indirectly insist upon* that similarity, demonstrates the growing importance of Africa to medieval England.

Africa is for the most part portrayed as utterly different, and the Africans as inhuman savages, so it makes little sense that Mandeville would attempt to reconcile their conception of Christianity too closely with his own. Yet the text's colonialist desire also generates points of congruence, spaces in which there exist the possibilities of similarities as well as difference. It is not enough that there is wealth in Africa, and that the Africans are weak; the later eighteenth and nineteenth-century discourses of colonialism were driven largely by the fiction, or more generously the belief, that the colonizing power was, in reality, helping the colonized peoples. For that to be possible, though, similarities *must* exist; there must be a way for the colonized to be helped and so it becomes necessary that, although the Africans have a king who worships an ox, there also exist within those lands seeds of Christianity, however heretical and blasphemous. It might be possible to take a man who worships an ox and make him into a Christian, but it is certainly easier to do so to people who already have an inkling of the faith. Thus it is also important that a nest of Nestorians resided there, and still persist in some places; however misguided, they too are Christians, and as such represent a moment of similarity between cultures, a gap which can be widened and exploited. Indeed, Mandeville tells us that there is even a Christian relic in Ethiopia, the hand of Saint Thomas the Apostle, which the locals use for magical purposes.[27] So while the Africans are certainly not as ambiguously constructed as the Saracens, they are certainly portrayed in a way which makes them less starkly other than commentators of this text have tended to argue; the Bodley author is careful to construct the Africans as extremely different, even monstrous at times, but not so monstrous that their fascination disappears.

This focusing on similarities, or saming, what Heng calls 'recuperations of otherness', works by domesticating 'all otherness by narcissistically reproducing oneself, and the image of one's culture, even while ostensibly speaking of otherness'.[28] This concept wholly informs the work of the Bodley redactor. Iain Higgins argues that we should, in fact, 'read *The Book*'s depictions of cultural and religious diversity as so many small mirrors in which "over there" at once differs from and resembles "over here", and consequently both reflects and reflects critically on Christianity'.[29] The text dwells on both difference and similarity, 'using difference to reassert Christianity's superiority, and similarity to expand Christendom *in potentia*'.[30] These other cultures, these mirrors, offer distorted reflections that are nevertheless recognizable, and what they tend to reflect, as Fleck, Heng and Higgins all recognize, are proto-Christian societies. The construction of these societies in this carefully proto-Christian way, this process of saming, deals with foreign cultures by effectively 'incorporating them into the fold of a vastly expanded, if also discontinuous and largely imagined, proto-Christian community'.[31] This, of course, makes it much easier to imagine and justify their eventual conversion and subjugation. As Heng argues, *The Book*'s conception of a world 'made up of places where a Christian European subject might not feel wholly alien – might, indeed, feel at home because of religion – theorizes the possibility of relocation'.[32] Indeed, she goes on to argue, the continual insertion of the familiar into every foreign society, '*invites* relocation: urges forth the directive to explore, expand, and even to settle. Identification with otherness, and participation in otherness, ultimately have the secondary effect of inviting the relocation of Europeans'.[33] *The Book of John Mandeville* works precisely to invite this relocation, by suggesting to its audience that even the most remote strangers are, in the end, rather similar; Paul Strohm argues that 'this confidence in ultimate sameness bolsters confidence in the possible conversion of the rest of the world'.[34] Akbari concurs, suggesting that Mandeville creates 'the image of a unified and harmonious world, shaped by the wisdom of its maker'.[35]

By constructing the Africans as both similar and dangerously different, Mandeville simultaneously suggests to his audience that they must be contained, and that they are similar enough to his audience, so that that containment can actually be accomplished. He suggests, in other words, a fairly radical idea at the time; that the savage Other is already partly contained within the Christian Self, and can thus more easily be incorporated into that Self.

2 NAMING THE OTHER, CLAIMING THE OTHER IN EARLY MODERN ACCOUNTS OF FIRST ENCOUNTERS: FROM MANDEVILLE TO JOHN NICHOLL (1607) AND RICHARD JOBSON (1623)

Nicholas Myers and Ladan Niayesh

René Descartes considered that 'travelling is almost the same as conversing with people from other centuries'.[1] This quote underlines the extent to which an enterprise of discovery of new lands is a historical endeavour as much as it is a geographical one. Indeed, to discover a place which is distant in space seldom fails to amount for explorers to searching for a place that is also distant in time. This causes them to expect an encounter with a more 'primitive' culture by the standards of their own, or allot (more or less consciously) a new location to myths and legends of otherness pertaining to their own culture.[2] Compared with and brought back to a better-known cultural reference, alterity can thereby be explained, classified and ultimately appropriated by travellers who view it, not with innocent eyes, but with selective ones, looking out for a confirmation of the beliefs and expectations with which they had set out on their journey. Likewise, armchair travellers reading their accounts back home often nurse the same double expectation vis-à-vis the narratives which they 'explore', insofar as they look both for the pleasure of novelty and a place for such novelty in their own framework of cultural assumptions.

In this chapter, we intend to focus on names and naming as a *locus* for this encounter between selfhood and difference in early modern narratives of exploration. After a general introduction on the moral background of medieval taxonomy and its incidences on early discoveries, we will concentrate on the case studies of one narrative of American exploration, followed by one of African exploration.

To the extent that culture can be defined as 'an organized system of differences',[3] taxonomy and naming play a decisive role in any experience of apprehending otherness. The Adamic assumption that the name is the key to the nature of things and beings presides over much of the pseudo-geographic and pre-ethnographic writings of the Middle Ages, of which Isidore of Seville's *Etymologies* is a good example. As indicated by the treatise's title, the Church Father makes extensive use of known etymologies to account for the distant marvels and monsters that he lists, harnessing and controlling otherness by linguistic means. Thus the Greek roots *aith* (meaning 'burned') and *ops* (meaning 'face') forming the word 'Ethiop' suggest to him that, for better or worse, the Ethiopians' colour is the result of their close proximity to the sun, while they can indifferently be located in Africa or in India. In the same manner, the Cyclops (literally the 'round-eyes'), the Cynocephali ('dog-heads'), the Amazons ('without breast'), the Hermaphrodites (a conflated version of the physical attributes of Hermes and Aphrodite) or the Anthropophagi ('man-eaters') can be diversely located or displaced at will, as long as they remain in the margins of the known world being, as they are, creatures of the extreme, both in their bodies and in their habitat.[4] The appellations given to these and other monstrous races by Isidore and his predecessors (Ctesias, Pliny, Solinus, etc.) have no geographical basis, but are entirely dependent on physical appearance, diet and sexual practices.

It follows that the monstrous races' names make them figures for vices or, more rarely, for virtues in the didactic and moral – rather than properly speaking geographical – works in which they appear. Thus, for example, according to the *Gesta Romanorum*, a collection of pseudo-antique tales composed by an English Franciscan friar before 1342, the *Blemmyes* have their eyes and mouths in their breasts because they are humble, while the *Panotii* have big ears so as to better listen to the word of God; and the notoriously handsome *Pygmies* are a living testimony to how an enterprise that begins well may nevertheless be curtailed.[5] In the highly didactic and moral geography of the Middle Ages, monstrous races stand true to the double etymology of the word 'monster', insofar as they serve to 'show' (*monstrare*) as well as to 'warn' (*monere*).

Traces of this geography of dogma and imagination abound in medieval cartography, as well as in the works of medieval travellers and pseudo-travellers, such as Sir John Mandeville, who in his *Travels* frequently provides explanations for the mores of the inhabitants of the exotic lands he is supposed to have visited. Let us take as an example the curious ways of the Christian inhabitants of the Isle of Lamory. Those people go naked, Mandeville reports, 'for they say that God made *Adam* and *Eve* all naked', and they copulate freely because 'they say that God commaunded to *Adam* and *Eve* and all that come of him saying: *Crescite et multiplicamini et repleti terram*'.[6]

The European discovery of the New World was to a large extent a rediscovery of this moralized medieval background in a new locale. This is how in 1522 Hernán Cortés sent to Charles V of Spain some bones supposedly belonging to Plinian Giants, while in 1540 Francesco de Orellana named the river Amazon after a European legend which he thought he had located in America. As for Walter Ralegh, he asserts the existence of Amazons and *Blemmyes* in Guiana, a discovery which makes him believe in the authenticity of Mandeville's *Travels* at the surprisingly late date of 1596:

> Such a nation was written of by *Mandeville*, whose reports were held for fables many years, and yet since the *Indies* were discovered, we find his relations true of such things as heretofore were held incredible.[7]

Reportedly equipped with a volume of Mandeville's *Travels*, Christopher Columbus did not just discover the New World, he also invented the term 'Cannibal', which became one of the chief stereotypes associated with America in the minds of its early travellers and settlers. A linguistic deformation of the name of a warlike native population, the *Caribs* or *Canibs* of whom the Admiral had heard during his first journey in the Lesser Antilles in 1492, the appellation made him formulate some Isidorian etymological hypotheses of his own. To him, 'Can' in 'Canib' appeared suggestive of *canis*, meaning 'dog' in Latin, which made Columbus suppose he had found the trace of the terrible *Cynocephali* of Plinian and Mandevillian fame in the islands he had just explored. Alternatively, he considered that 'Can' could stand for the Great *Khan*, whose kingdom he hoped to reach. As a result, his 'Cannibal' becomes a name haunted by many presences of diverse historical and geographical provenances, all of them equally ferocious, as in the following report made by Peter Martyr de Anghiera, who compiled the first account of the Columbian journeys:

> The wylde and myscheuous people called *Canibales* or *Caribes*, which were accustomed to eate mannes fleshe (and called of the olde writers, *Anthropophagi*) molest them [meaning the *Arawaks*] excedyngly, inuadynge theyr country, takynge them captiue, kyllyng and eatyng them.[8]

A geography which equates Caribbean natives with the Anthropophagi (legendary inhabitants of Mount Caucasus) is a geography that takes little account of the compass, mapping out a mindscape more than it does a landscape. This is how the term 'cannibal', despite its being originally derived from the name of an existing ethnic group, is gradually divested of its ethnicity, becoming first a noun and then an adjective that despite being associated with the New World frame, is not necessarily related to the native Caribs. Such is the case in the following excerpt, from Ralegh's *Discovery of Guiana*, written nearly a century after Columbus' discovery, and in which the term 'cannibal' appears as a synonym for man-eater and is applied to Europeans:

> The Spaniards to the end that none of the people in the passage towards *Guiana* or in *Guiana* itself might come to speech with us, persuaded all the nations, that we were man eaters, and *Cannibals* ... [9]

What we have just said of the linguistic odyssey of the term 'Cannibal' could equally apply to a variety of other appellations, e.g. 'Amazon', which starts as a legend relocated in America, before becoming a descriptive noun, and eventually a chief stereotype associated with the American continent, and appearing alongside the charge of cannibalism in most of the allegorical representations of the New World. Associated together, the figures of the Amazon and of the Cannibal embody the same fear of a hungrily absorptive other, filling New World accounts with what Gaston Bachelard calls 'the homeopathic function of terror'.[10] More than referring to ethnic groups, such terms as 'Amazon', 'Cannibal' or simply 'Savage' name a fear or a fantasy, which makes them hover somewhere in the unstable zone separating the Self and the Other.

To illustrate the ideological instability of such categories, we suggest we follow the linguistic odyssey of the term 'Cannibal' in the first known account of English presence in Saint Lucia, which is the unfortunate story of a shipwreck and ensuing hardships in a hostile environment, taking place in 1605. The account was written by John Nicholl (of whom little is known, except that he was one of the few survivors of the expedition) and published in 1607 under the title *An Houre Glasse of Indian Newes*. The full title of the work, appearing on the title page of its first and only known full edition, gives a summary of the adventures narrated therein:

Houre Glasse of In-
dian Newes.
OR
A true and tragicall discourse, shewing the
most lamentable miseries, and distressed Calami-
ties indured by 67 Englishmen which were sent
for a supply to the planting in Guiana in the yeare. 1605.

Who not finding the saide place, were for want of vic-
tuall, left a-shore in Saint Lucia, an Island of Caniballs,
or Men-eaters in the West-Indyes, vnder the Conduct of Captain Sen-Iohns, of all which said
number; onely a 11. are supposed to be
still liuing, whereof 4. are lately
returnd into Eng-
land.
Written by Iohn Nicholl, *one of the aforesaid*
Company.

This title page does not only provide us with a summary of the contents, but equally resorts to nomination in order to arouse an expectation and establish an interpretative pact. Here, 'Saint Lucia' appears half Spanish and half English, linguistically disputed between those two claimants long before the territory itself could become an object for dispute. Meanwhile its being defined as 'an Island of Caniballs, or Men-eaters' leaves us to wonder if 'cannibal' appears here in its ethnic sense (since the island is located right in the midst of the Caribbean Sea) or in its moral sense, as is suggested by the would-be synonym provided: '*or* Men-eaters'.

The promised account of cannibalism in the West Indies appears as an answer to the other expectation aroused by this title page, i.e. the one contained in the term 'Guiana', a name evoking the 'large, rich and bewtiful kingdome' of Raleghan fame, referred to in the first pages of Nicholl's narrative as 'the great and mightie kingdome of *Guiana*', 'reputed to be the chiefest place for golde mines in all the West India'.[11] Between them, the fear contained in 'Cannibal' and the fantasy contained in 'Guiana' epitomize the two sides – monstrous and marvellous – of the New World experience.

Such a title undoubtedly leaves the reader to expect the unfortunate English sailors' odyssey to be transformed into a 'digestive odyssey'[12] through the man-eaters' entrails. But the author of the account surprises us by his repeated waverings between an expected cliché and the utterly different experience that he faithfully records. Witness the *coup de théâtre* taking place during the scene of the English crew's first landing on the island:

> And so hauing beene seuenteene weekes at sea … we were brought to an Iland in the West *India* somewhat distant from the maine, called *Santa Lucia* … inhabited onely with a companie of most cruell Caniballs, and men-eaters, where we had no sooner anchored, but the *Carebyes* came in their Periagoes or Boats aboard vs with great store of Tobacco, Plantons, Potatoes, Pines, Sugar Canes, and diuerse other fruits, with Hens, Chickens, Turtles, & Guanas.[13]

We may note here the doubling of the appellation, 'Caniball' referring to the natives in their man-eating role, and 'Carebye' referring to them as traders selling wholesome food. The passage telescopes the two images around the same preoccupation with nourishment. As often in New World accounts, the good Indians and the savage Indians juxtaposed here are the same Indians, viewed differently. Treating them as if they were naked in their culture just as they were found naked in their bodies, such narratives project onto the natives their own fears and fantasies motivated by a hostile environment, thereby claiming, if not the natives themselves, at least what the natives could be made to represent.

In Nicholl's account, as well as in most accounts of early American discoveries, we do not find the natives' point of view, only whatever point of view is attributed to them by the European mediator reporting the encounter and ventriloquizing the natives' discourse. Witness the following passage, corresponding to the Europeans' decision to leave the island as a result of deteriorating relationships with the Indians:

And wee concluded, rather then wee would stay and dye so miserably at the *Car-rabies* hands, who thirsted for nothing but to eate our flesh, and drinke our blood, as they had done with many other of our fellowes, wee promised vnto the LORD . . . to betake our selues vnto his mercy, and doubted not but that hee would guide vs safely to some Christian Harbour.[14]

How can the narrator know whether or not the Caribs, whose language he does not speak, 'thirst for nothing but to eate' his flesh? Despite the assertion 'as they had done with many other of our fellowes', none of the English sailors of this account gets eaten by the natives. Here the pronoun 'they' becomes a generic appellation, reaching well beyond those particular natives, referring to a more or less fabricated savage type rather than to individuals actually encountered.

In the words of Pierre Chaunu, 'the Cannibal does not speak of himself, he speaks only of us; the Cannibal is us'.[15] Significantly enough, an account which capitalized on fears of native cannibalism finally materializes those fears among Europeans alone as, stranded on another island with no provisions left, they consider that possibility and come very close to actually practising it, before their final rescue by the Spaniards. Coming nowhere close to claiming either native land or natives themselves, the English sailors of this account seem to have claimed and appropriated only an appellation, 'cannibal', an accusation which comes from them and eventually returns to them and them alone.

'I is an other', Arthur Rimbaud wrote in a famous letter to George Izambard.[16] Considering this and such like fear-stricken, fantasy-laden accounts of American encounters in which the natives are ultimately either forgotten or flattened out into a stereotype produced by and for Europeans, this formula might be aptly reversed into 'The other is an I'. But could the same phenomenon be reproduced closer to home and in a better-known cultural frame? This is the question to which we shall turn our attention now, by examining a narrative of a first encounter in Africa, *The Golden Trade*, originally published in 1623, by one Richard Jobson.[17]

Jobson describes his voyages to Ethiopia and the Gambia River during 1620–1. About the man himself, very little is known. The references to Ireland in his account, some of which show a fairly detailed knowledge of conditions there, may indicate that he was the Jobson who worked for the Lord Admiral of Ireland years before, but this is not certain. This development will be limited to two aspects of the work – the ethnic divisions in the area he visited and the question of religion – since we argue that they bring to the fore the interpretative difficulties which the observing gaze itself is subject to in encounters with cultural material which is recalcitrant to assimilation into known cognitive frameworks.

The exact title of his piece is *The Golden Trade, or A Discovery of the River Gambra, and the Golden Trade of the Aethiopians*. This last term, it will be remembered, had been used in the vaguest way for centuries to refer to an area stretching right across northern Africa. The river Gambia in effect cuts Senegal in half and gave its name to the country which was, much later, formally colonized by the British. Although Jobson's account took book form, and was published two years later in an abridged version by the compiler Samuel Purchas, it was ostensibly addressed to the gentlemen and merchant adventurers who had founded the Guinea Company. Thus its intention, like much travel writing of the period, is exhortative, to encourage the Company's investors to continue to finance exploratory voyages of just the sort that Jobson had led in 1620–1. The 'gold' of the title turned out to be very elusive. When he was far upriver the author heard from a Mandinga trader of a town in which the houses were said to be covered with gold, but this is of course exactly the kind of fabulation that merchant adventurers commonly used as leverage with their backing investors. In any case, Jobson came back with very little. What *is* certain is that Jobson gives the most detailed account in English or indeed any other language of the ethnic communities along the Gambia in the early modern period.

Appearing well on into the seventeenth century as it does, however, the question arises as to what extent Jobson's narrative concerns a first encounter in the pristine sense of the term. Strictly speaking, it is nothing of the kind: the Portuguese had been trading up and down the coast of West Africa since the middle of the fifteenth century. Indeed, a mulatto race of Afro-Portuguese, whom we shall come back to, had long lived in scattered communities alongside the indigenous ones. The English themselves had sent the first tentative expeditions to Senegal in the 1550s. However, upriver it was a different situation, and Jobson is at pains to claim that his party formed the first white people that upriver Africans had encountered. Notwithstanding this, the shock of cultures in evidence here must be sharply distinguished from the experience of the Americas. The issue of the effective enslavement of indigenous communities in the New World, which famously generated enormous theological and political debate, particularly in Spain, was not an issue in Africa, insofar as it was a pre-existing fact of life. Indeed, although Jobson was not in the Gambia to take part in the slave trade, and explicitly refused it, African traders he encountered made it clear that slaves would have been the most precious commodity he could have offered them, along with the salt which he did profitably barter. It cannot be said that Jobson *claims* anything as a possession by *naming* it, certainly not in the way that Columbus and the conquistadors who accompanied Cortés and Pisarro did.

From a cultural perspective, though, the interest of Jobson's account lies precisely in the mishearings and misreadings which characterize it and effectively give his efforts to interpret what he observes a shifting, trial-and-error feel. Culture, as much as Nature, abhors a vacuum: when Jobson's knowledge of local conditions, whether concerning language, culture or religion, comes up short, as it frequently does, exegesis rushes in to attempt to make something out of nothing – transparency out of opaqueness – and effectively 'domesticate' strangeness for his readers. At certain points his account is coloured with what might be termed an irony of stance, the irony of assuming oneself to represent the norm, and in fact being a stranger in a strange land, and this is no less true for the fact that Jobson himself is only uneasily aware of it.

An instance of this is the episode in which he has to strip off and get into the water because the Mandingas whom he had hired as rowers flatly refuse to do so, for fear of the crocodiles. Seeing his example, and survival, they consult together and decide to follow him in at the next difficult passage in the river. When he asks them to explain their change of heart, he learns to his surprise that they had reasoned that, as they put it, 'the white man shine more in the water ... and therefore if Bumbo come, he would surely take us first'.[18] The narrative immediately places the requisite distance between their reasoning and his by assuring the reader that at no point was any member of his party, black or white, attacked by crocodiles. Partly, this is self-representation by Jobson as a sort of prototype of the unflappable Englishman abroad, but more importantly, it immediately re-establishes the proper hierarchy of rationalities, if not a simple mutually exclusive opposition: pragmatic rationality against unreason and superstition. Yet – and this is the irony – what the narrative unwittingly highlights is that here he is confronted with his *own* strangeness. *His* skin makes him singular and even monstrous in this landscape.

The problem of nomenclature is common to all travel narratives, of course, and Jobson's is no exception. The river itself, he notes, is variously referred to as Gamba, Gambia, and Gambra; but what is most disorienting for the mental habits of taxonomy and classification that Jobson represents is the fact that most of the indigenous populations do not denote it by a name at all, but simply by the common noun, *gee* used for all types of river.

Problems of description extend to the various ethnic communities. Jobson's party encounters three distinct ethnic groups. The Mandingos, dominant in the area, who are referred to interchangeably as Blackmen or Ethiopians; the Fulbe, herders who are described as being 'a tawny people', resembling 'Egiptians' (that is, gypsies); and the mainly mulatto Afro-Portuguese, referred to as 'Portingales'.[19] This last group emerges as particularly unplaceable in its cultural identity and practices. A number of years after Jobson's journey, a French traveller known as the Sieur de la Courbe confirmed his judgement on this point, commenting that 'most of them say neither Christian nor Muslim prayers, and others say both'.[20] Their failure to observe the proper liturgical boundaries is taken by Jobson to be symptomatic of a general treacherousness characterizing them, and it is clear that he finds it easier to respect the steadfast, if mistaken, piousness of the Muslims.

Towards the herding Fulbe, Jobson exhibits a measure of sympathy for a group whom he considers to be exploited by the Mandingo, tempered in a complex way by revulsion for their bestiality. He notes, for instance, that they do not even bother to whisk away the flies which swarm thickly over them. An important implication lies behind the apparently insignificant detail: husbandry, for Jobson, far from leading to assimilation between man and beast, as here, emphasizes the unbridgeable distance between the two in the society he comes from. On the other hand, in a passage in which he describes bartering with the Fulbe women for their dairy products on the river bank, he compares their standards of cleanliness to those of the Irish, who, he claims, follow very much the same way of life. And the comparison is much to the latter's disadvantage. Of course, such exemplary even-handedness towards an indigenous African community must also be read as a judgement on the completely irrecuperable nature of the Catholic Irish who remained, for the incipient imperial project of Elizabethan and Jacobean England, perhaps the most recalcitrantly 'barbarous' of colonized subjects, representing a direct threat for the Crown and English Protestantism in a way that no other colonized subjects did.

It is in his encounter with the local forms of Islam that the weak points in Jobson's frame of reference, and his attempts to shore them up, are most evident. Displaying a degree of ignorance that is surprising, even for a European, he appears to assume that familiarity with figures such as Eve, Moses and David indicates acquaintance with the Old Testament, whereas of course they are mentioned in the Koran. The marabouts, familiarized for his English readership as 'Mary-buckes', he considers as priests, although at this period it is more accurate to think of them as lay scholars of Islam, who were dedicated to spreading their faith, certainly, but who also doubled as traders in the mid-river area. The Arabic scripts which he saw he takes to resemble Hebrew. Naturally, Jobson uses the only cultural categories he has to hand. Anthony Pagden has analysed the extent to which, in the New World especially, the problem of recognition, which entailed a very rough procedure of analogy from the new to the old, was simply blind to local particularities.[21] A particularly flagrant instance of this is to be found in the episode in which Jobson attempts to describe a marabout at prayer, in which he claims that he faces east initially but then turns west.[22]

Of course, all such distortions are recuperated and diminished within the providentialist framework which, in more than one sense, authorizes Jobson's presence. In discussion with the marabouts he learns that, for Islam, Christ is recognized as a nabi – a great prophet – but notes also the Muslims' scepticism as to His being the son of God. Serenely, he records their admiration of the superior technology of the visitors as evidenced in the ocean-going vessels and navigational skills which had brought them there. Without its being said in so many words, he leaves the reader to conclude that these are signs of God's special favour, recognized as such even by the as-yet unconverted. For that is how he sees them:

> Thus like humaine creatures in darknesse they argue, being barred from that glorious light, which shines in the east, whereof though they have heard, they have not yet made use but no doubt when the fulnesse of time is come they shall; for amongst themselves a prophesy remains, that they shall be subdued, and remaine subject to a white people: and what know we, but that determinate time of God is at hand, and that it shall be his Almighty pleasure, to make our nation his instruments, whereof in my part I am strongly comforted in regard of the familiar conversation ... and the faire acceptance I received.[23]

If it is a truism that much travel writing is characterized by an anxiety to maintain proper thresholds between the civilized, as localized in the Self, and the barbaric, as exhibited by the Other, it is equally true that the ambivalence of such narratives arises from the tension between repulsion and fascination, the felt-yet-resisted temptation to allow the boundary of the Self's cultural identity to dissolve as one is sucked into the vortex of the unknown that the Other represents.

Marlow's familiar remark in *Heart of Darkness* about taking the earth away from those who have flatter noses not being a pretty thing unless it be redeemed by 'the idea' is pertinent here. What Conrad calls 'idea', we would probably now call the ideology which underwrites appropriation. In our analysis of accounts of first encounters in both the Caribbean and West Africa we have sought not only to demonstrate that ideology is the sustaining pillar in the observer's construct of the Other, but also to touch on a few nodal points of manifest uneasiness and ambiguity in the process of naming that demonstrate the tensions to which that pillar is subjected.

3 FALSE PLAY AND DUMB SHOW IN *THE WORLD ENCOMPASSED BY SIR FRANCIS DRAKE* (1628)

Sophie Lemercier-Goddard

When at the end of *The Tempest* Prospero is asked to tell his former enemies of his preservation on his strange island, he dismisses their request as untimely but provides instead a 'wonder'[1] to content them: the sight of Ferdinand and Miranda's false play at chess, with the two characters looking at the company gazing at them, their own eyes similarly caught in a wonderful vision. The discourse of 'wonder' is an essential element of travel narratives: it marks the encounter with difference, when in the course of a long journey the Self comes across the Other. The narrative which results from such encounters purposes to tell readers at home about different people and exotic places, and above all to make them experience astonishment or admiration.

In *The World Encompassed by Sir Francis Drake* (1628), which relates the circumnavigation accomplished by Sir Francis Drake between 1577 and 1580, the rhetoric of the wonderful is particularly needed, as the navigator can hardly boast of any major discovery at the end of his three-year voyage. When he returns to Plymouth Harbour in September 1580, Drake may be the first *Englishman* in history to have sailed around the earth, but he comes second to Magellan, whose men had accomplished the first circumnavigation more than half a century earlier (1519–22), entering what they called the *Mar Pacifico*, i.e. the Pacific Ocean, from the 'Strait of Magellan', which the Portuguese explorer discovered in 1520. Though difficult to navigate, this route, sheltered by mainland South America and the Tierra Del Fuego archipelago, is still safer than the 'Drake Passage', which the Englishman discovered after passing through the Strait, and where one of his three remaining ships was lost far South (September 1578) while another was forced to turn back to England. Throughout his journey, the English navigator follows in the steps of the Spanish, or the Portuguese.

The text published in 1628 is the first comprehensive account of the voyage, although it should always be kept in mind that its author is not Francis Drake himself, but the navigator's nephew, also named Francis Drake (1573–1634), who plays on his homonymy in his title, *The World Encompassed by Sir Francis Drake*, to suggest falsely that his compilation is the firsthand account of his famous uncle. Unlike Columbus before him, or Pigafetta, the diarist of Magellan's voyage, Drake failed to publish the tale of his adventures immediately after his return. The continuous plundering of Spanish ports and vessels along the coast of South America probably explains the lack of publicity given to his otherwise remarkable achievement. For though the number of men who came home safe and sound was never specified, Drake's company fared much better than their predecessors: out of the 270 men who had left Spain with Magellan in August 1519, only eighteen had survived the expedition. A short account of Drake's circumnavigation had first been published in 1589 in Richard Hakluyt's *Principall Navigations*, in the form of twelve unnumbered pages, a late addition to Hakluyt's anthology which may have reflected Drake's sudden renewal of favour at Court after his successful participation in the defeat of the Great Armada in 1588. Drake's 'Famous Voyage' had then been inserted in the second edition of Hakluyt's *Navigations* in 1600, and an almost identical version had again been published in 1625 by Hakluyt's successor, Samuel Purchas, in *Purchas his Pilgrimes*.

I argue that, given its unusually late publication for a travel narrative, the 1628 text – again, a compilation of Hakluyt's text, incomplete diaries and various reports, edited by Drake's nephew – uses the discourse of wonder to make up for the delayed presentation of events which had taken place fifty years earlier. The wonderful is also part of a legitimation process, toning down the mercantile objectives of the voyage, presenting instead a geographical survey of the globe, backed up with an anthropological and religious dimension. After a century of expeditions to the New World, Drake's voyage thus proposes to redefine the category of the Other, ranging from the similar and yet monstrously abject other, to the wonderfully different 'alter ego'. A close reading of the account shows that towards the end of their journey, when the English company come across the Indians of North California, meeting the Other in fact implies a new communicational strategy. I show that the discourse of wonder, based on dumb shows – to be understood here both as sign language and false play – leads to an apparent communion between Self and Other, a supposedly intimate fellowship which binds the two parties through faith, while enacting the sharing and eventually the translation of the Indians' lands and possessions.

As Steven Greenblatt argues, the style of travel narratives combines the simplicity of a monotonous prose and the production of wonder thanks to a deliberate rhetorical strategy: the 'realist' streak guarantees the authenticity of the events related by non-professional writers, while the 'wonderful', or 'marvellous', sustains the interest of the reader, thus providing 'an aesthetic response in the service of a legitimation process'.[2] In the 1628 edition of *The World Encompassed*, the flat description of the travellers' progress is punctuated by the insistent repetition of the adjectives 'wonderful' or 'marvellous'. However, such adjectives are found less as symptoms of the exotic than as generic markers: for instance, they serve to qualify the long, eventless crossing of the ocean, 'the vast gulph, where *nothing* but sea beneath us and aire above us was to be seene, as our eies did behold the *wonderfull* workes of God in his creatures';[3] or conversely, they come into play to undermine the violence of some of the first encounters with the Indians on the Peruvian coast: 'The General himself was shot in the face, under his right eye, and close by his nose, the arrow piercing a marvellous way in, under *basis cerebri*.[4] Hostile action which might have imperilled the whole voyage – and actually cost the life of two men – becomes a 'wonderful' scene in its own right.

As a point of fact, the whole world is made to appear 'wonderful'. When they sail across the equator, Drake's men enter a land of plenty where resources are not only abundant but easily gathered, with birds or fish landing naturally on deck. The world is turned upside down, and a reverse logic seems to prevail. Mogador, off the coast of Morocco, the first sight of land after the company's departure from England, already signals a shift to a world of deceiving appearances: the Moors welcome the navigators in a very friendly way, but soon prove to be deceitful when they seize one of the Englishmen unawares. The natural kingdom also seems to be upside down, as when flying fish are spotted.[5] Dainty and wholesome fruit is found in January on the northern coast of Africa, but in summer, on the western coast of America, the travellers find a squalid and barren country which they call 'the frozen zone'.[6] The face of the earth thus appears to be 'deformed': 'Besides how unhandsome and deformed appeared the face of the earth itself! Showing trees without leaves, and the ground without greenes in those months of June and July'.[7]

As a consequence, economic rules seem to have been turned upside down as well. Men and women are bought like merchandise, while water is sold to the natives of Cape Blank at a very high price, in containers meant for liquor.[8] On the western coast of South America, Drake's men even discover that it is easier to find gold than fresh water:

> they lighted on a Spaniard who lay asleep and had lying by him 13 barres of silver, weighing in all about 4000 Spanish ducats ... Our search for water still continuing, as we landed again not farre from thence, we met a Spaniard with an Indian boy, driving 8 lambs or Peruvian sheep: each sheep bore two leathern bags, and in each bag was 50 pound weight of refined silver, in the whole, 800 weight.[9]

The English later come across a Portuguese ship laden with 'fruit, conserves, sugars, meal and other victuals, and (that which was the especial cause of her heavy and slow sailing) a certaine quantitie of jewels and precious stones, 13 chests of rials of plate, 80 pound weight in gold, 26 tons of uncoyned silver', but they are still searching for 'some convenient place, wherein to trim our ship, and store ourselves with wood and water and other provisions as we could get'.[10] Such lines also suggest to what extent even the traditional economy of plundering is revisited by the discourse of wonder. Within two weeks of their arrival off the coast of North Africa, Elizabeth's privateers had already seized three Spanish fishing boats and two caravels. But Drake's men do not *seize* or *chase* Spanish or Portuguese ships; they simply *find*, *take* or *meet* them. The 1628 text thus systematically erases all the traces of the violent colonial competition between the European nations which the first account of the voyage in 1589 had underscored. Suffice it to compare the two following accounts of the same event:

> Being before this Island, wee espied two ships under sayle, to the one of which *wee gave chase*, and in the end *boorded* her with a ship boate without resistance which we found to be a good Prize.[11]
>
> On the South-west of this Iland [St Iago] we *tooke* a Portugall laden the best part with wine, and much good cloth, both linnen and woollen, besides other necessaries, bound for Brazill, with many gentlemen and Marchants in her.[12]

The rhetoric of the wonderful serves still another purpose, since it also manages to root the text in a Christian perspective. The first sight of land after leaving Plymouth is Cape Cantine in Barbary and, as the text is very careful to underline, it occurs on 25 December. The name 'Barbary' seems henceforth to be taken to mean the site of 'barbarity', and the allegorical dimension of Drake's relation of events clearly emerges, for instance, when the travellers go ashore to find doves assaulted by hawks and 'such like birds of prey', or when south of the island they spot great stores of 'very wholesome but very ugly fish to look to'.[13] The strange coincidence of the Christian calendar and of the materialization of Muslim territory thus functions as a filtering grid for Drake's perception of the coastal regions of North Africa, inciting readers to inscribe his voyage within a Christian pattern, and therefore to bestow upon his men some kind of divine 'mission'. This is later confirmed by the interpretation the text makes of the date of Drake's return to England:

> And the 26. of Sept. (which was Monday in the just and ordinary reckoning of those that had stayed at home in one place or countrie, but in our computation was the Lords day or Sonday) we safely with joyfull minds and thankfull hearts to God, arrived at Plimoth, the place of our first setting forth.[14]

The difference between the travellers' calendar and that of their fellow citizens evinces the discrepancy between the manifest purpose of the voyage – Drake brings back enough treasure to pay off the entire national debt, and the Queen knights him – and its supposedly concealed religious motives, as if the booty the pirates are bringing home were only meant as a cover-up for the missionaries' spiritual agenda. One may very well argue that Drake's arrival in the New World is marked by a similar example of Christian symbolism.

Out of the five ships that make up the English fleet, the *Pelican*, the *Elizabeth*, the *Marigold*, the *Swan* and the *Christopher*, it is the latter, literally the 'Christ-bearer', which gets lost when they come in sight of the Brazilian coast. The fleet is immediately spotted by the Indians who light what the English crew take to be sacrificial fires. The *Christopher* is found again nine days later – only to be severed from the rest of the fleet a second time three weeks later – and the temporary loss of such an aptly named ship seems to suggest that the Indian fires were not meant to protect the natives from the Europeans as potential invaders, but rather to emphasize both the tragic fate of the heathen tribes and the arrival of the English as the coming of Christianity to America.

But this sense of wonder is not limited to the rhetorical devices or religious topoi used in Drake's description of the New World. It is presented from the very outset as the very purpose of the expedition, except that the English do not start with the ambition to *see* the wonders of the world, or to admire unknown lands and their strange inhabitants; Drake and his men set on their journey with the objective of *becoming themselves objects of admiration*. As the narrator of *The World Encompassed* explains:

> Neither had [Francis Drake] omitted to make provision for ornament and delight, expert musicians, rich furniture ... and divers shows of all sorts of curious workmanship, wherby the civilitie and magnificence of his native country, might amongst all nations whithersoever he should come, *be the more admired*.[15]

This reversed feeling of wonder may call to mind a famous drawing, 'America' (*c.* 1575), by Jan Van der Straet, better known as Johannes Stradanus, a Flemish painter. Stradanus describes the Florentine navigator Amerigo Vespucci – whose transatlantic trips to the New World at the very end of the fifteenth century had inspired cartographer Martin Waldseemüller to label the new continent after Vespucci's Christian name – as he sets on the shores of 'America'. The drawing is intensely allegorical, Vespucci being represented as engaged in a ritual of interaction with a naked feminine figure named 'America'. Strangely enough, Vespucci's composed gaze and self-assured countenance are met by what looks to us more like a look of wonder on America's part, than a possible gesture of apprehension:[16] the naked allegory looks at the intruder with parted lips, and she holds up her hand not in a defensive way, but as if she were about to touch the explorer and test his reality.

Of course, the feeling of wonder is more often than not generated by natural elements, rather than by the people encountered: the lush vegetation on Mucho

Island off the Chilean coast anticipates further and greater riches ('besides ... it is thought to be wonderfull rich in gold');[17] mountains in Tierra del Fuego are 'of so rare a height, as they may well be accounted amongst the wonders of the world'.[18] Once natural resources have been listed, however, the description of the inhabitants follows, usually pointing out the natives' 'comely' proportions and harmless disposition, as if it were of the greatest importance that the discourse of wonder be reserved either for the natural beauties of the New World, or for the English gentlemen themselves.[19]

Even the Indians' partial nakedness and the widespread custom of body painting are seen not as tokens of otherness, but as familiar signs recalling the otherness of those other strangers at home, women: 'some paint their whole bodies black, leaving onely their neckes behind and before white, much like our damosels that weare their squares, their neckes and breasts naked'.[20] Resemblance, more than difference, is emphasized by the narrative, which therefore derides the fiction of the giants of Patagonia described by Magellan: 'they are nothing so monstrous, or giantlike as they are reported'.[21] On the northern Californian coast where they settle for a month, in a place they name 'Nova Albion', the travellers note the patriarchal organization of Indian society, and they underscore the pliant characters of the women, 'very obedient to their husbands, and exceeding ready in all their services; yet of themselves offring to do nothing, without the consents or being called of the men'.[22] As a consequence, the English do not hesitate to present themselves as the Indians' 'friends'.[23]

The Other is indeed less the Indian than the Portuguese or the Spanish, whose colonial influence in America is harshly indicted for having subjected the natives to the 'most miserable bondage and slavery'.[24] Whenever the English undergo an attack, as at Cyppo, on the Chilean coast, the text is anxious to draw a distinction between the innocent Indians and their Spanish tormentors:

> [One Englishman] whose dead body being drawn by the Indians from the rock to the shore, was there manfully by the Spaniards beheaded, the right hand cut off, the heart plucked out, all which they carried away in our sight.[25]

The Spaniards are also denounced for their 'most filthie and loathsome manner of living ... wherein (amongst other the like Spanish virtues) not only whoredom, but the filthiness of Sodom, not to be named among Christians, is not common without reproof'.[26] Particular emphasis is laid on their cruelty when dealing with the Indians:

> [The Spanish] suppose they show the wretches great favour when they do not for their pleasures whip them with cords, and day by day, drop their naked bodies with burning bacon: which is one of the least cruelties, amongst many, which they universally use against that Nation and people.[27]

The fried bacon is a potent symbol, which reverses the traditional accusation of cannibalism associated with the American Indians. No instance of anthropophagy is ever recorded in Drake's narrative; nor is it completely wiped out from the text. A generic feature of white colonist fiction of the Other,[28] hints of cannibalism are in fact displaced: by suggesting that the Spaniards break down the frontier between pork meat and human flesh, the text turns the European Catholics into the true barbarians. The construction of the Indian as alter ego of the Protestant gentleman goes hand in hand therefore with an 'otherization' of the monstrous Catholic. The expedition does not only serve thus the political interests of England; more importantly, the text suggests that English colonization is needed to save the souls of the Indians, whose fine bodies are a clear sign of divine election:

> They have cleane, comely and strong bodies: they are swift of foot, and seem very active. Neither is anything more lamentable ... than that so goodly a people, and so lively creatures of God, should bee ignorant of the true and living God ... having in truth a land sufficient to *recompence* any Christian Prince in the world, for the whole travell and labour, cost and charges bestowed in that behalfe: with a wonderfull enlarging of kingdome, besides the glory of God by encreasing of the Church of Christ.[29]

Drake does not pose as a conqueror ready to take the riches of the land, but as a true Christian ambassador, whose efforts can only be rewarded by the gratefulness of the natives.

But although the Indian other may be a 'friend', he is hardly a fully recognized alter ego, or an equal. Whenever a meeting is planned between the Indians and their visitors, men are exchanged as a pledge to guarantee the safe return of their fellow countrymen. The same equation always applies, with one Englishman standing for two natives. In Mogador already, two Moors had come onboard while one Englishman had been left on land as a pledge of their return. Non-Europeans, however, do not uniformly arouse the same benevolence as that induced by the Indians. The Moors encountered along the northern coast of Africa are descried for their inhuman manners: 'in eating ... their manner was not only uncivil and unsightly to us, but even inhumane and loathsome in itself'.[30] Not only are the Moors presented as different, but the balanced syntax which yet seems to posit cultural relativism and anthropological neutrality ('uncivil and unsightly *to us*') fails to produce anything but a fundamentally alien category ('inhumane and loathsome *in itself*'). No attempt is made here to look at the Other with an unbiased eye, unaffected by cultural or moral prejudice. The discrepancy between the white man's benevolent discourse on Native Americans and his scornful indifference to the Moors therefore alerts us to the nature of Drake's ideological posture: it is easier and more profitable to be the champion of human rights where lands are still waiting to be claimed, rather than in the Old World where the domination of the Spanish and Portuguese is already complete.

Having redefined both the Indians as victimized alter egos and themselves as benevolent saviours, the English travellers seek to promote further encounters in the hope of developing trade. Communication between the explorers and the natives always proceeds along the same three successive steps. The two parties first establish contact by exchanging visual or oral signs, as on Mogador Island, when Moors 'by signs and cries made show that they desired to be fetched aboard'.[31] Once contact has been made, objects are exchanged. The third stage is that of verbal communication. Each step presents its own difficulties, but contrary to all expectations, it is the third and final stage, that of conversation, which proves to be the easiest mode of interaction.

The sign language Europeans and American Indians develop is quite elaborate. Some signs can have ambivalent or even opposed meanings. For instance, a fire can be a worrying sign, a 'sacrifice to devills', designed to wreak havoc among the English fleet when they are lit by Indians along the coast of Brazil;[32] or it can be just the opposite, a friendly beacon, for instance when, a month later, Drake goes ashore and lights fires in the hope of retrieving his missing ships, the *Christopher* and the *Marigold*.[33] The encounter which takes place with an Indian South of Valparaiso attests to the complexity of this language: 'we showed him, partly by signs, and partly by such things as we had, what things we needed, and would gladly received by his meanes, upon exchange of such things as he would desire'.[34] Sign language includes mime and the presentation of objects which make up for words (a glass or a bottle may easily translate as 'water' for instance). But we reach here a further degree of subtlety, as objects do not necessarily stand for themselves, but for their opposites: 'by such things as we had, what things we needed'. This first stage segues into a courteous conversation which curiously seems to be unhampered by linguistic difficulty: 'So he offered himself to be our pilot to a place ... where, by way of traffic, we might have at pleasure, both water, and those other things which we stood in need of. This offer our general very gladly received'.[35]

The English explorers seem to be fluent in sign language on both sides of the Atlantic, communicating with Moors or Indians alike. In their first encounter with non-Europeans, on Mogador Island, the English already show a remarkable command of this new language:

> They that came aboard were right courteously entertained, with a daintie banquet, and such gifts as they seemed to be most glad of, that they might thereby understand that his fleete came in peace and friendship ... This offer they seemed most gladly to accept, and promised, the next day, to resort again, with such things as they had to exchange for ours.[36]

Once on board, the exchange includes gifts, then mime (the verb 'seem' shows their guests reacting with signs of contentment, or joy), and ends with the promise to return the next day. Though here again we may imagine the Moors resorting to sign language to express their solemn arrangement (possibly with their hands on their hearts, or respectfully bowing with clasped hands?), the very notion of 'promise' – a performative utterance that cannot exist outside language – signals a shift to verbal communication. What the text fails to mention, however, is that a man who 'had attained to some use of the tongue' was also present on board, a detail which is recorded by Francis Fletcher, chaplain to the expedition, in his diary.[37] The presence of the translator explains how some elementary conversation could complement the sign language and pantomime. By keeping silent about the presence of such a mediator, *The World Encompassed* gives the impression that the English and the Moors communicate in a natural and universal language; that they have the ability to understand one another beyond the language barrier, no longer miming but simply trusting the rhetoric of the body – gestures or voice inflections. Assuming that foreign words can almost naturally be turned into transparent signifiers, the narrative thus entertains the illusion that the discovery expedition is also a journey back in time, transporting Europeans into a 'wonderful', prelapsarian world, as if the curse of Babel could indeed be removed.

The skirmish that follows this favourable first encounter confirms this interpretation. Though the two parties have agreed to meet the next day to exchange more commodities, the second meeting turns out to be an ambush in which an Englishman, one John Fry, is captured. Fletcher interestingly notes here that Fry happens to be the apprentice translator. Fletcher does not, however, conclude that Fry is kidnapped because of his economic value, but rather that his linguistic skills directly explain his rash behaviour: Fry 'had attained to some use of the tongue (and therefore the bolder) did suddenly but unadvisedly leap out of the boat onshore'.[38] In Fletcher's account, linguistic translation is more of a liability, exposing men rather than helping them to communicate; bilingual literacy only impedes the *natural* communication which can exist between the Europeans and the natives. On Mucho Island, Drake's first stop after sailing through the Strait of Magellan, the English fall into another ambush because of a single word. After agreeing to supply them with fresh water, the islanders suddenly turn against the visitors:

> The cause of this force and injurie by these Ilanders, was no other but the deadly hatred which they beare against their cruell enemies the Spaniards … And therefore … (suspecting us to bee Spaniards indeed, and that the rather, by occasion that though command was given to the contrary, some of our men in demanding water, used the Spanish word Aqua) sought some part of revenge against us.[39]

In Drake's narrative, Spanish words are for the English as many traps laid by their enemies, like the name given to the Pacific ocean, 'called by some *Mare pacificum*, but proving to us rather to be *Mare furiosum*'.[40] The name chosen by Magellan seems to be specifically designed to deceive the English navigators, as the three ships which make it through the Strait are carried off course by contrary winds and tempests for several weeks. This, and the incident on Mucho Island, only confirm the travellers' distrust of words when they cease to be the transparent signifiers of some kind of natural language. Linguistic bilingualism is clearly not a prerequisite to communicate with the natives of the New World.

The climactic episode of Nova Albion reveals then the full potential of this pre-Babel, both natural and 'wonderful' language. The navigators stop on the West American coast – somewhere in the San Francisco area –[41] to trim their ships after an unsuccessful attempt to find the Northwest passage (they probably sailed as far north as the area that would become the United States–Canadian border). They befriend the local tribe, and this is where their dumb shows prove the most effective. For after a month of regular encounters, the Indians eventually relinquish all their rights to their land, and willingly offer their kingdom to Francis Drake, whom they greet as their new king.

The first encounter gets off to a very good start. An Indian emissary is sent to welcome the visitors, delivering three successive orations, which though 'long and tedious', are the prelude to an offering of a feather headdress.[42] The text insists on the feeling of wonder experienced by the Indians when they first see the English, 'wondring at [them] as at Gods', 'as men ravished in their mindes'[43] – though no precise description is given to substantiate this assertion. The god-like nature of the Europeans, a commonplace in travel accounts of the Americas since Columbus, Vespucci and later Cortés, is presented as a delusion, but the travellers, who at first are intent on freeing their Indian hosts from such a misconception, gradually seem to fully endorse their new identity, as is suggested by the subtle shift of meaning of the preposition 'as'. Used first to draw a comparison, 'as' eventually indicates capacity and identity: 'their errand being rather with submission and feare to worship us as gods'.[44]

During the third encounter, the Indians set up a strange ceremony in which the men, after another 'long and tedious oration', come to their visitors loaded with presents, while their women tear their flesh, cry and shriek 'in a monstrous manner'.[45] To put an end to what they think is a bloody sacrifice, Drake and his men respond with a religious ceremony of their own:

> This bloudie sacrifice (against our wils) beeing thus performed, our Generall with his companie in the presence of those strangers fell to prayers and by signes in lifting up our eyes and hands to heaven, signified unto them, that that God whom we did serve, and whom they ought to worship, was above.[46]

The mechanical gesticulation is followed by the reading of chapters from the Bible and the singing of psalms, which are reverently listened to by the Indian audience:

> In the time of which prayers, singing of Psalmes ... they sate very attentively: and observing the end at every pause, with one voice still cryed, Oh, greatly rejoycing in our exercises.[47]

In this strange pantomime, Christian devotion becomes a dumb show in which religious fervour is replaced by outward signs, meant to engage the attention of the Indians and divert them from their own practice. The new performance combines Indian and Christian rituals, as is the case with the exclamation 'Oh', earlier described as a common Indian response during their leaders' orations. The Indians also use the word '*Gnaàh*, by which they entreated that we should sing.'[48] This improvised spectacle shows not only the Englishman's capacity for 'empathy', so typical according to Greenblatt of the Renaissance Western explorer, using improvisation and 'psychic mobility' as a tool of colonial power,[49] but also Drake's ability to rewrite the other's ritual into his own scenario, predicated on the assumption of the possibility of immediate, transparent communication, unimpaired by linguistic difference.

The success of this pantomime leads to a second ceremony, held within a week of the sailors' arrival. The natives again deliver several long orations before renouncing their land:

> the king and divers others made severall orations, or rather indeed if wee had understood them, supplications, that [our General] would take the Province and kingdome into his hand, and become their king and patron: making signes that they would resigne unto him their right and title in the whole land, and become his vassals in themselves and their posterities: Which that they might make us indeed beleeve that it was their true meaning and intent; the king himselfe ... set the crown upon his head ... These things being so freely offered, our Generall thought not meet to reject or refuse the same ... for that he knew not to what good end God had brought this to passe, or what honour and profit it might bring to our countrie in time to come.[50]

The phrase 'if wee had understood them' temporarily exposes the false play of the English dumb show: the hypothetical proposition unveils the linguistic incomprehension on both parts, while simultaneously transcending it since the sentence claims that linguistic competence is not needed, as the English fully comprehend the *intentions* of the Indians, and the crown set on Drake's head comes only as a confirmation of the ritual. A combination of sign language and verbal communication based on the rhetoric of the body, the 'natural' language devised in the New World thus produces a colonial discourse of wonder: the Indians are represented as freely resigning their lands, their selves and their history to the representatives of the English sovereign's nascent Empire – a scene reminiscent of Miranda's acceptance of the false play of her sweet lord: 'Yes, for a score of kingdoms you should wrangle,/ And I would call it, fair play'.[51] Like Columbus before them, the English therefore take possession of Nova Albion thanks to a linguistic performance.[52]

A plaque is then erected to commemorate the transfer of authority, described as 'a plate of brass, fast nailed to a great and firme post', which presents the Queen's portrait to her new subjects thanks to an English six-pence coin.[53] To the English, the coin is to be taken literally, as the concrete sign of the commercial transaction, and it also functions as an assurance to future explorers that good bargains are there for the taking. Its meaning is also metaphorical, as it ceases to bear any monetary value to become the visual symbol of the distant political power it represents. Drake's use of the Queen's head, a simple representation of an absent reality endowed with quasi-magical powers, is emblematic of the 'theatre of wonder' which travel narratives gradually generated, giving priority to the body to produce the emotional and intellectual experience of wonder, at the expense of the natural wonders of the world.[54] The six-pence coin, as a metaphorical and visual sign, but also as a literal joke which is lost on the Indians, thus clearly shows that the discursive economy of wonder is based on dumb show and false play. But false play is not only at the expense of the American Indians. No colonization project ensued, as the attempts at founding an American colony were soon to focus on the eastern coast of North America. And the plaque itself was never found, an absence casting serious doubt as to the reality of the whole episode. The dumb shows produced by the first encounters between the American natives and the English travellers thus reveal the complexity of interaction between the travellers themselves and their fellow countrymen at home.

One should indeed guard against seeing the dumb show strategy as a one-sided fooling of the native population: English culture was then marked by fears and misgivings, as much as by confidence, and all parties in these dramas were uncertain about the outcome of such relationships.[55] As the visitors' stay draws to a close, a final dumb show is organized: the Indians begin with their usual sacrifices, lighting fires, tormenting themselves, and Drake's men, eager to stop this heathen practice, respond again with their own Christian pantomime. This time, the Indians follow suit and start replicating the Englishmen's behaviour through a curious play of mimicry: 'suffering the fire to go out, and imitating us in all our actions; they fell alifting up their eyes and hands to heaven as they saw us do'.[56] The show of course delights the white man. But on the day of the English crew's departure, the Indians take their farewell by lighting fires all along the coast. *The World Encompassed* does not linger on the episode to determine whether their mimicry had been false or fair play.

4 'WATERALI' GOES NATIVE: DESCRIBING FIRST ENCOUNTERS IN SIR WALTER RALEGH'S *THE DISCOVERY OF GUIANA* (1596)

Line Cottegnies

In a letter to his wife dated 14 November 1617 and written from the Cayenne river on his second ill-fated voyage of exploration in Guiana, Sir Walter Ralegh writes: 'To tell you that I might be here King of the *Indians* were a vanitie; but my name hath still lived among them; here they feed me with fresh meat, and all that Countrey yields, all offer to obey me'.[1] This was not a lie. In fact, travellers report that both the words 'Waterali' and 'Gualtero' are attested in the seventeenth century in local Amazonian dialects as honorific titles, enduring well into the eighteenth century.[2] This extraordinary fact reveals the impact Ralegh made on political consciouness and oral traditions as early as his first 1595 expedition, and how, while he was dealing with what Lévi-Strauss would call 'cold cultures' – i.e. societies which do not possess a written culture – his own memory (or a shadow of it) was preserved through oral transmission. One of the purposes of this paper is to try and assess the significance of this incorporation of Ralegh's name into local cultures, even though his exploration failed to advance the English presence in Guiana. In 1595, Ralegh promised the Indians he would be back with an army to free them from the Spaniards, but he had to delay his expedition until 1617, where divisions among the Indians and new skirmishes between the English and the Spaniards caused his men to set fire to a Spanish town – in direct contradiction with James I's instructions. In the process, he lost his son Wat, and his trusted friend and captain Lawrence Keymis committed suicide. He sailed back to England only to be sent to the scaffold.

In his edition of the 1596 *Discovery of the Large, Rich, and Bewtiful Empyre of Guiana*, Neil Whitehead describes the narrative as an 'enchanted text', whose magic appeal derives from its unique 'blending of the factual and fictitious',[3] which might account for the enduring attention it has received over the years. Informed by the topoi and myths elaborated through the 'fantastic ethnography' of classical and modern authorities,[4] *The Discovery of Guiana* also reflects

Ralegh's precise knowledge of previous travellers' accounts, mostly Spanish, which he lists at the end of his own text. Neil Whitehead confirms how carefully Ralegh's ethnology is informed by his predecessors' narratives. But he also reads the text as 'proto-ethnography', because more than is usually the case in these documents, it tells us about Ralegh's empirical quest for a real dialogical encounter with local indigenous cultures and practices; in Whitehead's words, it 'strongly registers native culture'.[5] This is manifest, for instance, in the place and status he grants the indigenes of Orinoco and their own discourse in the text, recording his various interviews with them, which leads to the hybridization of colonial discourse that Young describes in *Colonial Desire*.[6] What Ralegh's narrative eventually reveals is, in Whitehead's words, the 'symbiotic nature of cultural construction and the two-way, mutual character of cultural transmission, even from colonized to colonizer'.[7] This essay will focus on Ralegh's encounters with natives in their linguistic aspects, to show that while they are fraught with ideological and ethical anxieties, they also manifest a genuine desire to communicate with the Other, with all the 'miscommunication' this implies.[8] As will be apparent, these encounters result in a kind of mutual 'colonial mimicry',[9] whereby the colonial discourse accommodates (and is accommodated by) indigenous languages and practices.

Intriguingly Ralegh consistently configures his meetings with the Indians as 'first' encounters with unspoilt natives – irrespective of the fact that the whole area had been in contact with the Spaniards for close to a century. This is more, it seems to me, than just a political stance aiming at somehow making up for the English absence in the area until then. It can be interpreted instead as a desire to symbolically recast these encounters as virgin of all previous associations, at a time when the Spanish settlement was meeting with increasing opposition among the local tribes. Ralegh's text is in fact motivated entirely by its wish to undo and unwrite the Spaniards' previous 'discoveries'. The narrative is striking, for instance, for its permeability to and accommodation of vernacular toponyms and patronyms. In direct opposition to the Spaniards who usually renamed places and cities, baptized the Indians they befriended or employed, and gave them Christian, Spanish-sounding names, Ralegh tries to record the local names and toponyms, transcribing them phonetically. He does not take up Captain Keymis's suggestion to rename the Orinoco River *Raleana*, after his own name,[10] for instance. Through this, he shrewdly acknowledges the anteriority of the natives' presence on the land, but also avoids using Spanish names altogether, thus occulting their having taken possession of the country. Throughout the text, Ralegh defines his conduct as systematically contrasting with the Spaniards'. For instance, like Drake before him, he insists on the Spanish cruelty to the natives, and pits it against the 'temperance' and 'respect' with which he and his crew treat them. His attitude to naming places and people is part of the same strategy. Michel de Certeau, commenting on Theodor Galle's engraving representing Vespucci and America, after the famous drawing by Jan van der Straet, writes: 'what is initiated here is a colonization of the body by the discourse of power. That is *writing that conquers*'.[11] Stephen Greenblatt has described how, for Columbus, 'taking possession is principally the performance of a set of linguistic acts: declaring, witnessing, recording. The acts are public and official'.[12] But it is the Spanish conquest at large that was carried out through a series of pragmatic, illocutionary procedures: the drafting of records, acts, deeds and precise maps, and then through massive campaigns of evangelization and schooling – including the teaching of the Spanish language. By recording native names in his text and drafting a map that includes Indian toponyms,[13] Ralegh, who presents himself to the Indians as an official ambassador from the Queen, establishes a unique colonial bond between England and the tribes he meets, as he offers himself both as a liberator from the Spanish yoke and as a reporter-cum-transcriber of their reality. This he thought possible because of the identity of his translator and interpreter, an Indian whom he had brought from England, and with whom he seems to have established a close enough relationship that he felt communication with the natives could be transparent. Ralegh seems in fact to have developed strong friendships with several natives. It is perhaps not wholly surprising that he should have later been followed in the Tower by two Indian servants, named Ragapo and Harry, who, as tradition has it, seconded him in the kinds of 'chemistry experiments' that his contemporaries viewed with much suspicion – and which might have had something to do with coca.[14] In a typical passage of his 1596 narrative where he details the brutal treatment of natives in the hands of the Spaniards, Ralegh even presents himself as a hero of the Indian cause, telling the reader how he delivered five 'caciques' – a local word which he appropriates and uses very freely in his text – whom he says 'are called in their own language *Acarewana*' – an actual Carib word for 'King'; and he adds: 'now of late since English, French, & Spanish are come among them, they cal [sic] themselves *Capitaynes*, because they perceive that the chiefest of every ship is called by that name'.[15] This is a wonderful example of the reciprocal hybridization of discourse (or two-way mimicry) in the kind of colonial, dis-cursive context Whitehead and Young describe: Ralegh appropriates an Indian word, '*Cacique*', but he simultaneously gives us what turns out in fact to be an accurate transcription of a local title, attested by other sources. Meanwhile, the locals, inspired by the naval hierarchy of their invaders, reciprocally appropriate a European title ('*Capitaynes*'), which they see as equivalent to theirs, although it is not clear if the word was used phonetically by the Indians or if this refers to the way the Europeans came to call the indigenous lords. This two-way process, I would like to claim, applies to most of the situations described by Ralegh, as his text focuses on mimetic, or what I call '*transitive*', exchanges.

Ralegh consistently offers a phonetic transcription of his interlocutors'
indigenous names, and this is an equivalent, in many respects, to cartography: it
is not simply an 'effet de réel' to guarantee the veracity of his narrative in the eye
of a disbelieving English reader. It is a means of drafting a living picture of the
country at a given moment, fixing the forces present on the spot in the perspective of a further implanting of the English, since Ralegh is hoping at that stage
for a prompt return – hence the stress on the garnering of information from all
quarters:

> [O]f al these I got som knowledge, & of manie more, partly by mine own travel, &
> the rest by conference: of som one I lerned one, of others the rest, having with me
> an Indian that spake many languages, & that of *Guiana* naturally. I sought out al the
> aged men, & such as were greatest travelers. And by the one & the other I came to
> understand the situations, the rivers, the kingdoms from the east sea to the borders of
> *Peru*, & from *Orenoque* southward as far as *Amazones* or *Maragnon*, and the regions
> of *Maria Tamball*, and of all the kings of Provinces, and captains of townes and vil-
> lages, how they stood in tearms of peace or war, and which were friends or enimies
> the one with the other, without which there can be neither entrance nor conquest in
> those parts, nor els where . . .[16]

This explains for instance why he transcribes the names of the captive Indian
chiefs in full, as well as many other Indians' names: 'Those five *Capitaynes* in
the chaine were called *Wannawanare, Carroarori, Maquarima, Tarroopanama,
& Aterima*'.[17] The litany of names again serves to emphasize the contrast with the
Spaniards who are shown, on the contrary, to be set on obliterating the memory
of the indigenous past by killing the elderly leaders, burning out villages, deport-
ing the population and renaming young captives. We know they also burned
many age-old Indian codeces throughout South America, in order to force the
population to learn Spanish. In this context, Ralegh's inclusion of native names
could be read as a diplomatic act of recording the history of the vulnerable societies he was planning to save and rule.

A similar strategy of mimicry is used by Ralegh when he impresses the Indians with the greatness of his Queen, describing her as 'the great *Casique* of the
north, and a virgin, and had more *Caciqui* under her then there were trees in
their Iland ... an enemy of the *Castellani* in respect of their tyrannie and oppres-
sion'.[18] This the indigenes translate in their turn – and Ralegh's attempt at
transcribing this Indian version of Elizabeth's title is extraordinary – as '*Ezrabeta
Cassipuna Aquerewana*, which is as much as *Elizabeth*, the great princesse or
greatest commaunder'.[19] This instance shows Ralegh's talent (or his interpreter's,
or both) at making himself mimetically comprehensible by the natives; but it
also demonstrates, I think, how conscious Ralegh was of the symbolic import
of name assimilation. The assimilation of his own name in a phonetic neologism

('Waterali'), although not mentioned in his own text, can be seen as part of the same strategy of 'attuning' English names to Indian ears.

The 'assimilation' process always goes both ways with Ralegh, and he in turn records in his narrative the stories of various Indian chiefs with whom he has established a special relationship, above all the old Topiawari whom he meets twice during this trip. This in turn allows him to record the alleged 'surrender' of the Indians to the English. The scene of the first encounter with Topiawari is powerfully illustrated by a plate Theodore de Bry inserted in his 1599 *Americae pars VIII,* a volume which includes an abridged Latin version of Ralegh's text adorned with seven plates.[20] The image, reproduced in Whitehead's edition,[21] illustrates the scene of Ralegh's reception of the chief under his own tent – a scene reminiscent of other diplomatic encounters, such as the famous meeting between Henry VIII and Francis I at the Field of the Cloth of Gold in 1520:

> we arrived at the port of *Morequito,* and ankored there, sending away one of our Pilots to seeke the king of *Aromaia,* uncle to *Morequito,* slaine by *Berreo* as aforesaide. The next day following, before noone he came to us on foote from his house, which was 14 English miles, (himself being a 110. yeers old) & returned on foote the same daie, & with him many of the borderers, with many women & children, that came to woonder at our nation, and to bring us down victuall, which they did in great plenty, as venison, porke, hens, chickens, foule, fish, with divers sorts of excellent fruits and rootes, & great abundance of *Pinas,* the princesse of fruits, that grow under the *Sun,* especially those of *Guiana.* ... After this old king had rested a while in a little tent, that I caused to be set up, I began by my interpretor to discourse with him of the death of *Morequito* his predecessor, and afterward of the Spaniards ...[22]

The illustration captures a wonderfully equivocal moment, which I would like to describe as expressing the transitivity of exchange that I have been pointing out: Ralegh, with his baton of commander, is obviously entertaining the chief in a courtly fashion, treating him as a foreign head of state by having him sit 'in state' next to him, under the canopy. The fact that they should be sitting on a stool and facing the audience is itself an European posture of power – the illustrator was obviously a very astute reader of Ralegh's. But the scene becomes visually reversible, as the Chief is shown pointing out the offerings brought by his people, subtly inverting the perspective: the performance of hospitality is obviously Indian, and he seems to be entertaining the English, who are clearly shown as the recipients of *his* gifts. We can contrast the huddled English men – some, curiously, with Spanish helmets, probably spoils of war –, with their hands on their swords (strutting perhaps, or looking slightly nervous), and the group of confident, pacific natives with their arms full of gifts of food. The ambivalence of the moment is also captured by the unspecificity of the witnesses' physical traits, as some of the natives are made to look very European, as is obvious, for instance, in the women's headstyles. We can further note the similarities between the elaborate design of Ralegh's costume and the chief's feathers, and the intimacy with which Ralegh's arm and baton seem almost to rest on his neighbour's arm: the picture perfectly illustrates the special relationship that Ralegh claims to have established with Topiawari. The background vignette illustrates another scene, however: the farewell scene between Ralegh (recognizable thanks to his sword), who is leaving for England again with the chief's son, as will be seen later. What is striking in this vignette is the absence of Ralegh's soldiers: the scene concentrates instead on the singular relationship between Ralegh and the Indians, who are here featured as an ordered army, albeit with 'native' weapons: this is meant to illustrate the military alliance Ralegh claimed he had achieved with Topiawari against the Spaniards.

The mature Ralegh obviously warmed to the old chief: at one point in his text he transcribes a long narrative of Topiawari's – a unique moment which the anthropologist Neil Whitehead reads as an intense ethnographical transcript of an actual conversation. In this passage, Ralegh interprets the Indian's tale as a historical narrative alluding to the invasion of the regions by Inca warriors in the previous century, while Whitehead has in fact recently deciphered it as a mytho-poetic creation tale about the conflict between the spirits of water and of rain.[23] However, the place and status granted Topiawari and his speech in Ralegh's text is striking, all the more so as it ends with the Englishman's expression of his admiration for the old man:

> This Topiawari is held for the proudest, and wisest of all the *Orenoqueponi*, and so he behaved himselfe towards me in all his answers at my returne, as I marvelled to finde a man of that gravity and judgement, and of so good discourse, that had no helpe of learning nor breed.[24]

A few pages later, he includes another long interview with Topiawari, in indirect speech, which ends on a striking moment of immediacy when Ralegh is caught literally transcribing the Chief's own words in direct speech in the first person – in a process of ventriloquization:

> [A]nd because said hee, they [the Spaniards] woulde the better displant me, if they cannot lay handes on mee, they have gotten a Nephew of mine called *Eparacano*, whome they have christened *Don Juan*, and his sonne *Don Pedro*, whome they have also apparrelled and armed, by whome they seeke to make a partie against mee in mine owne countrey ...[25]

This second interview ends with a solemn alliance, and Ralegh's promise to come back a year later with an army; it is then followed by a deeply symbolic exchange:

> [H]e freely gave me his onelie sonne to take with me into England ... and I left with him one *Frauncis Sparrow*; a servant of captaine *Gifford*, (who was desirous to tarry,

and coulde describe a cuntrey with his pen) and a boy of mine called *Hugh Goodwin*, to learne the language.[26]

Ralegh thus returned to England with the Chief's son Cayoworaco, and, if we are to believe Whitehead, with the two servant boys who would later spend some time with him in the Tower.[27] Once again, the difference between the Spaniards' strategy of forced assimilation (implied in the renaming of the Chief's nephew and his son) and Ralegh's assimilation of Indian names is striking. As was reported later, Francis Sparry (not 'Sparrow') was quickly captured by the Spaniards and Goodwin was attacked by four jaguars in the jungle – an episode which Whitehead explains anthropologically as having to do with a ritual killing; as far as the three Indians were concerned, they seem to have eventually found their way back to Guiana.[28] The extraordinary moment of the 'exchange of sons' ('a boy of mine') is probably one of the most emblematic instances of the mimetic structure of exchange that I have underlined in the text. It also, incidentally, testifies to Ralegh's deep understanding of the value of exchange in native societies, which has since then been amply documented by Marcel Mauss. In *The Gift*, Mauss showed how giving and exchanging were the basis of many primitive societies, and that the practice of exchanging was governed by a series of obligations that could be considered as the basis for a moral system. Interestingly, in the various rituals of exchange to which Ralegh partakes, he shows an acute awareness of these native obligations. This might be accounted for by the fact that Ralegh had perhaps carefully read his predecessors' accounts, or that his translator was a good go-between, or because the economy of the gift in an aristocratic society was not so dissimilar. However, these obligations are: the obligation to receive gifts (which shows respect to the giver) and the obligation to give, and even to return gifts – which establishes the giver or the recipient of the gift as an honorable person, deserving respect. Most of the contacts with Indians ritually begin with gifts of food, which are highly symbolic of power, particularly when the country in unknown by one of the parties; but Ralegh is constantly shown to reciprocate, and he even knows to anticipate by giving first. At one point, he comes across a group of Arwacan natives, allies of the Spaniards, who are terrified by the English because they have been told that they are cannibals.[29] Shrewdly, Ralegh gives them food and trinkets without demanding anything in return, which results in their defecting to the English. The anecdote points to a fascinating reversibility here: by participating in the local economy of giving, Ralegh enters into dialogue with native culture; but it is also clear that his strategy is not devoid of self-interested calculation, and the gifts of trinkets themselves reflect common colonial practices. With Topiawari, the practice of exchange even takes on the competitive and strategic aspect that Mauss describes and that finds its most extreme variant in the Potlatch – a north-west coast Native American form of competitive exchange that eventually leads to the destruction of costly gifts. In fact, Ralegh finds himself caught up in a spiral of conspicuous consumption, and he clearly ends up giving more than he receives:

> For I did not in any sort make my desire of golde knowen, because I had neyther time, nor power to have a greater quantitie. I gave among them manye more peeces of Golde then I receaved of the new money of 20. shillings with her Majesties picture to weare, with promise that they would become her servants thenceforth.[30]

In a society whose economy is based on exchange, coins become fetish-like gold medals, precious because they are rare gifts, while remaining instruments of colonial domination that allow the Queen's portrait to be displayed and passed around. Interestingly, Ralegh expresses here the ambivalence of his colonial motivations, by contrasting his strategy of giving with the strategic dissimulation of his desire for gold. In his approach to the natives he appears constantly torn between mimetic sympathy and his colonial quest, the object of which is the gold of the Indians, a pursuit he is aware of sharing with the Spaniards: 'we came both for one errant'.[31] Nevertheless, his clever mimetic participation in the gift culture, which ultimately leads to the symbolic exchange of sons – and which his own son's death will tragically echo twenty years later – can explain why his memory could live on, years after he had left.

At the very end of his narrative, Ralegh reports an Inca prophecy which he has heard from his Spanish counterpart (and nemesis), the governor of Trinidad, Antonio Berrio. This prophecy heralds the restoration of Inca rule and the final victory of the English over the Spaniards in South America:

> And I farther remember that *Berreo* confessed to me and others (which I protest before the Majesty of God to be true) that there was found among prophecies in *Peru* (at such time as the Empyre was reduced to the Spanish obedience) in their chiefest temples, amongst divers others which foreshewed the losse of the said Empyre, that from *Inglatierra* those *Ingas* shoulde be againe in time to come restored, and delivered from the servitude of the said Conquerors.[32]

This 'Peruvian' prophecy seems to come to Ralegh as a sudden afterthought ('I *farther* remember'), after he has already expanded his vision of an English empire rivalling the Spanish one. It very aptly serves his final plea for a full-scale English colonization of Guiana:

> The countrey is alreadie discovered, many nations won to her Majesties love & obedience, & those Spanyards which have latest and longest labored about the conquest, beaten out, discouraged and disgraced, which amonge these nations were thought invincible.[33]

By having his worst enemy report the prophecy, and by having him do so in public ('Berreo confessed to me and others'), Ralegh hopes to convince his readers, and foremost among them, Queen Elizabeth, to support further expeditions and settlements. But Ralegh's anxiety about the extraordinarily apt status of the prophecy to bolster his case is clearly perceptible in his additional resort to a solemn asseveration: 'which I protest before the Majesty of God to be true'. It could be argued that the Knight protests too much. The source of this 'prophecy' is unclear; it is most likely that Ralegh made it up. It does not feature in any of the histories of the Incas of the period. A prophecy that did feature in these histories, however, is another, more famous one, which Ralegh alludes to here: the supposedly age-old prophecy that foretold the fall of the Inca empire and was interpreted retrospectively as announcing, and justifying, the arrival of the Spaniards. In his popular 1607 history of the Incas, *Comentarios reales de los Incas,* the Inca-born Spanish writer Garcilaso de la Vega interviews an old chief about the fatalism of Inca leaders in the face of the Conquistadors: if the Incas relinquished all their power so easily to a handful of Spaniards, he is told, it is because of an old prophecy according to which 'at a certain period of Years after the succession of such a number of Kings, there should come a sort of people from far remote Countries, never seen, or known before in those Regions, who should take away their Religion and subvert their Empire'.[34] Garcilaso de la Vega shows how this prophecy, supposedly transmitted from generation to generation, was taken to be fulfilled by the coming of the Spaniards. It was even alleged to have caused one of the last Inca Kings, Huaynac Capac, to legate his Kingdom to the Spaniards.[35] If the actual existence of the prophecy before the arrival of the Spaniards is dubious – although these kinds of prophecies were widespread in highly ritualized societies and oral cultures as ways of making sense of history – it is interesting here to see just how a political prophecy was put to use both to comprehend an overwhelming experience and justify the present political situation.

To the best of my knowledge, Ralegh's 1596 narrative is the earliest text to record a 'prophecy' that establishes a link between the future of the Incas and the English. It is obviously modelled on the better-known prophecy justifying the Spanish rule. The irony of this extraordinary textual moment is that it did take up a life of its own, with a little help from native leaders. As early as 1597, a Dutch expedition is told that an oracular fire-spirit, Wattopa, spoke to a 'captain' of Caribs who was about to be hanged by the Spaniards and foretold 'deliverance through the Dutch and English'.[36] The 'prophecy' is attested again in the eighteenth century, as in the preface to the second, 1723 edition of de la Vega's *Comentarios reales* published in Lima, which was censored by the colonial authorities as seditious.[37] A a matter of fact, the eighteenth-century editor of de la Vega's text – Andrés Gonzalez de Barcia Carballido y Zuniga – quotes Ralegh as his source, in the Latin version of the text that was published in 1599 by Theodore de Bry in his collection of voyages.[38] It is this Latin version of Ralegh's text

that circulated widely in the seventeenth and eighteenth centuries rather than
the English one. In the eighteenth century, in fact, the prophecy was used by the
Inca revolutionary movement as part of a campaign to organize resistance to the
Spaniards.[39] As such, it contributed to the gradual emancipation of Southern
America from the Spanish yoke and it facilitated the return of the English in the
region. In 1769, the explorer Edmund Bancroft tells us in his *Essay on the Natural History of Guiana in South America* that almost two centuries after Ralegh's
first trip, the natives of the region still retain the memory of his promise that
from England would come an army that would free them from the Spaniards:

> they retain a tradition of an English chief, who many years since landed amongst
> them and encouraged them to persevere in enmity of the Spaniards, promising to
> return and settle amongst them, and afford them assistance: and it is said that they
> still preserve an English Jack, which he left them, that they might distinguish his
> countrymen.[40]

This anecdote wonderfully illustrates how Ralegh's 'prophecy', tailored for an
oral tradition on the model of pre-existing similar prophetic utterances, can be
read as emblematic of the two-way 'assimilation', or mimeticism, that is characteristic of Ralegh's colonial encounters. His stroke of genius, as a master
myth-maker, was to author the prophetic statement *in print* for the benefit of
future ages – de Bry's and Hakluyt's extraordinarily successful collections of travels were of course instrumental in publicizing it beyond its immediate English
readership.[41] Finally, one can perhaps point out that Ralegh was himself a poet,
with a keen ear for sound effects, and this it is obvious in his attempt to link the
destiny of the Incas (or 'Ingas') with that of the inhabitants of 'Inglatierra'. The
quasi homophony between 'Ingatierra' and 'Inglatierra' (with a one-letter *dif-
férance*) obviously played a part in his forging the prophecy, as well, perhaps, as in
its extraordinary subsequent fortune. This also illustrates, incidentally, another
form of hybridization, ironic this time, with the language of the Spanish enemy,
which is used here to undermine their own power.

What *The Discovery of Guiana* reveals, ultimately, is the mutual entanglement of languages and practices in colonial milieu, which I have described as a
mimetic, transitive exchange. One illustrious reader at least was not convinced.
When Ralegh was sent to the Tower by King James on his return from his second
trip, he kept with him a list of items that can finally be interpreted as metonymic
tokens of his engagement with an idealized form of 'Indian-ness' with which he
had become deeply fascinated: 'a 'Stob' of gold, a Guiana idol of gold, a 'plott'
of the river Orinoco',[42] not to mention his beloved pipe. With these items as
talismanic emblems of his symbolic possession of Guiana, 'Waterali' could still
imagine himself as 'King of the Indians'. It is to be wondered if Ralegh ever owned
the kind of pipe that became known in England and Holland around the mid-

seventeenth century as a 'Sir Walter Ralegh pipe', because it bore a human head vaguely reminiscent of Ralegh's on the bowl (seemingly watched by an open-mouthed crocodile, carved on the stem). Such pipes were made both in Holland and in England and seemed to have been very popular around the middle of the century.[43] These pipes represent to me perfectly hybrid, 'entangled objects', to use Whitehead's phrase;[44] and as such they perfectly exemplify the mutual 'colonial mimicry' at work in the encounters described above: the characteristic shape of the clay Dutch and English pipe, subverted by native decorative motifs – in the present case a stylized crocodile – makes for a totally hybrid object, half-way between the two cultures. There is no better emblem for the unique ambivalence of *Waterali* in *A Discovery of Guiana*.

5 DOMESTICATION AND RECOGNITION OF THE OTHER IN JOHN LAWSON'S *A NEW VOYAGE TO CAROLINA* (1709)

Robert Sayre

In this essay I will discuss the encounter experience of the English colonizer John Lawson with North American Indians, as textualized in *A New Voyage to Carolina*, published in London in 1709. I will attempt to show how this narrative of encounter pictures a highly 'unstable zone', one in which, in the representation of the confrontation of Self and Other we see deployed first and foremost many patterns of domestication of the Other. But at the same time a process of destabilization of the comfortable certainties thereby established comes into play, leading ultimately to some real recognition of the specificity and value of the Other, albeit partial and contradictory.

Next to nothing is known for sure about Lawson before his arrival in Carolina in 1700. His birth date has not been established with certainty, though there is some indication it may have been 1674. The main problem confronted by biographers insofar as his English period is concerned, is the commonness of both his first and last names in England at the time. He probably came from a well-to-do family (though nothing designates it as a noble one), and he seems to have received a university education. Concerning his reasons for going to America, Lawson explains in the introduction to his book that, desiring to travel he spoke with a man 'who was very well acquainted with the Ways of Living in both Indies; of whom, having made Enquiry concerning them, he assur'd me, that *Carolina* was the best country I could go to'.[1] Lawson soon thereafter shipped out from London, and arrived in Charles Town (Charleston, SC) after a stopover in New York. He spent several months there, and then set out on an expedition to explore the interior of the country, in regions little known to the English at the time. He may have been commissioned to undertake this trip by the governors of the province, or by an English collector of botanical specimens whom he met in London, though these are only suppositions as there is no sure indication of the motives for Lawson's trip.[2] Whatever the case may be, this first foray lasted about two months, from December 1700 to February 1701, and covered some 500 miles (although Lawson claims a thousand miles in the subtitle of his book).[3] Lawson was accompanied by five other Englishmen, and four Indians (one of whom was a woman) to serve as guides. Their course of travel took them in a wide curve to the west and north. Then, with some of his fellow travellers, Lawson returned to the coast, but far north of Charles Town, near the Virginia border.

He settled in this area, which was inhabited by only a small number of settlers, with Indian tribes (particularly the Tuskarora) still located nearby. Lawson mainly remained there during the eight years preceding publication of his book, returning briefly to London to arrange for publication, but also making repeated trips into the interior and visiting the Indians of the region. He engaged in various activities in this period: botanizing for the English collector for whom he may have made his initial trip, surveying (he was named 'Surveyor General' of the province in 1708), fur trading and above all real estate speculation. He was instrumental in the founding of several new towns: Bath, the first town of North Carolina, incorporated in 1706, and, several years later, New Bern. So Lawson was very centrally involved in the British colonization effort in the area. As such, he was clearly perceived to be a threat by his Indian neighbours, for he was captured and put to death by Tuskaroras when on an exploratory trip that almost certainly was made with a view to new settlement.

This brief sketch of John Lawson's activities in the Carolinas provides a context for understanding the dynamics of domestication of the Other in his travel account. The latter includes both a narration of his first trip ('A Journal of a Thousand Miles'), and a section in which he presents his general reflections on Indians ('Exact Description and Natural History of That Country'), as he had come to know them over the longer period. These two elements are often found, sometimes in separate parts, sometimes intermingled, in accounts of encounter with North American Indians.[4] In the term 'domestication' I mean to include, on the one hand, expressions of possession and control of the Other by the Self (here the Self is a collective one: the colonial subject), but also the symbolic transformation, through language, of the Other into the Self, the 'de-othering' of the Other, as it were. We find ample illustration of both aspects of domestication in Lawson's discourse on Indians in *A New Voyage to Carolina*.

The work is dedicated to the 'Lords Proprietors', the governing body of the province; 'I here present Your Lordships', Lawson tells them in the dedication, 'with a Description of your own Country'.[5] Lawson proposes, then, to reveal to the possessors their possession, hitherto largely *terra incognita* to them, inhabited by alien Others. In this sense the text as a whole can be seen as an instrument of domestication. Moreover, a rhetorical figure recurs regularly in the account of the first expedition, which imagines future, concrete appropriation of the land by the English. We might call it 'prospective vision'. As the traveller gazes on land now occupied by Indians, he sees in his mind's eye what that land could become in the hands of the English. Lawson describes, for example, a valley that is perfectly adapted to cultivation and well irrigated by rivers that are 'very convenient for the Transportation of what Commodities this Place may produce';[6] in another passage, he says of the site of an Indian town that it 'would prove an exceeding thriving range for Cattle, and Hogs, provided the English were seated thereon'.[7] Also, as if to buttress these prefigurations of English possession, Lawson often emphasizes the fidelity and submission to the British settlers of the Indian tribes he visits. Very near the beginning of the narrative, for instance, he claims that 'they [the English settlers] have an entire Friendship with the neighbouring Indians of several nations, which are a very warlike People, ever faithful to the English ... and are a great Help and Strength to this Colony'.[8] So, although Lawson points out at one point that 'the Savages do, indeed, still possess the Flower of Carolina, the English enjoying only the Fag-end of that fine Country',[9] his text asserts present control, and strongly projects a future possession by the English that has not yet been fully accomplished.

If we look now at the other aspect of domestication, the 'de-othering' of the Other, we might first point to a striking linguistic practice, apparently adopted by the group of travellers as a whole and echoed in Lawson's text. The individual Indians with whom he and his fellow travellers develop particular relations (most often the chiefs that host them), are designated by familiar English nicknames, such as 'Santee Jack', 'Keyauwees Jack' and 'Enoe Will'.[10] Thus, the Indians' self-designated names are replaced by attributed Anglo-Saxon names. The kind of Anglo-Saxon name given, well illustrated by the example of Jack, which is used several times, makes especially acute the loss of identity by the Indian Other. For here a unique, invented Indian name (this was the common practice of North American natives) is replaced by a particularly commonplace, quasi-anonymous English one. In the case of chiefs, the renaming would also have the effect of removing the aura of moral authority that was inherent to their position and integral to their identity.

But this refusal of alterity goes beyond naming and often permeates the style of the narrative. For Lawson often translates what he observes of Indian life into an English frame of reference, forcing what he sees into familiar moulds that eliminate the specificity of difference. This can be seen in his choice of vocabulary in portraying scenes involving Indians, and interactions with them. In describing a ceremony, for instance, Lawson speaks of a 'ditty' being sung; the best hunters are termed the 'chief Sportsmen'; and Lawson calls the woman with whose family he was lodged on one occasion his 'landlady'.[11] Beyond isolated vocabulary, this tendency can infect an entire narrative sequence. Lawson recounts one incident in which another of the Englishmen in his party becomes interested in having sex with an Indian woman and gives her gifts to gain her assent before going off with her. When he returns she has taken some of his things and disappeared. But the story is told in a jovial, burlesque style, in the tones of an English picaresque novel, with the two protagonists called 'Mr Bridegroom' and 'Mrs Bride' and their coupling a 'Winchester-Wedding' (probably a forced marriage, as Lefler suggests in an editorial note). The story ends in mock pathos, with the author waking early to see a melancholy figure

> who in less than 12 Hours, was Batchelor, Husband, and Widdower, his dear Spouse having pick'd his Pocket of the Beads, Cadis, and what else should have gratified the Indians for the Victuals we receiv'd of them. However, that did not serve her turn, but she had also got his Shooes away … Thus dearly did our Spark already repent his new Bargain, walking bare-foot, in his Penitentials, like some poor Pilgrim to *Loretto*.[12]

This tendency to translate the experience of the Other into familiar frameworks of the Self often seems to stymie Lawson's attempts to understand what he witnesses. For he is confronted with an overall culture that is entirely alien, in which particular elements that superficially resemble elements of his own culture in fact take on entirely different meanings. Thus, in the above scene Lawson seems to treat the Indian woman's act as pilfering qua taking repayment for the food offered by the Indians to the English, though such a motive would be entirely inimical to the Indian ethic of hospitality. Similarly, in another passage the sexual freedom of girls before marriage is called 'Whorish' ('the more Whorish, the more Honourable', Lawson exclaims,[13] and the women who play a diplomatic role in giving their favours to visitors are described in language suggesting actual prostitution: 'They are mercenary, and whoever makes Use of them, first hires them, the greatest Share of the Gain going to the King's Purse, who is the chief Bawd'.[14] Here the emphasis is also on the monetary. Coming himself from a thoroughly commercial culture and society, Lawson often depicts Indian society in mercantile terms. According to his account Indian brides are 'sold', and Indians can 'buy off' a murder with wampum, 'their Mammon' as he once calls it.[15]

While in this way he changes many observed aspects of Indian social relations into the currency, often in a literal sense, of his own social background, in the realm of religion Lawson is confronted with practices entirely alien to English Protestantism, that call forth other domesticating strategies. Lawson in fact hesitates between two alternative means of bringing the Indians' religious rites and beliefs into sync with his own spiritual worldview. In a few passages he suggests that Indians may be devil-worshippers, thus bringing their practices into the Christian universe of discourse but as blasphemous negation.[16] He seems to have trouble believing this explanation, though, and more often opts for a debunking approach, also couched in his own cultural terms. Often myths and legends become simply 'lies' – he treats in this way, for example, the tale of how a tribe came to possess lightning in the form of a partridge[17] – and shamans are 'quacks' or 'cunning knaves' who are purposely fooling a credulous people.[18] In addition to these 'de-othering' devices applied to the religious domain, Lawson also attempts on several occasions the spiritual equivalent of domestication as possession/control: he tries his hand at proselytizing, attempting to convert to Christianity one of his guides, as well as one of the chiefs he spends some time with, albeit with ambiguous results.[19]

There are, however, a considerable number of points in Lawson's narrative, starting from early on, at which destabilizing elements are introduced that question this affirmative message of domination and absorption of the Other by the superior Self. At one point he acknowledges, for example, that he owes his life to the canoeing skill of one of the Indian guides on the expedition,[20] guides otherwise complacently referred to as 'our' Indians.[21] Also, in spite of his scornful debunking of Indian beliefs and magical practices in many instances, his responses in this area are in fact contradictory and hesitant, for he informs the reader that he has been witness to, and has been told of, efficacious Indian cures, and concedes that they compare well with European medecine.[22] Even more puzzling and disquieting – since the cures could be explained, without abandoning European medical principles, by the use of effective herbs – are instances in which he sees a prophecy fulfilled or seemingly supernatural control exercised by a shaman over a natural phenomenon – in one case, a thunder storm.[23] Lawson appears to be at a loss to account for these occurrences within the terms of his system of belief and understanding, and is reduced to reporting them without commentary.

At the same time Lawson shows signs of frustration in his desire to understand more fully. For the Indians refuse to answer certain questions that he asks, especially those that involve their religious beliefs and practices. In one instance, Lawson observes several Indians approaching a concave stone, placing tobacco in it and spitting; they remain silent when he asks them why.[24] Lawson also becomes curious regarding the Indian custom of circumcision, but tells the reader that 'if you ask them, what is the Reason they do so, they will make you no Manner of Answer; which is as much as to say, I will not tell you. Many other Customs they have, for which they will render no Reason or Account; ... for there are a great many of their Absurdities, which, for some Reason, they reserve as a Secret amongst themselves ...'[25] Lawson's irritation seems palpable in this passage. He cannot understand why his interlocutors will not simply explain everything straightaway. This irritation would seem to reveal a real fear and frustration at not being able to control the Other fully through forcing it to give up its secrets, and at not receiving a 'Reason' for its 'absurdities' that would provide a translation of the Other into the Self.

These passages show chinks in the armour, so to speak, but others seem to point toward a more active questioning of stereotyped certainties of European superiority. Moral superiority, first and foremost, for Lawson has found 'amongst some of them, great Observers of Moral Rules, and the Laws of Nature; indeed, a worthy Foundation to build Christianity upon ...'[26] A worthier one, perhaps, than was to be found in his English compatriots, whose cheating of the Indians Lawson castigates, leading him to the admission that 'if we do not shew them Examples of Justice and Vertue, we can never bring them to believe us to be a worthier Race of Men than themselves'.[27] More generally, the superiority of the English way of life is brought into question in one passage in which Lawson alludes to the many cases, of which he has personally known several, of English-men who have chosen to remain among the Indians, 'without ever desiring to return again among the English, although they had very fair Opportunities of Advantages amongst their Countrymen'.[28]

Lawson's narrative of encounter even moves beyond these doubts and questionings in some passages, to arrive at a modicum of what I will call 'recognition', a term that has both cognitive and evaluative aspects: cognitive insight into the nature of the Other, and willingness to attribute positive value to the Other. In fact, from the start Lawson expresses a desire to write truly and justly about the Indians, claiming in the introduction to his work to be a rectifier of errone-ous conceptions propagated in the past by English traders, who were generally uneducated and self-seeking, and who, although on their travels 'they often spend several Years, are yet, at their Return, uncapable of giving any reasonable Account of what they met withal ...'[29] Yet he also indicates, in one passage, that he is aware of the great difficulty of comprehending and appreciating radical otherness, claiming that the Indians' 'way of living is so contrary to ours, that neither we nor they can fathom one anothers Designs and Methods'.[30]

In spite of this general difficulty, and in spite of the many ways in which his cultural 'blinders' get in the way, Lawson does at points seem to show a lucid awareness of a number of areas of Indian culture, perceived as significantly differ-ent from English (and European) modes of thought and behaviour. In surprising contradiction to his commercialization of Indian culture elsewhere, in certain places in his text Lawson develops the idea that Indian money, means of meas-urement and sense of time and work are all fundamentally different from those of Europeans, and that these are interrelated. The Indians never push themselves to work so as to accumulate goods or wealth, he claims, but only do as much as is necessary to provide subsistence; when travelling or hunting, though, they often exert themselves enthusiastically and tirelessly because these activities bring both pleasure to them and practical advantage to their group.[31] Lawson points out in another place that the production of wampum is extraordinarily painstaking and time-consuming, but since the Indians 'never value their time ... they can afford to make them'.[32] He also makes the related observation that the Indian method of measuring the length of a wampum belt is to extend it from the elbow to the little finger, but '(t)hey never stand to question, whether it is a tall Man, or a short one, that measures it'.[33] What he is pointing to here, clearly, is that the standardized quantification of commercial transactions does not hold with the Indians.

Lawson's text often also points to an underlying principle of Indian societies which is at loggerheads with English and European ones: the tight-knit, integrated nature of their communities. Although often belied by the textual practices I have illustrated above, Lawson does often emphasize, in portraying the Indians, egalitarian sharing of material goods, deep attachments, generosity and mutual aid, the predominance of the common good over that of the individual, etc.[34] This adds up to a striking lack of dissension, as Lawson comments: 'They never fight with one another, unless drunk ... They say, the Europeans are always rangling and uneasy, and wonder they do not go out of this World, since they are so uneasy and discontented in it'.[35] Although ostensibly just reporting what Indians say, Lawson seems to be speaking with them as well.

Here cognitive insight seems to be mixed with strong sympathy. Some commentators have gone so far as to speak of a thematics of the 'noble savage' and of a New World Eden.[36] My analysis here attempts, however, to reveal the complexities and contradictions in Lawson's work. And indeed, particularly in the last section of his work which gives a general portrait of the Indian peoples he has known, Lawson expresses admiration for many specific aspects of Indian society (the lenient treatment of children, and funeral customs that do not include burial of the body, for example). More significantly, the generalizing section, and with it the work as a whole, culminates in an overall praise of, and plea for the Indians:

> They are really better to us, than we are to them ... We look upon them with Scorn and Distain, and think them little better than Beasts in Humane [*sic*] Shape, though if well examined, we shall find that, for all our Religion and Education, we possess more Moral Deformities, and Evils than these Savages do ... these Indians are the freest People in the World, and so far from being Intruders upon us ... we have abandon'd our own Native Soil, to drive them out, and possess theirs; neither have we any true Balance, in Judging of these poor Heathens, because we neither give Allowance for their Natural Disposition, nor the Sylvian Education, and strange Customs, (uncouth to us) they lie under.[37]

It is true that this passage occurs in the context of final recommendations to the settlers (and Lords-Proprietors) as to how to 'make these People serviceable to us, and better themselves thereby',[38] that is, to civilize and convert them, and extend British rule. Lawson recommends doing so by persuasion and intermarriage rather than by force and trickery, but this does not change the nature of the goal. In spite of the imperial context, though, this statement as well as a good many passages preceding it, stand in strange contrast to the discourse of domination and de-othering that I have discussed.

The reader is left, finally, with a puzzlingly dissonant impression. How can the blatant contradictions in Lawson's text be explained? I can only, in conclusion, suggest some tentative possibilities. One involves the fact, already hinted at, that insight and sympathy are most strongly concentrated in the generalizing section, in contrast with the travel account. We might hypothesize that in the account of the voyage Lawson remains too close to lived experience to escape his conditioned responses, whereas the framework of the treatise provides him with greater intellectual distance. Moreover, only in the final summation of that section does Lawson become fully conscious of a point toward which he tended previously. But while this may explain the distribution of the dissonant elements in the text, we still would need to try to understand how a man so energetically engaged in the colonial enterprise, and whose prose is so often permeated with that perspective, could in the same text rather forcefully question and subvert it. In this regard I would suggest that perhaps Lawson's text can stand as an illustration of a general principle:[39] the potential (only a potential, but a potent one) for transcendence of the Self's conditioning in the experience of travel encounter itself.

6 THE (HE)ART OF FIRST ENCOUNTER AT TAHITI: SAMUEL WALLIS'S CONFLICTS OF INTEREST (1767)

Sandhya Patel

The writing of travel and its publication has served various ideological ends over the centuries. Prominent among those is the production of a newly discovered Other, both place and person, but also of a rediscovered Self, that of the traveller himself. In 1598, Richard Hakluyt initiated a compilatory trend – 'pioneering in its scope' in Bohls and Duncan's words[1] – which contributed to the undertaking of empire and importantly paved the way for a national archival memory-making and for the invention of a national identity rooted in maritime exploits, articulated not in poetry but in prose narratives, in the language of the common man: 'What the old epics were to the royally or nobly born, this modern epic is to the common people'.[2]

In his conceptualization of the narrative of exploration, MacLaren identifies four stages, the first of which is the logbook entry made en route. The journal then gives body to the log entry, 'informing it with continuity and purpose': whereas the log entry may display tentativeness, in the journal, the use of the past tense and retrospection generates orderliness and consistency. This production is central in the emergence of an author, as the narrative is also shaped by the potential audience's exigencies. The third and fourth stages, the draft manuscript and the publication itself, are similarly subject to the demands of the audience.[3] The nature of the texts I will be examining here draws attention to the log entry itself as a site of ambivalence – which the navigator explores and fully exploits.

Commander Samuel Wallis was the first Englishman to have more than a fleeting encounter with the inhabitants of what is known today as the Tuamotu archipelago. Furthermore, his discovery of the Society Isles in the South Pacific, specifically Tahiti, is the earliest documentary record of the encounter between Europeans and Polynesians. Unlike his successors, though, Wallis did not write a journal onboard ship; his log may nevertheless be interpreted as a key text in elucidating relationships between Self and Other, in that it attests to first encounter in an account which has not been reworked to suit the tastes of a reading public. Little academic attention has been paid to the Wallis texts precisely because of this form. In the major studies on the Wallis material, such as Pearson's article on the scope of John Hawkesworth's emendations in *An Account of the Voyages ... performed by Commodore Byron, Captain Carteret, Captain Wallis and Captain Cook*, only the log held at the Public Records Office (hereafter PRO) in London is referred to.[4] The PRO holds a log written most probably by Wallis himself, according to Hugh Carrington who published George Robertson's journal. Robertson was Master onboard the *Dolphin* and his text is accepted as being the most authoritative account of the ship's sojourn at Tahiti. Another Wallis log exists, however, archived in Australia at the Mitchell Library in Sydney.[5] Importantly, this document is similar but not identical to the one in London, and I argue that the differences between the two epitomize tensions between conflicting representations of Self and Other in the South Pacific. Wallis's manuscripts were significantly both logs, not a log and a journal, but the disparities between the two transcribe in their short message form the intricacy of the politics of first contact in this part of the Pacific.

A comparative study of the two documents must necessarily be based on two assumptions – firstly a supposition as to whom the authors were, and secondly a premise as to which log was written first. The handwriting and the signature confirm at first view that both logs were written by Wallis. I propose on the strength of this that the Australian text, which I will call 'the first log', was Wallis's first impression. The London text, which will hereafter be referred to as 'the second log', seems to have been written afterwards. My proposal is based on the encapsulatory dimension of the first log (the Australian text) and the relatively more elaborate stylistic turn of the second (the London text). Some passages in both logs, though importantly more so in the London log, are not in abbreviated note form and are narratives in the fashion of a journal, with hypotactic characteristics. This is so when Wallis deliberately decides to devote two or three pages to descriptive purpose, though the first, Australian log also contains descriptive passages. Encapsulation – short sentences, sometimes nominal, with little punctuation and few conjunctions, and simple syntax – characterizes most of the Australian log entries. Thus, going from notes to narrative appears more likely than going from narrative to notes. Exactly when the second, London log was written remains to be seen and needs to be determined. Most research (very little as compared to work on Cook or the Forsters) has been done on this second log and none, as far as I know, on the first.

The objective here is to minutely identify and explore this initial reworking by Wallis, well before Hawkesworth committed himself to the task. Wallis's two logs display a revealing production and promotion of Self and Other which, though not as outright as various editors' reworking of narratives of exploration, is largely significant. Even the inventorial form of travel writing then may be understood as a self-conscious form of recuperation in the interests of collective and personal enterprise.[6] Greg Dening argues that 'when [the explorers] tried to describe what they saw, they themselves were revealed. Their own values, the structures of their consciousness and the categories of their mind were present in the things they selected to describe'.[7] Bhabha interrogates what he terms as the formulation of strategies of representation and empowerment in the context of competing communities.[8] His 'dynamics of writing' acquire additional significance in the pre-colonial context, as they also transcribe to some extent the socio-politics of first encounter, clearing the way for future action, namely annexation and appropriation, conquest and colonization. Thus, Wallis's texts recounting the encounter with one group of the Pacific peoples seem to lend themselves particularly well to a type of close reading which may be considered as revealing these 'sites of ambivalence'.

This study will specifically focus on how Wallis negotiated his representations of situations of conflict. Greg Dening's conceptualization of this contact, very appropriately described as taking place on a beach and therefore symbolic of a meeting of worlds at the frontier – us and them, good and bad, familiar and strange – is relevant here. Dening argues that difference can be so great that the only means of control is violence. He calls attention to an oversight in this understanding of contact – it patently overlooks the aggression inherent 'in the presumed right to possess the land'.[9] Interestingly, the identities of the assailant and defender are not posited as firmly in Wallis's first log as in the second. Thus, his observations in the latter attest to a gradual polarization of initially uncertain categories, which emerge more clearly sparing the Englishmen any blame for the violence of contact. They are the defenders and the Tahitians, the assailants. The disparities between Wallis's two texts seem to illustrate the materialization of this 'managerial process', which is also a process of stereotyping.[10] The typology I propose comprises three modes of disparity between the two documents, namely: discretionary diction (by which I mean a sometimes weighted choice of words in order to convey a specific view of events), strategic oversights/additions, and questions of chronology. These modes work together sometimes in single entries and inform a discussion of the politics of the South Pacific and specifically Tahitian contact zones, based on that which Wallis himself wrote up as the first Englishman to sail across these islands.

Pinaki in the Tuamotu archipelago is sighted on 6 June 1767, the first sign of land in the Pacific for weeks. On 8 June, after having precariously secured meagre supplies at Pinaki, Wallis sails on to the second nearby atoll, Nukutavake. There, the second log performs its detailing deed in providing elements which expand the telegraphic form of the first log into a more narrative form. These added details weight the polemical aspect of the very first potentially antagonistic encounter between the islanders and the English, which the observations in the first log do not, as the following example shows. In the second log, the boats are manned and armed because Wallis sees fifty natives 'drawn up' and 'running about with long Pikes and fire brands'.[11] This is inserted in the second log in brackets, as a justification for arming the men. The dynamic confrontational dimension of the Tahitians' response to the longboats coming within the reach of the shore is accentuated by verbs such as 'drawn up' and 'running about', and of course by the reference to their weapons. Wallis takes pains to point out that any aggression on the English side is to be avoided at all costs. The English are 'civil', attempt to 'persuade', and endeavour not to give offence, and by these civil and civilized means, are to obtain fruit and water. But the natives stand guard and do not suffer them to land, up in arms.

The first log is rather less categorical in its representation of the events. The diction does not produce an image of any offensive in the offing, and there is no mention of natives up in arms. No running about either, implying disorganized martial frenzy, but simply 'great many inhabitants on the beach', and a short: 'They would not suffer the people to land'.[12] Here, the violence of contact is significantly less apparent as compared to its palpable presence in the second log. The power relations are most definitely weighted on the Tahitians' side, as the Tahitians refuse to let the boats land. The second log, though, imbalances the relationships in terms of control, and this through recourse to what may be qualified as a considered addition of detail, which stresses the strength and serenity of the British manoeuvres in the face of this potential assault.

As the contact zone takes shape, the language in the second log does indeed take on a more narrative form, though not in terms of literary artifice. More details are added, through parentheses and longer sentences, and the construction of collective Self is privileged as contact is prolonged and structured. The rational rationale of contact on the British side emerges more firmly. These tendencies are illustrated in the first log, in which Wallis includes an interesting and rather decisive detail of this first encounter, namely that two members of the expedition do indeed try to force a landing: 'They would not suffer the people to land – except two who they soon put into the boat again'.[13] In the second log, the incident is entirely glossed over, and the aggressive stance of the Tahitians is thrown into relief: 'they stood on their ground with long Pikes & would not suffer the people to land'.[14] This is going somewhat against the pacific ethics of encounter as detailed in the instructions to Lieutenant Furneaux in the first few lines of the entry in the second log: '... endeavour to traffic with them for fruit water or anything that might be useful to us at the same time not to give them offence but endeavour by civil means to get refreshments from them'.[15]

In view of this strategic oversight in the more narrative second log, where adding detail is undoubtedly one of the textual functions, the relating of the nature of the encounter is modified from the first to the second log. The violent landing – the necessary encroaching on a land which constitutes 'incomprehensible extravagance'[16] – is effaced in the second log, preserving the symbolic representation of the civilized means of contact employed by the British. This representation thus produces a polarization effect of the 'us' and 'them' – defender and assailant – dichotomies. The islanders then leave, and the English being in need of sustenance proceed to help themselves to the food and water on the island. They take on supplies until the 11 June, not being in any way disturbed by any lingering islanders who in the second log are described as having 'fled' Nukutavake.[17] While the islander is thus produced as assailant, the second log also confusedly attempts to characterize the 'native' as cowardly or ineffectual, which may also work towards attenuating the power of the Other, associated with being the aggressor, and reinforcing that of the Self, consolidating further the categories established on first contact by the writing strategies just discussed.

Wallis's second log institutes thus a categorial confusion, whereas the first 'impression' continues in a more composed strain which elides to some extent the production of colonial discourse. On the 11 June, when the *Dolphin* approaches Lord Egmont Island, the first log describes the situation thus:

> At ½ past 3 the New Island Bore from the East End of it [Charlotte Island] SE about one mile – at this time we were abreast of 8 Sail of Double Canoes that were hauled upon the beach and were the same People that left Charlotte Island, the people all sitting on the Beach, their things just taken out of their Canoes.[18]

This description represents the Tahitians as resting, or waiting for ensuing events. The image evokes serenity, peaceableness and a certain watchfulness. The second log then transforms this visual encounter and further grounds the image enunciated initially in this South Pacific context on 7 June:

> We saw the Canoes with all the Inhabitants by them that had fled from Charlotte Island, there were not any Hutts but the people had hauled up their Canoes upon the Beach and placed their Weomen & Children under them and they came down close to the waterside with big Pickes in their Hands, & some with Firebrands making a great noise and dancing in strange manner. There were 7 or eight Double Canoes with about Four score Men Weomen and Children.[19]

Here the representation is at odds with the ambiance of Wallis's initial notation. In effect, the islanders' belligerent intentions are made clear. They are brandishing weapons, their women and children are safe under the canoes, out of harm's way, implying that they expect to wage war. The 'strange' manner in which they are dancing constructs these potential enemies, and the categorial strategy further 'fixes' the production of their otherness – an important feature of colonial discourse.[20] Thus in the second log, the discursive practice of repetition of the hostile posturing of the islanders may very well be understood as a means of 'othering', based on proximity to or distance from violence. Wallis thus sails from Lord Egmont, and from the putatively aggressive islanders, taking care to point out (but only in the second log) that there was 'little likelihood of refreshment to be met with on it'.[21]

The reworking of powerplay is thus identifiable in the minute details of these first encounters. It is based 'on a manipulation of relations of force'.[22] Seemingly insignificant details then acquire particular importance in this respect. For example, it may be inferred from the entry on the 18 June in the second log that the Tahitians are somewhat in awe, and retreat to the safety of the shore on just 'seeing' the boats: 'Severall canoes coming off put back on seeing our boats'.[23] In the first log, Wallis is clear: Lieutenant Furneaux goes 'very near three or four canoes – who all pulled for the shore'.[24] The threat emanates in the first log from the Englishmen, and the withdrawal of the Tahitians is its result, which is not the case in the second. The second log seems to downplay the potentially aggressive gestures on the part of the longboat crew. Which version is true is of little importance here. What is significant is the polysemic representations of this encounter by the same man. The play of influence is indeed rooted in representations of relations of force. The potentially vulnerable position of the Englishmen faced with the islanders on their home ground, in need of nothing and apparently aware of the violence of the contact zone, is the backdrop to this oscillation in the attempt at manipulating the relations of force. Wallis in the second log may thus be understood as seeking authorization for strategies which will inevitably justify conquest in terms of a mode of violent appropriation.[25] The exigencies of the situation require that the process of discovery and learning apparent in the first log be subjugated to the 'signifiers of stability' inherent in stereotypical discourse – namely those of courage and daring displaced by otherly cowardice and treachery.

Thus, the Englishmen in the boat are forced to throw the Tahitians a rope in order to make an attempt at trade; the Tahitians in turn attempt a hijacking of the boat, according to the second log. The firing of a warning shot puts an end to the endeavour as the Tahitians let go of the rope; the hijacker swims away and the boat returns to the ship.[26] No mention is made of this episode in the first log, in which the Englishmen are quite frankly shown to be at a disadvantage. The fact that it is described in the second seems to re-establish the rather disrupted order of things in the first log. What matters for posterity, and therefore for the nationalist enterprise, is that the Englishmen be shown to have parried an unjustified attack without loss of life, saving the collective Self from any humiliation. The sixteenth-century image of 'the chiefest Captaines at sea, the greatest Merchants, and the best Mariners of our nation', in Fuller's terms, is thus preserved in the second log.[27] As Dening puts it, 'it was neither the nail nor the life that was important but the theatre of discipline and right order'.[28]

In the first log, on the contrary, the ship sails away from the island with no victuals, the natives having refused trade relations and the woods being inaccessible: 'they made signs that they would bring Fowles CocoaNutts Hogs &ᶜᵉ. But after waiting severall Hours not one came & the woods being inaccessible the Boats Returned and we Sailed from the Island'.[29] Discretionary diction and strategic oversight thus produce an ambiguous account. Accordingly, the rather genial description of the Tahitians in the first log – 'The Inhabitants were about two Hundred Men Weomen & Children – all well look'd Stout people – the Weomen Handsome & dress'd in white ...'[30] – disappears in the second entirely, as if the empathy (between Self and Other) of this description could disrupt the rather more polemical politics of encounter identifiable in the second long, justifying the use of firearms and lauding the success of the men in bringing off fresh fruit and vegetables in spite of the attack on them by hostile Tahitians.

The next encounter is of a different nature. As HMS *Dolphin* sails along the shore on 19 June 1767, the ship is surrounded with a hundred or so canoes, and the Tahitians, empty-handed, are invited onboard. This time, both logs focus on the 'thievish' quality of the people.[31] Together, the logs also represent the people as 'hallowing and Shouting that we could scarce hear each other speak' and as setting up 'a great Hallow'.[32] These descriptions thus use what can be described as the repetitive mode as they mutually reinforce the representation of the islanders as being iniquitous and belligerent.

The wider and ongoing pattern of differentiation is consolidated the next day when the site of encounter is again at sea, not on land, and the English have still not managed to land with or without the permission of the islanders; they have not been able to find anchorage, and are overwhelmed as the Tahitians surround the boats and this time attack. The encounter is related in the two logs in quite different ways. In the first log, Wallis recounts how the boats are prevented from getting close to a 'fine bay' both by the breakers and by a concerted attack with stones by a fleet of canoes. Wallis's men react by firing once, which does nothing but incite the Tahitians to continue their attack, and then they fire a second time. The shot wounds one of the islanders, on which the assailants pull off, which allows the marines to row back to safety. Wallis as Captain plays no role in the management of the crisis, the responsibility of using firearms being left in the hands of Furneaux who is directly under threat :

> the inhabitants came off in their Canoes & was beginning to pillage them & throw stones there being near one hundred Canoes about them so they fired a musquet clear of them to let them see on which they set up a great Hallow & came close to the Boat on which they shot at one & wounded him for they were quite surrounded & expected they would [illegible] in a moment on which they pulled off at a distance & never came near them again & they got safe onboard.[33]

In the second log, Wallis allots himself a rather more active part in the whole affair. For example, it is the Captain who orders the boats to come onboard on observing that hundreds of canoes have surrounded them. He also orders the first warning shot to be fired, but takes no responsibility for the second shot, which is fired by the mate and wounds a Tahitian:

> They then stood round to an Opening when they were surrounded with a vast number of Boats [illegible] and at the same time made the signal for them to come Onboard, the Boats did then attempt to board Ours and threw stones at them on which I ordered a shot to be fired over them and the Mate that was in one of the boats found that if he suffered them to come nearer he should not be able to defend himself fired a Musquett with Buck shot and wounded a Man who was then standing up ready to jump onboard in the Shoulder on which they all moved off and suffered the boats to return to the Ship without any molestation.[34]

What is also interesting here is the omission Wallis makes. In the first log, while his longboats are being attacked, Wallis is busy trading (rather ineffectually) with the islanders in another hundred canoes amassed around the ship:

> at the same time we had some hundreds of Canoes about the ship – to whom I gave nails & some Trifles but they brought nothing in exchange & so thievish that they clambering up the side & taking everything they could lay hand on.[35]

This, in terms of tactics, may well have been a diversionary strategy on the part of the Tahitians. In the second log this reference to trading at the same time is entirely omitted. By not including this episode, Wallis lets yet another occurrence of trade gone bad, but this time under his direct command, pass. More importantly still, Wallis saves himself from any possible accusation of neglect of duty or mismanagement: trading while his men are being attacked is hardly 'the right order of things'. Thus, in the second log as noted, Wallis's management of the crisis comes to the fore as long as his strategy is in keeping with his peaceful mission. When a Tahitian is wounded, the mate is responsible and though justified in his action, is not obeying Wallis's orders. The second text, whilst recounting some failure (to land, to obtain food, to find anchorage), nevertheless builds up Wallis's authority through his successful direction of a crisis situation. In view of these examples, the second log produces the effect of a classification, using the defender/assailant categories to preclude a certain form of victimhood more apparent in the first. Victimhood in the first log does not allow representations of supremacy or control, which are seriously compromised as the boat's hopes of landing and finding anchorage are continually dashed.

These first encounters then set the scene for further conflicts of interest with the discovery of Tahiti. After sailing from Mehetia on 20 June, the island of Tahiti comes into view, holding promises of a tropical paradise: 'The shore pleasant beyond imagination full of inhabitants Millions of CocoaNutt Trees fine Cascades running off the Mountains'.[36] The relation of ensuing events raises interesting questions of chronology. In the first log, the armed encounter is described thus:

> at 9 Ordered the Master with the Boats Mann'd and Arm'd to land along the Shore to the Westward and look after a Watering place there were at this time severall hundred Canoes about the Ship and the Shore & when the Boats came near the Shore several Boats that were very large laid the Barge Onboard & threw stones at them and the Other Boats were coming up with them fast that they could by no signs make them keep off not even by firing Musquets over them & two more large sailing Canoes full of men coming [illegible] for the Boats and it would have certainly sunk her he fired & wounded two which made them all shoar off and they made no more attempts so the Boats continued Sounding in Shoar and looking out for a good watering Place. The Canoes about the Ship brought off Cocoanutts, plaintains, a few Fowls and some small Hogs & other Refreshments which they bartered for Nails &cc.[37]

In the second log, the order of events is reworked:

> as soon as we had secured the ship, sent the Boats to sound along the shore and to look at the place where we saw the water at this time a great number of boats came of from the shoar to the ship and brought of with them Hogs, Fowls & plenty of fruit which we bought of them for Nails and such like things; but when our boats pulled toward the shore, most of the Natives went at them and after them keeping at a Distance, but as the boats drew nigher The natives grew bolder and on a sudden three large Sailing boats ran at the Cutter and carried away her Outlicker and stove her quarter, more coming down they fired two Muquetts over them, which they only laught at and attempted the barge who fired at the Boat that was laying her onboard and much wounded a Man on which they desisted and went away to Leeward, and other returned to the Ship again and traded.[38]

The writing strategy by which the categorial effect is produced here is based on recourse to discretionary diction and to the chronology of the reporting. In the first log, Wallis describes the stone-throwing as a reaction to the boats approaching the shore. The last sentence refers to the trading which takes place during and after this skirmish. In the second, the Englishmen's attempt at landing is reworked somewhat. In the first log, Wallis orders his men to land, while in the second they are sent in simply to reconnoitre the location of the river and sound. The objective in this second 'system of recordation'[39] is more reasonable than ordering a landing after days of hostility. Further, the consequent attack is contextualized by a presentation of the equitable abundant trading before the boats approach the shore line (the subsequent attack by the Tahitians is thus represented as unreasonable). This slight revision of diction and chronology is significant as it elides any British confrontational stances in the second log as, for example, setting out to land. This elision works towards reinforcing the categories which have been taking shape since first contact. In the second log, the British are first attacked, and fire once they have suffered material damage. Even then the Tahitians are presented as ignoring the warning justly given by the Englishmen according to the right order of things, negligently laughing at such prevision (again consolidating the image of hostile show or blustering on the part of the islanders). This is not the case in the first log: warning shots are fired as the Tahitians approach in their canoes before any contact.

All these skirmishes come to a head on 24 June 1767. The ensuing struggle is for the Tahitians their final but failed attempt at sea to resist the British onslaught. The details of the naval battle between the two adversaries are reported in the two logs in broadly similar ways, but again strategic omission is identifiable in the second, which unobtrusively operates as an 'apparatus of power'.[40] In the build up to the battle, the first log relates an overture of peace which the second does not:

> At ½ past Nine a boat with a large Company over the Middle & brought a large Plaintain tree with a bunch of various coloured feathers & a Pig & a Man who sat on the top of the Canopy made motions of peace & pointed to himself and then to the Ship is tho' twas to be given to the Superior.[41]

These motions of peace are not recorded in the second log and this important event thus loses its significance without the qualification detailed in the first log:

> At last a Man sitting on a canopy that was fixed on a large double canoe made signs to let him come near the Ship which I allowed him to do when he gave a Bunch of red and yellow feathers to one of our People to bring to me and then put of.[42]

Similarly, the two logs do not necessarily concur as to the actual rather telling particulars of the battle itself. The first log details two charges:

> every Canoe set up a Halloo & threw such a Shower of Stones at all parts of the Ship that was astonishing, on which I ordered the People to fire on them, they persisted sometime but some of our Great Guns breaking a few of their Large Canoes & the QuatorDeckGuns fired loaded with Musquetts that made them sheer off. however they Kept hovering at a Distance & Throwing Stones – things which they did with Great Judgement and hurt many of our People. They on our ceasing fire after a Pause made a Second effort and came on with a Great Resolution but on their coming near & slinging stones we fired a few Loaded with Great Guns and Grape at them and they all pulled for the Shore so that at Noon there was not a Canoe to be seen.[43]

In the second log, Wallis describes a rather more heated battle, with the Tahitians attacking three times. The effect of their first volley of gunfire only 'puts them into some confusion'.[44] Another bout of shooting pushes back the second Tahitian onslaught. The Tahitians finally retreat after a third attempt which ends in the destruction of one canoe: 'I ordered them to be fired on and one of the schott hit the Canoe that had called the others to him and cut it asunder, on seeing which they immediately disappeared that in half an hour there was not a canoe to be seen'.[45]

This representation of the battle details a more measured approach as compared to the description in the first log, in which firing into the crowd is an immediate reaction to the initial rush. In the second, in effect, the Englishmen are forced to fire amongst the canoes only after three concerted raids, and the result is the destruction of only one canoe. Further, the fact that it is the one from which the chiefly figure proclaims the commencement of hostilities is particularly propitious (not detailed in the first log), justifying conquest as a means of appropriation. In the second log, Wallis himself acquires presence and prestige as the battle progresses. In the first log, he refers freely to his feeble condition and to the fact of his being in the gallery, following events from there by looking out of the window. This detail is omitted in the second log and the Captain's active presence on deck is substantiated. His more frequent use of the personal pronoun in the second log corroborates this more operational representation of Self.

Wallis's logs may be considered as being, then, at the heart of the South Seas construct and as laying bare the fragility of these representative artefacts. The texts attest to an intricate process of workmanship exacerbated by the fact that up until the arrival at Tahiti, Wallis is himself transcribing reports that have been brought to him by Lieutenant Furneaux. In other words, even Wallis's firsthand reports are in fact secondhand. This initial interpretative process, associated with the subsequent transcriptive writing up of the two logs discussed in this paper, highlights the intricacies of the process of representation by operations of language, even at this early textual stage. In Saïd's view, the distinction between representation and misrepresentation without positing a pre-existing 'truth', may very well be a matter of degree.[46] When the language is in its most basic form, as in the first log, representation seems less ideologically inclined. The degree of deformation increases as the language becomes subject to distorting factors, namely the cultural and political ambience. Though all captains claimed that their need for food and water overrode all other claims for territoriality, ownership, or sacredness, Dening argues that the question of power, or self-image countermanded all others.[47] The Wallis texts qualify this analysis somewhat in that in his first log, without the subtext inherent in a more narrative archival form, Wallis may well have expressed some sense of seemliness, perhaps less troubled with considerations of command or control.

7 DISTANCE AND PROXIMITY IN JAMES COOK'S FIRST VOYAGE AROUND THE WORLD (1768–71)

Anne Dromart

In 1766 the Admiralty and the Royal Society jointly planned an expedition to the South Seas. If the Admiralty had territorial ambitions, and hoped to establish the existence of the mythical *terra australis incognita*, the continent that many Europeans thought existed as a counterweight to the Northern hemisphere's continental masses,[1] what came across as the apparent aim of the exploration was the Royal Society's scientific mission to observe the transit of Venus across the sun, due on 3 June 1769.

Captain James Cook was appointed to command Her Majesty's Bark the *Endeavour*, and the expedition left Plymouth on 26 August 1768, with official instructions, both from the Admiralty and the Royal Society, underlining the importance of astronomical measurements and geographical exploration, as well as the necessity of establishing contact with the indigenous peoples.[2] The island of Tahiti was both the place where the scientific calculation of the distance from the earth to the sun was to be carried out, and an opportunity for supposedly easy commerce with distant populations who had already been in contact with Europeans. The ship was then to sail further west and south, in search of the hoped-for continent, taking this opportunity to draw maps of New Zealand, at the risk of entering into contact with native tribes as yet unknown to European explorers.

Cook himself did not write the narrative through which his exploits came to be known in 1773. John Hawkesworth, a writer of miscellaneous essays, plays, stories and journalism, and a one-time friend of Dr Johnson, was commissioned by the Admiralty to edit the explorer's papers, a work for which Hawkesworth is said to have received the huge sum of £6,000.[3] Hawkesworth's text was therefore the authorized edition of Cook's logbook. In this paper, references to Hawkesworth's text will be made through dates of entry, as they appear on the 'South Seas' online edition of the 1773 official record held by the National Library of

Australia[4] and references to Cook's own logbook will be to Beaglehole's 1968 edition.

As is well known, the record published by Hawkesworth caused quite a sensation in Britain. Among the causes for the uproar was Hawkesworth's tale of the way the islanders innocently indulged in free sex, which was widely condemned on moral grounds.[5] What interests me here, however, is how Cook's journal, as rewritten by Hawkesworth, reveals not promiscuity, but tension: the tension that both Europeans and non-Europeans – whether Tahitians or Maoris – seem to have experienced in deciding how close or how distant from each other they actually wanted to be.

What I argue, furthermore, is that this issue of physical distance between the two groups made manifest the *cultural* issues involved in exchange. The search for an ideal ground of exchange, both in terms of trade and mutual understanding, was constantly frustrated by the realization that spatial arrangements could in fact only be determined through shared cultural codes. As it thus invites the Europeans to question their own attitude towards the Other, suggesting that common cultural grounds are the cornerstone of effective communication, Hawkesworth's edition of Cook's logbook introduces a timid awareness of the meaning and role of cultures in interaction, a notion of culture which surprisingly seems to break away from the Enlightenment 'uniformitarian view' of human nature as a shared universal.[6] But what a close reading of Hawkesworth's rhetoric also reveals, however, is that such encounters seem to be worth describing in Hawkesworth's view only insofar as they produce an unequal relationship between the navigator and the islander. The values of the white man constitute the filter through which various events are interpreted. Gunpowder then becomes not only a talisman of power, but also a cultural tool used to regulate distance and proximity on the model of a hierarchical structuring of relationships.

At first view, Hawkesworth's narrative seems to express no fear of, or contempt for, the South Seas islanders. The narrative is not centred on the Europeans only; it allows room for the natives, as is constantly suggested by the verbal forms used. For instance, the natives are very often allowed to become the grammatical subjects of verbs, as if the narrator of the Journal were willing to grant them the dignity of being centres of perception and thought, to the extent that the 'savages' are metamorphosed into enigmas to be understood: 'They had with them a pig, which they would not part with.'[7] Hawkesworth's choice of 'would' clearly suggests the perception of a will which remains opaque to the visitors and consequently kindles their curiosity. The reader nevertheless perceives a contradiction here. Cook must establish peaceful relationships with the islanders, but he cannot allow the natives any pre-eminence if he wants to remain in control of the situation of interlocution. The aim of the voyage was indeed to acquire a better knowledge of new territories and cultures, but it also aimed at enlarging England's 'network' of wealth and power.[8] Cook is certainly careful to follow the Earl of Morton's recommendations, 'to exercise the utmost patience and forbearance with respect to the natives of the several Lands where the Ships may pass',[9] but he is equally mindful not to risk having his boat dismantled by the Tahitians – Cook was fully aware that when Samuel Wallis, who had arrived back in England just in time to pass on navigational information to the Admiralty, had made landfall at Tahiti in June 1767, he had been attacked by the Polynesians. Cook's concern, therefore, is both to protect the natives from his men, and to protect his men from the natives. Hawkesworth's record is very careful to underscore this mixture of benevolence and mistrust:

> A proper person or persons will be appointed to trade with the Natives ... and no officer or seaman or other person belonging to the Ship, excepting such as are so appointed, shall trade or offer to trade.[10]

The Admiralty and its representatives recurrently find refuge in such specific rules, aimed at securing safe relationships between the European visitors and the South Seas islanders. If such rules prove necessary, is it not because exchange between civilized and uncivilized is thought to be potentially risky for both sides? The implicit assumption here is that the British common sailors might be tempted to act with the islanders as with an inferior species, perhaps even as with animals (as will indeed appear further down), an attitude very likely to cause trouble for the two parties. Rules therefore restrict exchanges to a highly coded form of 'trade', thus delineating the scope and nature of contact. They also suggest both that the natives, however different, are human beings who should be treated as such, and that the Europeans are entrusted with a mission that makes sense only if their supremacy remains unquestioned throughout the ritual of interaction. As is implied by the necessity of the permanence of such rules, Cook and his crew are thus repeatedly confronted with a major difficulty: they must choose how close to, or how distant from the natives they want to be.

Hawkesworth's narrative first describes such relationships in terms not of cultural exchange, but of 'territoriality' – the ground each covers in the presence of the other party, so that the right distance between the two is maintained.[11] The Journal is replete with notations concerning the spatial distance that separates the two groups, whether at Tahiti, in New Zealand or in Australia. An apt image of the gap between the savages and the civilized is thus to be found in the stretches of water lying between Cook's ship and the Maoris' canoes: 'At this time we saw several canoes standing cross the bay',[12] 'About fifty of them seemed to wait for our landing, on the opposite side of the river'.[13] In Australia and in New Zealand, what is immediately noticeable about the natives' attitude is their obvious, whether real or pretended, lack of interest in the newcomers, with the unforeseen result that direct, face-to-face contact cannot in fact be established.[14] Cook is very eager to bridge the gap and 'establish an intercourse with them',[15] but there is nothing in the narrative that suggests that the other party is interested in communicating or exchanging with the Europeans. So that when Cook and his men decide to bridge the distance and approach the islanders, diffidence is replaced with violence, and territoriality becomes a hot issue.

The meeting ground is seen as a highly unstable zone, in which proximity may be a source of danger, to both sides. At one point, in New Zealand, a sailor, feeling threatened by the attitude of the islanders, fires his musket over the natives' heads, meaning to scare them off, and thus to re-establish a safe distance between the two parties. But these tribes have never seen white men before, and know nothing consequently about gunpowder; still undeterred, they move closer, which causes the marine to shoot this time at a native and kill him.[16] Hawkesworth's text strongly suggests that the attack on the marines had been premeditated and that the islanders were the aggressors, not suspecting once that encroaching on native land without having been formally invited to do so might have been perceived as a form of aggression. His account draws a vivid picture of savages rushing out of the woods, brandishing lances: 'When we had got some distance from the boat, four men, armed with long lances, rushed out of the woods ... in a few minutes [they] renewed the pursuit, brandishing their lances in a threatening manner'.[17]

Once more, Hawkesworth's grammatical choices serve to underscore the spatial movements in which communication seems to be caught, implicitly reshuffling the uncertain ground of interaction into two distinct, antagonistic communities. When they hear the sailor's musket, the Europeans huddle together and become a compact 'we' facing the indiscriminate 'they' of the Maoris: 'they went back, dragging after them the dead body, which however they soon left, that it might not incumber their flight. At the report of the first musket we drew together, having straggled to a little distance from each other, and made the best of our way back to the boat'.[18] What Hawkesworth's narrative also suggests is that the 'we' of the Europeans is welded together by values – solidarity, respect for the dead – which do not seem to prevail among the fierce savages.

The narrator's 'I' – Cook's assumed voice – only reappears in Hawkesworth's account when he has Cook remember his instructions and decide to re-establish contact:

> As I was desirous to establish an intercourse with them, I ordered three boats to be manned with seamen and marines, and proceeded towards the shore, accompanied by Mr. Banks [Joseph Banks, the naturalist and botanist of the expedition], Dr. Solander, the other Gentlemen, and Tupia [a Tahitian serving as guide and interpreter]; about fifty of them seemed to wait for our landing, on the opposite side of the river, which we thought a sign of fear, and seated themselves upon the ground: at

first, therefore, myself, with only Mr. Banks, Dr. Solander, and Tupia, landed from the little boat, and advanced towards them.[19]

This time again, the grammar of the text is symptomatic of the predicament in which Cook and his men find themselves. Whereas the Europeans are clearly identified and named, the savages are only referred to through an unspecified, collective 'them'; what is more, 'I' and 'them' are repeatedly positioned at opposite ends in the sentences. The Europeans' hesitations are marked both by the shifts from the 'I' to the 'we', indicating intense debate in the boats between Cook and his companions, and by the verb inflections which express the doubts with which the 'Gentlemen' seem to be agonized ('seemed to', 'we thought'). Finally, the narrowing of the distance between the two parties, as Cook and his men advance towards the islanders, is a source of suspense, the outcome of the meeting being marked by its utter unpredictability.

This tension between distance and proximity raises therefore an even more fundamental issue as to the dialectics of first encounters: the uncertainties of the Gentlemen as they land on the beach where the natives are seated are due mainly to the fact they are unsure whether their interpretation of the 'signs' ('which we thought a sign of fear') addressed to them by the islanders is the correct one. Is 'seating oneself on the ground' to be analysed as a show of fear and submission on the part of the natives? Is this new spatial arrangement an invitation to initiate exchange? It seems the toning down of the tensions inherent in questions of territoriality, and the promise of proximity between the two parties, do not suffice to settle the question of the proper distance to be adopted.

By dramatizing first encounters in the way it does, Hawkesworth's narrativization of events seems thus to offer the necessary basis for a study of the interactions, vocal and non-vocal, among representatives, not of different nations or races, but of various cultures. Hawkesworth's narrative of Cook's unstable positioning vis-à-vis the islanders suggests that successful communication is necessarily predicated on the ability to discern which communication acts and codes are important to groups of different cultures, what types of meanings groups apply to different communication events, and how such codes provide insight into particular cultural communities. In sum, it seems that Hawkesworth's narrative, precisely by virtue of its being a narrative, lays bare the necessity of an 'ethnography of communication'.[20]

The islanders are first described as refusing verbal exchange. Nonverbal communication, however, does takes place, notably in the form of gesture, of voice inflexion or of various other clues present in the context in which the interaction takes place. For example, Tupia the interpreter assumes the Maoris, whose distant, indifferent attitude to the visitors is deemed intolerable, may be addressed in the Tahitian language, but the sounds he forms do not seem to elicit the expected response from the Maoris:

> Tupia called to them in the language of Otaheite; but they answered only by flourishing their weapons, and making signs to us to depart; a musquet was then fired wide of them, and the ball struck the water, the river being still between us: they saw the effect, and desisted from their threats; but we thought it prudent to retreat till the marines could be landed.[21]

When Tupia starts speaking, his appearance, together with the meaning of his utterances, articulated in a language of the South Pacific, are assumed to be clear enough messages of goodwill and peaceful intentions. But it seems this message, be it in form or in content, is somehow unacceptable to the islanders. Whether the Maoris understand Tupia or not remains so far an enigma; all that can be said on reading Hawkesworth's relation of events, is that what characterizes the exchange is a misunderstanding of some sort. And it is indeed this cultural difficulty that determines each party's recourse to some kind of primitive nonverbal exchange – flourishing weapons, firing muskets – aimed at reasserting each party's territoriality, with water functioning once more as a reassertion of distance.

But Hawkesworth's account is more subtle here than it appears. The passive structure of the clause 'a musquet was then fired' seems to suggest that firearms are used by the white men almost by accident, perhaps even against orders, as if to suggest that the abolition of distance for the benefit of mutual understanding is indeed the primary objective of the European explorer. The adverb 'then' implies that the use of the musket is in fact a direct consequence of the Maoris' aggressive behaviour. Still – and the narrative is very careful to insist on this – since water lies between the two antagonistic groups and the bullet does not hit anybody, no harm is done, threats stop, and the possibility of peaceful exchange is restored. The British even manage to set up some trade with a few Maoris, as if the principles of European civilization and culture – the following of strict rules of conduct, the assumption of universal benevolence, the inevitability of trade and commerce – could eventually prevail over the natives' instinctive, or cultural, reactions of diffidence and violence.

But trade itself is a source of tension:

> But after some time they took what was handed down to them, without making any return; one of them who had done so, upon being threatened, began to laugh, and with many marks of derision set us at defiance, at the same time putting off the canoe from the ship: a musquet was then fired over his head, which brought him back in a more serious mood, and trade went on with great regularity. At length, when the cabbin and gun-room had got as much as they wanted, the men were allowed to come to the gang-way, and trade for themselves. Unhappily the same care was not taken to prevent frauds as had been taken before, so that the Indians, finding that they could cheat with impunity, grew insolent again, and proceeded to take greater liberties.[22]

The British blame the Maoris for not respecting the fundamental, supposedly universal, rules of commerce. Again, Hawkesworth's text, by focusing on the white man's perception of the transactions, and by choosing to interpret certain clues as marks of 'derision' and 'defiance', suggests that the fault is entirely the Maoris', whose culture is clearly indicted as being one of 'cheating'.

Hawkeworth's other accounts of similar exchanges seem to point in the same direction. In Tahiti, reciprocity seems to have been the first rule of interaction: the visitors and islanders meet on firm land and exchange gifts; then the Tahitians go on board for another exchange of presents; finally Cook and a few Englishmen visit the local chiefs,[23] so that it even becomes somewhat unclear in Hawkesworth's narrative who the host is, and who the guest, as if the two parties were caught in some kind of spiral of imitation, from which the interlocutors emerge as two potential alter egos. Visitors and natives even exchange items of clothing, which partly erase external signs of difference.[24] But then a 'theft' – or rather what appears to be a theft and is indeed interpreted by the narrative as 'pocket-picking', is taken very seriously by the Europeans, which inevitably impairs the harmony between the two communities:

> Just at this time, Dr. Solander and Mr. Monkhouse complained that their pockets had been picked. Dr. Solander had lost an opera glass in a shagreen case, and Mr. Monkhouse his snuff-box.[25]

Feeling they have been cheated, and even assaulted, the Europeans are terribly upset: 'Complaint of the injury was made to the Chief'. The impersonal phrasing of Hawkesworth's account underscores the purely legal turn of the relationship. What then happens is particularly telling. In order to compensate for whatever deperdition or confusion of meaning the translation of the complaint addressed to the chief might entail, gestures are used by the Europeans to reformulate their message and make it even more explicit. To make sure the white man's anger is carried across to the native, 'Mr. Banks started up, and hastily struck the but end of his firelock upon the ground'.[26] The text then mentions a rush to get out, shouting, noise and tumult. Only the chief and his wife remain with the Europeans when every other native has run away, so that the two groups are distant again, and 'territoriality' is disputed again, spatial distance translating the cultural misunderstanding that has just taken place.

The episode is particularly significant in that it shows the cultural gap between the two groups concerning ownership. Hawkesworth's rendering of this scene suggests that civilization clearly distinguishes between giving and taking, as well as between offering and selling, in a way that is apparently not meaningful for the Tahitians, who may also have imagined, after receiving various gifts from their visitors, that the Europeans did not value ownership. This is something Hawkesworth's narrative does not acknowledge, and each group thereafter remains locked up in their own cultural references and in their respective constructions of the other group's motives. Mutual understanding has proved impossible, having failed to take place as 'a cultural performance', i.e. as the enactment of a common culture, where gestures and attitudes are foreseeable according to shared codes.[27]

The text nevertheless insists that the Europeans' indignation is taken into account by the Tahitians, as if the natives were in turn beginning to grasp the full scope of cultural codes as potential sources of serious conflict. Hawkesworth describes the local chief, Toubourai Tamaide (with whom the Europeans have signed a peace treaty), endeavouring to find a solution 'with a mixture of confusion and concern', which reads in fact like a validation of the Europeans' values.[28] Hawkesworth's narrative suggests that the Europeans also use the theft incident to get the upper hand again, and regain a position endangered by the mimetic spiral of exchanges. His text obviously takes this opportunity to place the white man in the position of a privileged observer, whose central presence is again that of the ethnographer in first contact zones:

> It will not perhaps be easy to account for all the steps that were taken in the recovery of this glass and snuff-box; but this cannot be thought strange, considering that the scene of action was among a people whose language, policy and connections are even now but imperfectly known.[29]

Finally, what the text implies here is that neither the details of the steps taken by the chief, nor the real substance of the words exchanged among the Tahitians, are of any importance. What matters is that the Europeans' indignation should have been acknowledged by the islanders, as a token of their awareness of cultural issues in matters of interaction. It remains, however, that the islanders are implicitly expected to share the white man's values; not once does the Journal allude to the Tahitians' reaction to the Europeans' attitude. Implicit to Hawkesworth's narrative, therefore, is the normality of a situation of unequality whereby the Europeans feel entitled to annex foreign territories, while feeling the right of strongly, perhaps even disproportionately reacting to the 'theft' of small European belongings.

As a point of fact, according to the Journal, the Europeans' failure to tune in with the Tahitians is matched by the islanders' attitude towards them. Nobody seems to be willing to learn more about the other's way of life and customs, let alone adopt them. The two groups remain locked within two widely different cultural systems, the existence of which is gradually acknowledged, as a form of mutual recognition, but which do not seem to be destined to communicate. There is a good deal of curiosity, but it mainly serves the purpose of trade, no more. Even mimicry seems to be a form of minimal politeness, meant to secure the white man's good opinion of the natives. This is most manifest when Cook invites the Tahitians to attend a religious service:

[Mr Banks] placed himself between them, and during the whole service, they very attentively observed his behaviour, and very exactly imitated it: standing, sitting, or kneeling, as they saw him do: they were conscious that we were employed about somewhat serious and important, as appeared by their calling to the Indians without the fort to be silent; yet when the service was over, neither of them asked any questions, nor would they attend to any attempt that was made, to explain what had been done.[30]

The tragic result of this communicational failure is the constant threat of renewed violence. For what Hawkesworth's account systematically foregrounds is not the difference of cultural outlook, of the kind the cultural relativism of Montaigne's essays had evinced as early as the end of the sixteenth century, but the discrepancy between the antagonistic systems of values in the two groups, with the ignorance of the other's thoughts and intentions being a permanent threat to the safety, and dignity, of each. When he chooses where to settle camp, Cook literally draws a line on the ground and forbids the Tahitians to cross it:

Having marked out the ground that we intended to occupy, a small tent belonging to Mr. Banks was set up, which had been brought on shore for that purpose: by this time a great number of the people had gathered about us; but, as it appeared, only to look on, there not being a single weapon of any kind among them. I intimated, however, that none of them were to come within the line I had drawn.[31]

In a striking parallel, Hawkesworth relates that the Tahitians ask the English not to go into the nearby forest. The atmosphere is thus fraught with reciprocal distrust and lack of mutual respect: each party's territory is forbidden ground to the other. But the English, convinced that cheating and lying are essential to the Other's culture, believe they are kept away from the forest because there is game hidden there, and therefore resolve to trespass. Meanwhile, one of the natives decides to overlook Cook's interdiction, and crosses the line to steal a musket. The transgression is quite similar, with the English and Indians being represented as interchangeable actors in the tragedy of violence, but the consequences are quite different, if only because the white man can use powder to impose respect and restore his supremacy. The islanders who have followed Cook into the forest are scared by the noise of a gun fired at ducks; the thief is shot dead.[32] The similarity between the two scenes is striking, Hawkesworth seeming to imply that natives and animals are treated in a similar fashion by the European visitors.

What the narrative perhaps unwittingly underlines, however, is that firearms are used by the British to defend their material possessions, which dehumanizes both the Europeans, who give the impression of being more attached to the possession of objects than to the preservation of life, and the Tahitians, who may be killed as easily as game. Hawkesworth's account does indeed take a tragic turn, as error, distrust and greed, in equal measure on both sides, now widen a gap which first presented itself simply as cultural and linguistic. Firearms are thus made into a potent symbol of this utter failure in communication, as they widen the gap between the two groups, both literally and symbolically. At this stage, reminiscences of Defoe's and Swift's fascination with, or indictment of, gunpowder in contexts of cultural contact may be perceived in the narrative,[33] and one may even wonder whether such intertextuality is not a crucial dimension of Hawkesworth's decision to dramatize this event. One may indeed wonder whether by referring his British readers to famous textual antecedents where gunpowder is made into an essential ingredient of contact zones, Hawkesworth's narrative, as it emphasizes the tragic inescapability of violence in first encounters, is not also seeking to justify and even 'naturalize' the lethal use of firearms.

But again, the narrative is more subtle than it may appear. The islander is systematically turned into the aggressor, the consequence of this being that whenever a white man is led to use gunpowder, the context, much more than the essential brutality of the European, is to blame:

> the petty officer, a midshipman, who commanded the party, perhaps from a sudden fear of farther violence, perhaps from the natural petulance of power newly acquired, and perhaps from a brutality in his nature, ordered the marines to fire; the men, with as little consideration or humanity as the officer, immediately discharged their pieces.[34]

Hawkesworth's long sentence seeks to be mimetic of what in his view took place. The tragic order of the midshipman is reduced to its briefest linguistic form ('ordered the marine to fire'), an utterance reported in such a way that it seems to be lost in the various possible explanations for the unfortunate shooting ('perhaps ... perhaps ... perhaps'), presented as the inevitable result of the extreme confusion in which the sailors were then caught. Seventeenth- and eighteenth-century authors – Behn, Swift and Defoe in Britain, Voltaire, Montesquieu and Rousseau in France – were often quick to underline the cruelty of Europeans towards innocent primitives, and modern anthropology has established the widespread phenomenon of violence as being 'integral to the process of contact and settlement'.[35] But Hawkesworth's narrative never represents the islanders as the innocent victims of European barbarity; what his text suggests, rather, is that gunpowder is a dangerous item per se, endowed with a life of its own, capable of wreaking havoc in specific contexts, especially in the presence of unruly primitives and when 'petty officers' are in charge.

From then on, even the friendly chief Owhaw takes distance from the Europeans:

> The next morning but few of the natives were seen upon the beach, and not one of them came off to the ship. This convinced us that our endeavours to quiet their apprehensions had not been effectual; and we remarked with particular regret, that we

were deserted even by Owhaw, who had hitherto been so constant in his attachment, and so active in renewing the peace that had been broken.[36]

Again, Hawkesworth's narrative strategy constrains the reader's perception of the events. The Tahitians are present only as the grammatical subjects of a passive form ('few of the native were seen'), which posits the visitors as the active centre of representation and thought, as the events described induce the white man to think about what has happened ('this convinced us'). But who is 'we' here ('we remarked with particular regret')? The pronoun seems to refer neither to the petty officer who gave the order of shooting, nor to the marines who immediately discharged their weapons, as if the text were drawing an implicit distinction between the panic-stricken reaction of the rank and file, and the more enlightened attitude of the leaders, thus transforming the whole affair into an unfortunate, but accidental incident. The narrative does not betray any feeling of guilt: on the contrary, Hawkesworth's account insists that the officers' efforts ('our endeavours') remain 'ineffectual', as if the islanders were the ones to blame for not wanting to make up for past errors and to resume dialogue; the phrase 'the peace that had been broken' uses a passive form with no agent, thus exonerating any particular individual of the responsibility for the tragic events.

Cook is now left with no other option but to bridge the gap again. Hawkesworth's text takes up the territorial metaphor, and shows how Cook chooses to bring the ship nearer the coast. The movements to and fro are resumed. Two local chiefs come on board to bring gifts, which is greatly appreciated (the chiefs are called 'our noble benefactors'). But the natives seem to have learnt a lesson and now ask the Europeans to keep at a distance. This is first made clear to Cook when he examines the body of the man killed by the sailor:

> I took notice that several of the natives observed us with a mixture of solicitude and jealousy in their countenances, and by their gestures expressed uneasiness when we went near the body, standing themselves at a little distance while we were making our examination, and appearing to be pleased when we came away.[37]

The distance the English required of the islanders after the theft is now required of the visitors by the Tahitians themselves, who in turn show every sign of feeling cheated and wronged. Hawkesworth's narrative, by implicitly equating the violence of the murder with the violence of the theft, points out the strangeness of the behaviour of the sailors *as perceived by the natives*. Only then is the theme of the 'noble savage' allowed to emerge in Hawkesworth's account:

> Upon this occasion it may be observed, that these people have a knowledge of right and wrong from the mere dictates of natural conscience; and involuntarily condemn themselves when they do that to others, which they would condemn others for doing to them.[38]

But any further development of this idea would inevitably imply an indictment of the white man's handling of the situation – and therefore of 'civilization' itself. Hence Hawkesworth's qualifications:

> Yet if we admit that they are upon the whole happier than we, we must admit that the child is happier than the man, and that we are losers by the perfection of our nature, the increase of our knowledge, and the enlargement of our views.[39]

Interestingly, as Edwards points out,[40] Hawkesworth will later omit what Cook's logbook has to say about Australian aborigines:

> They may appear to some to be the most wretched people upon Earth, but in reality they are far more happier than we, Europeans; being wholly unacquainted not only with the superfluous but the necessary conveniencies so much sought after in Europe, they are happy in not knowing the use of them. They live in a Tranquillity which is not disturb'd by the inequality of condition.[41]

Cook's thoughts here, unmediated by Hawkesworth's editorial processing, are reminiscent of Montaigne's celebration of primitive culture as a world of 'childhood' innocence.[42] In Hawkesworth's narrative, on the contrary, Cook is made into the perfect representative of arrogant eurocentrism, taking the superiority of European civilization for granted. The text admits, however, that if the Europeans are upset by the natives' thieving tendencies, the islanders for their part resent the brutal superiority gunpowder confers upon the Europeans. For instance, the Tahitians do not approve of cannons being mounted upon the fort built by Cook to observe the transit of Venus.[43] But the Europeans are not ready to do without gunpowder, which in Hawkesworth's account is gradually invested with the magical dimension of a talisman of authority, the wielding of which is the guarantee of the white man's superior status. When Tabourai Tamaide suddenly 'yields to temptation' and grabs Mr Banks's gun, the white man's reaction according to Hawkesworth is unequivocal:

> As it was of infinite importance to keep the Indians totally ignorant of the management of fire-arms, he [Banks] had taken every opportunity of intimating that they could never offend him so highly as by even touching his piece; it was now proper to enforce this prohibition, and he therefore added threats to his reproof.[44]

This time, the passage does not appear in Cook's log,[45] which is further indication that in Hawkesworth's view the issue of the *structure* of the relationship between colonizer and colonized is granted priority over that of its *nature*. 'Childhood' innocence needs to be preserved, not to bring the colonizer's methods of civilization into question, but to secure the explorer's superiority over the islander. For Hawkesworth, rituals of interaction do not therefore afford opportunities for communicative exchange; interaction produces nothing but power relationships, to the extent that any exchange of useful information between the white man and the native is perceived as being potentially dangerous for the success of the colonizing process. What matters for Hawkesworth is that the superiority of the European should be reasserted with the utmost vigour, as is suggested by the uncommon number of adjectives and adverbs used in his sentence ('infinite', 'totally', 'every', 'never', 'so', 'even'), a rhetoric which superbly ignores the Other's expectations in terms of cultural transmission, while at the same time implicitly condemning the unruly Other to obedient, acquiescing silence.

According to Watzlawick, Beavin and Jackson, all communicational interchanges are either 'symmetrical' or 'complementary', depending on whether they are based on equality or on difference: 'symmetrical relationships' are based on equality, with partners tending to have similar behaviours; 'complementary relationships' are unequal in power, with one partner taking a dominant role and the other a submissive one.[46] What I have tried to show is that Hawkesworth's narrative of Cook's exploration of the South Pacific islands evinces a very interesting tension between distance and proximity, when scenes of first encounters are marked by the hesitations of both visitors and islanders as to the nature of the ritual of communication that is about to take place. Spatial arrangements then allow for the possibility of 'symmetrical' interchanges, whereby trade but also other kinds of transactions are made possible. What gradually emerges, however, is the awareness that this initial quest for the right kind of distance between the two parties is in fact made impossible by the cultural systems regulating the attitudes and behaviours of each community. The gradual obliteration of any kind of anthropological ambition by a narrative which is henceforth intent on extolling the colonizer's values, to the detriment of issues of mutual understanding or of cultural transmission, ends up pitching the two camps against each other. Subtle narrative strategies are then used both to invalidate the myth of the innocent, noble savage, and to exonerate the white man's procedures of any wrongdoing. The tension on which Hawkesworth's narrative builds itself, finally, is that which looms behind the conflict for the control of firearms and gunpowder, and it appears the edition of Cook's logbook was meant primarily to reassert the challenged authority of the colonizer, whose status was being increasingly threatened in the contact zones. Through its rhetoric – choice of pronouns, point of view, verb forms, adjectives, adverbs and so forth – Hawkesworth's narrative makes sure that for the British public at home interaction seems to be viewed in terms of 'complementary relationships': the encounter is recorded only insofar as its narrativized relation may produce an unequal relationship between the English explorer and the Polynesian primitive.

8 WALKING IN THE CONTACT ZONE: GEORG FORSTER AND THE PERIPATETIC MODE OF EXPLORATION (1768–77)

Christian Moser

In the second part of *Les Mots et les choses* Michel Foucault points to the historical rift that separates the *episteme* of the *âge classique* from the modern order of knowledge.[1] The repercussions of this rift can be shown in many fields of scientific and (inter-)cultural practice, not least in the European discourse of exploration as it developed in the second half of the eighteenth century. The voyages led by the British explorer James Cook furnish a graphic example of the ambiguous state of transition between conflicting *epistemes*, for while most of the members of his scientific crew – and especially he himself – remain firmly rooted within the discursive order of the Enlightenment, others manifest an early awareness of innovative means to produce knowledge in the fields of natural history and anthropology. The most interesting among the latter is the Anglo-German scientist and writer Georg Forster, who accompanied Cook on his second voyage to the Southern Pacific and published the English version of his account, *A Voyage round the World*, in 1777 (the German version, entitled *Reise um die Welt*, appeared in 1778–80). By comparing the travel writings of Cook with those of Forster, the effect of the epistemic rift on the practices of exploration can be made visible. In particular, the comparison makes it possible to work out two different (Enlightenment and post-Enlightenment) modes of fashioning the first-contact situation as well as corresponding ways of constructing the 'contact-zone' in which the encounter between the European traveller and the non-European 'native' was to take place.[2]

Cook's *Journals* are generally held to be representative of the Enlightenment mode of exploration.[3] A characteristic of his account is the attempt to separate the report of what happened to him and his crew during his visits to newly 'discovered' places from the detached description of these places and their inhabitants. Cook distinguishes neatly between narrative and description. His descriptive labour depends on his ability to collect first-hand information while maintaining an outsider's position. This is made possible by the vehicle that Cook uses for his exploration – and for writing down his observations: the ship, a mobile home that allows the explorer to extricate himself from his involvement in the foreign culture, to decontextualize and objectify his data.[4]

Forster, however, employs a very different vehicle in his attempt to construct a specific type of knowledge about other cultures: the vehicle of his body. A remark made by Forster in his description of the *Resolution*'s initial visit to Tahiti appears, at first sight, to be rather harmless and insignificant. In fact, however, it provides a key to his specific mode of exploration:

> Our acquisitions in natural history being hitherto so inconsiderable, we had leisure every day *to ramble in the country* in search of others, as well as to pick up various circumstances which might serve to throw a light on the character, manners, and present state of the inhabitants.[5]

According to Forster, Tahiti does not have much to offer to the botanist or zoologist. There are hardly any unknown species that await the natural historian in order to be described and classified. Therefore, Forster has plenty of time to go ashore where, instead of studying plants and animals, he can focus his attention on the human inhabitants of the island. Thus, natural history is characterized as an activity that is primarily practised on board ship, whereas anthropology is defined as an activity that is practised primarily in the field, in immediate confrontation with the members of the foreign culture.

This opposition between the offshore practice of natural history and the inland practice of anthropology seems somewhat odd. One would expect botany and zoology to be disciplines that are practised in the field as well. Forster, however, seems to insist on the fact that natural history is, in large measure, a sedentary activity. Plants and animals are not to be scrutinized in their natural environment, but in the scientist's study. Here, the specimens collected in the field are to be analysed, described, put into order and classified according to a Linnéan taxonomy. In the German version of the passage quoted above, Forster is even more specific with regard to the sedentary components of the botanist's activity – he mentions 'Zeichnung und Beschreibung', the drawing and description of the collected items.[6] Thus, knowledge in natural history is generated by abstracting its objects from their original context and submitting them to the discriminatory gaze of the scientist. The ship is an instrument that is indispensable for the production of this kind of knowledge. It provides the neutral ground that enables the scientific gaze to operate, as well as the element of distance that allows for the objectification of natural phenomena. Isolated from its original context, the object can reveal its distinctive trait. By contrast, Forster seems to conceive of anthropology as a discipline that produces knowledge on the spot and in immediate communication with its object. In order to gain insight into a specific culture, Forster considers it necessary to study manners, customs, artefacts and institutions in their original surroundings. In his opinion, anthropology is not a sedentary activity, but is associated with a certain type of movement – a *rambling*, peripatetic movement in the field.

Before engaging in a further investigation of this movement, it is necessary to indicate how far Cook's mode of exploration differs from Forster's. Forster's distinction between natural history and anthropology is also what distinguishes him from his captain in terms of the production of knowledge. Whereas, in the case of Forster, it is only botanical and zoological data that need to be trans- planted on the ship in order to be transformed into knowledge, in the case of Cook, this applies, without exception, to all kinds of data, whether they pertain to the domain of Nature or Culture. According to Cook, the ship constitutes the privileged locus for the production of any kind of knowledge, including anthro- pology.

In his 1768–71 voyage to the Pacific, the journals dealing with the visit to Tahiti are neatly divided into two sections. The first section is headed 'Remark- able Occurrences at Georges Island'.[7] It constitutes a journal in the strict sense of the term in that it presents a day-to-day factual report of what happened to Cook during his stay in the vicinity of the island – his activities on board and ashore, his dealings with the members of his crew and with the natives, his move- ments in and around Tahiti. The second section is entitled 'Description of King Georges Island'.[8] It was written on board the *Endeavour*, after its departure from Tahiti. The combined spatial and temporal distance allowed Cook to abstract his data from the concrete instances of their observation and to arrange them according to a preconceived order. This order bears a striking resemblance to the one employed by Antoine de Bougainville in his *Voyage autour du monde*.[9] Obviously, both explorers follow a standard Enlightenment procedure. In fact, the scientific treatises published in the *Philosophical Transactions* by members of the Royal Society during the seventeenth and eighteenth centuries often exhibit the same bipartite structure – a succinct narrative account delineating the circumstances under which scientific insight was gained, combined with a static presentation of this knowledge, often in the form of *tableaus*, diagrams, maps, charts and algebraic formulae.[10] Cook and Bougainville do not employ such formulae, but arrange their material in a 'static' fashion, under the headings of geography, flora and fauna, and the people of Tahiti, the latter part of the description being subdivided into the physical appearance of the Tahitians, their character, clothing, customs, houses, economy, politics and religion. Concern- ing the moral character of the Tahitians, Cook, for example, gives the following account:

They have all fine white teeth and for the most part short flat noses and thick lips, yet their features are agreeable and their gate gracefull, and their behavour [*sic*] to strangers and to each other is open affable and courtious and from all I could see free from treachery, only that they are theives to a Man and would steal but everything that came in their way ...[11]

In the 'Remarkable Occurrences at Georges Island' Cook relates several concrete instances of (supposed) Tahitian thievery,[12] but refrains from analysing them within a moral or cultural framework. In the 'Description of King Georges Island', by contrast, he hypostasizes thievishness as a general trait that defines the moral character of the Tahitians. Since Cook deals with thievery under the heading of 'moral character' – and not, for instance, under the heading of 'customs' or 'economy' – he deprives himself of the opportunity to interpret Tahitian stealing as a cultural or economic practice. Thus, Tahitian 'thievishness' is essentialized – it appears to be as substantial and as blatantly visible as the whiteness of the islanders' teeth. This procedure is typical of the 'Description of King Georges Island'. The elements that make up Tahiti and the Tahitian society are not copiously depicted. Rather, Cook confines himself to isolating certain elements that are marked as distinctive traits. Thus, he produces a totalizing and timeless portrait of Tahiti that combines natural history with cultural analysis. By rigidly separating the temporal narrative of the occurrences and instances of observation, on the one side, from the taxonomic arrangement of the data gained thereby, on the other, Cook succeeds in isolating the marks that define Tahiti as a specific entity.

Cook generates knowledge by transferring the object of observation from its original context to his ship. The consequences of this procedure for the analysis of culture can be further illustrated by one more striking example taken from his second voyage. During the first voyage, Cook had gained the suspicion that the inhabitants of New Zealand were cannibals. He had not been able to verify this suspicion, because Maori cannibalism was integrated into a complex cultural and ritual context which made it less conspicuous. Therefore, in order to prove that New Zealanders were cannibals, Cook deemed it necessary to isolate the cannibalistic act 'proper' from its cultural context and transplant it on board the *Resolution*. In November 1773, while the *Resolution* anchored in Ship Cove, a group of officers walked through a Maori village and stumbled upon the remains of what they believed was a cannibalistic feast. The natives, so they reported, tauntingly offered them a bit of the human intestines, but the Europeans declined the offer, purchasing the victim's head instead. Subsequently, they exhibited this trophy on board the *Resolution*. Cook, taking advantage of the presence of some New Zealanders on his ship, availed himself of the opportunity and conducted, as Forster puts it in his narrative,[13] an 'experiment': 'I ... ordered a piece of the flesh (from the head) to be broiled and brought on the quarter deck where one of these Canibals eat [*sic*] it with a seeming good relish before the whole ships Company which had such an effect on some of them as to cause them to vomit'.[14] Thus, by transposing the act from its original environment, Cook fabricates a 'proof' of Maori cannibalism. He is not interested in discovering the cultural significance of this act, however. In his opinion, it suffices to establish the 'fact' in order to secure a definitive trait (the New Zealanders are 'cannibals') and, on this basis, to effect a classificatory move (the New Zealanders are 'savages' – 'savage man ... in his original state').[15]

Moreover, by transferring the cannibalistic act on board his ship, Cook turns it into a public spectacle.[16] Thus, he seeks to assure that the distinctive mark that allegedly defines his object of knowledge becomes visually perceptible. This emphasis on the visual manifestation of knowledge is, as Foucault argues, typical of the Enlightenment *episteme*.[17] It is for this reason that the discipline of botany serves as a paradigm for the production of knowledge. In the taxonomy developed by Linné, the sexual organs constitute a distinctive and visible trait that allows for the specification of plants. Similarly, Rousseau, in *Les Rêveries du promeneur solitaire*, praises the discipline of botany: in contrast to the mineralist who must penetrate and violate the earth in order to gain a knowledge that is concealed, the botanist deals with objects that adorn the surface of the earth and immediately reveal their distinctive properties to the eye of the observer.[18] Like Rousseau, Cook favours a mode of knowledge that scans the surface of the objects from which it seeks to extract visible marks. His gaze does not attempt to penetrate surfaces in order to take hold of hidden essences. Rather, it functions as a view from the outside that maintains distance and relies on the object's readiness to manifest its nature.

Cook's technique of knowledge-producing has consequences for his mode of exploration. Firstly, it impinges on the way he moves about in his field of investigation. Secondly, it affects the way he handles situations of first encounter with other cultures. In the first instance, it is conspicuous that Cook avoids penetrating the interior regions of the land that he explores. He prefers to hover in border regions, in liminal spaces like the beach, which always allows for a quick retreat to his ship. In his first voyage, the largest bulk of the narrative section, 'Remarkable Occurrences at Georges Island', is devoted to reporting his successful attempt at making 'the Circuit of the Island in order to examine and draw a Sketch of the Coast and Harbours thereof'.[19] Following the shoreline partly by boat and partly on foot, Cook circles around the entire island of Tahiti. Thus, he sketches the outline of the island and procures a totalizing view from the outside – the indispensable basis for drawing an exact map of Tahiti. Just as, in the descriptive section, the concrete instances of observation disappear into the taxonomy of distinctive traits, so the circuit around the island (and its narrative representation) vanishes into the map which allows the eye to take in the entirety of Tahiti and its salient features in a single view. The performative *parcours* – a tentative movement through space that can only be presented diachronically, by means of narrative – is absorbed by the possessive *carte* – the map that systematizes spatial relations into the synchronicity of a totalizing representation and that contains all possible movements through a certain terrain.[20]

In the second instance, it is striking how Cook strives to play down the importance of first-encounter situations. The passage in the 'Remarkable Occurrences' that deals with his initial landing in Tahiti is significantly terse and reticent. In this passage, Cook expresses his desire to gain absolute control over the first-encounter situation. He attempts to prepare himself for the encounter – on the one hand, by securing the services of a go-between, a native Tahitian familiar with Europeans, who is to mediate between the captain and the inhabitants of the island; on the other hand, by issuing a catalogue of strict rules that are to regulate the traffic between his crew and the natives.[21] The encounter itself seems to go off smoothly: 'No one of the Natives made the least oppossission at our landing but came to us with all imaginable marks of friendship and submission'.[22] Cook reduces the natives to objects of perception that display a multitude of visible signs. These signs are immediately legible and transparent; their understanding does not require the least hermeneutical effort. They belong to the repertoire of signs that are 'imaginable' to a European; they are part of a universal language. Thus, the first-encounter situation is not obscured by any cultural difference. The only difference that matters is the difference of power which elicits, on the side of the natives, seemingly transparent signs of submission. The relation of manifest power and domination allows Cook to maintain his detached position of the observer who is content to skim the surface of objects in his search for distinctive marks and self-explanatory signs.

Whereas Cook refuses to distinguish between the modes of knowledge applied in natural history and anthropology, Forster attributes a special status to the latter discipline. In his opinion, anthropological insight cannot be produced by abstracting the data of observation from their original environment. Rather, it is necessary to study manners and customs as parts of a larger cultural context. In order to do so, it does not suffice to view its elements from the outside and to scan its surfaces. On the contrary, the observer must strive to attain an *insider's* view; instead of circling around the object, he must penetrate it, get inside the natives' villages and dwellings – and, ultimately, inside their minds. The new paradigm for this hermeneutic mode of exploration is the walk. And indeed, Forster's account of Tahiti is based on a sequence of walks that lead him into the interior parts of the island.

Forster's preference for the peripatetic mode of exploration must be seen against the background of the bourgeois 'ideology of walking' that developed in the course of the eighteenth century.[23] A major site for the construction of this ideology was aesthetic theory, the new category of the 'picturesque' being conceived as a weapon against the topographical art associated with aristocracy and its use of the 'cavalier perspective', the static prospect from high above.[24] In his *Essays*, William Gilpin criticizes the aristocratic gentleman who abuses art for the sake of self-aggrandizement. He imagines a landowner who leads an artist to the highest point of his estate – 'the point of amplest prospect' – and gives him the following direction: 'Take thy stand / Just here ... and paint me *all* thou seest'. The work of art that results from this direction, however, is 'but a painted survey, a mere map'.[25] According to Gilpin, the aristocratic penchant for prospects betrays a possessive attitude that tends to reify Nature. Therefore, he considers it necessary to substitute the static, immobilizing view from above by the mobile and limited perspective of the walker. Gilpin advocates the artistic walker who produces a sequence of imperfect sketches instead of a totalizing map.

Significantly, Forster employs his walks on Tahiti and on other Pacific islands to sketch 'picturesque' views of the exotic landscape. The literary sketch of picturesque Nature constitutes an aesthetic counterpoise to Cook's geographical maps. Russell Berman draws a similar conclusion in his comparison of how Cook and Forster describe the *Resolution*'s sojourn at Dusky Bay in New Zealand: 'For Cook, Dusky Bay is a cartographic fact, a latitudinal item to be entered in the charts ... For Forster, it is an aesthetic experience as well as a natural fact ... The scientist Cook measures a geometric space whereas Forster encounters a life world'.[26] However, Forster's predilection for walking and picturesque views does not only signify a new aesthetic relationship between the bourgeois subject and Nature. It also implies a new attitude towards culture, as the walker condescends to move on the same social and cultural level as his fellow-beings, entering into an immediate relationship with the people he meets in his way, gaining intimate knowledge of their affairs. In Book IV of his *Confessions* (1782), Jean-Jacques Rousseau praises the virtues of walking. In particular, he relates how, during a long pedestrian tour that led him from Paris to Chambéry, he attained insight into the secret life of the French peasantry, presenting the walker as a figure who solves mysteries, discloses the concealed ills of society, and penetrates the secret thoughts and motives of his fellow-creatures.[27]

Rambling across Tahiti, Forster adopts the penetrating gaze of the bourgeois walker. He advances into remote parts of the island's interior and into secluded nooks, even though the Tahitians try to prevent him from trespassing into these areas. Above all, he enters the dwellings of the natives in order to study their ordinary way of life, family structures and social behaviour. Some of these pedestrian explorations lead him into first-encounter situations. For example, in the course of his most extended walk on the island, Forster and his companions enter a rustic hut whose occupants, a large family headed by a venerable patriarch, are engaged in a conversation:

They desired us to sit down on the mats among them, and we did not give them time
to repeat their invitation. Their curiosity, which had perhaps never before been gratified with the sight of strangers, now prompted them to examine our dress and our
arms, without bestowing their attention longer than a moment on any single object.
They admired our colour, pressed our hands, seemed to wonder that we had no punc-
tures on them, nor long nails on our fingers, and eagerly enquired for our names,
which when known, they were happy to repeat. These names, as they pronounced
them, were not so like the originals that an etymologist could easily have deduced
them, but in return they were more harmonious ... Forster was changed into *Matara*,
Hodges into *Oreo*, Grindall into *Terino*, Sparrman into *Pamanee*, and George into
Teoree.[28]

Whereas Cook, in his Tahitian first-contact scene, reduces the Other to a visual
display of transparent signs of submission, Forster is more wary in his assessment of the situation. His wariness indicates that, in his opinion, the signs
emitted by the Tahitians are not transparent at all, but demand interpretation.
Forster assumes that his hosts have never seen Europeans before – but this is no
more than a conjecture, a tentative interpretation of their behaviour. Instead of
maintaining distance, he tries to read the situation from the perspective of his
Tahitian hosts and so to enter their minds. Forster engages in a hermeneutics
of the native psyche. Thus, contrary to Cook, he attempts to create a situation
of reciprocity: the European desire to know the natives is, according to his
hermeneutical conjecture, matched by the native desire to know the Europeans.
However, this semblance of reciprocity masks a relation of power and domination that is no less threatening to the Tahitians than Cook's manifest scenario
of submission. Whereas European curiosity succeeds in penetrating the native's
skin and entering his mind, the European's skin constitutes an insurmountable
obstacle to native curiosity. Forster deciphers his hosts' psychological motives,
but the natives remain preoccupied with their guests' bodies – their 'outside': the
whiteness of the skin, the shortness of the nails, the absence of tattoos.

In fact, Forster too, in his first-contact scene, stages the hermeneutic superiority of the European explorer. The most graphic illustration of his alleged
superiority is the inability of the Tahitians to pronounce the European names.
By communicating this significant detail, Forster suggests that the natives are
locked into their own language and their own culture. Their culture is a static,
localized culture, strictly confined to its own specific environment, whereas the
European explorer claims the ability to walk around freely and to enter other
environments and cultures at will. Thus, Forster's account exhibits a penchant
that is characteristic of modern Western ethnography, which, according to the
Indian anthropologist Arjun Appadurai, proceeds from the assumption that
'natives are not only persons who are from certain places, and belong to these
places, but they are those who are somehow incarcerated, or confined, in those
places'.[29]

And yet, although Forster does not hesitate to stage his own hermeneutic superiority, he stops short of asserting a position of detached omniscience, a totalizing point of view. He claims that the walker's perspective is superior to the native's, but he also admits that it always remains limited, subjective and fragmentary[30] – as fragmentary as a sketch produced by the 'picturesque' traveller. For this reason, Forster refrains from classifying the results of his hermeneutic activity and from establishing an integrative portrait of Tahiti. Contrary to Cook, he does not separate the narrative of events from the description of the other culture. Instead, he attempts to combine his observations of Tahitian cultural practices with the account of how he procured his information. His narrative represents the process of collecting bits of knowledge about the other that never add up to a totalizing picture.

This mode of representation concedes the possibility of hermeneutic error. For example, the encounter with the patriarch and his family induces Forster to surmise that Tahitian society is still in a primitive state of equality. But one of the next stops in his walk robs him of this illusion: he enters a magnificent dwelling where he meets a Tahitian aristocrat who revels in luxury.[31] The knowledge gained by this encounter supplements and rectifies the impression received on the former occasion, but it does not cancel it out. Like a series of sketches, Forster's peripatetic exploration of Tahiti is structured according to the logic of supplementarity. In fact, Forster explicitly states that his representation of Tahiti aspires to be no more than a mere supplement of the account given in Cook's first voyage:

> All the merit of the preceding pages concerning the isle of Taheitee, must therefore consist in a few gleanings and elucidations on several subjects. However, I am in hopes that the particular point of view in which I have beheld, and consequently represented circumstances already familiar to the reader from former accounts, will not prove uninteresting, and may in several instances suggest new and valuable reflections.[32]

As a 'supplement' to Cook's voyage – a word I take here in its deconstructionist sense of a substitute which postpones that which it installs[33] – Forster's narrative adds something to Cook's account without completing it: his particular point of view rectifies and subverts Cook's portrait of Tahiti at the same time that it *defers* closure. Nevertheless, however subversive his text may be, it perpetuates the relation of power and domination that relegates the native point of view to a position of immobility and inferiority.

9 THE DISORDER OF THINGS: EMPIRICISM AND THE CARTOGRAPHIC ENTERPRISE, OR, THE OBSERVATIONS OF SAMUEL HEARNE (1795) AND ALEXANDER MACKENZIE (1801)

Cheryl Cundell

Prominent among the narratives of explorers whose overt purpose was the expansion of the territory and trade interests of the British Empire, were Samuel Hearne's *A Journey from Prince of Wales's Fort in Hudson's Bay to the Northern Ocean* (1795) and Alexander Mackenzie's *Voyages from Montreal on the River St. Laurence, through the Continent of North America, to the Frozen and Pacific Oceans* (1801). Although the two expeditions had similar purposes and their narratives were offered as contributions to empirical knowledge, a comparative study demonstrates that the narratives reflect extremes of empiricism that produce opposite attitudes to natural history and anthropology. I wish to argue that the extremes of empiricism articulated in these narratives therefore call into question Mary Louise Pratt's vision of the imperial enterprise of the time.

In *Imperial Eyes*, Pratt argues that '[f]or three centuries European knowledge-making apparatuses had been construing the planet above all in navigational terms,'[1] but that, in the second half of the eighteenth century, 'the descriptive apparatus of natural history' presented a new means for making 'global-scale meaning,'[2] and thus a new mode for justifying imperial expansion. Justifying imperial expansion was possible because natural history established the European-Self as the guarantor of meaning in relations with non-European Others, by positing the European as the culmination of a natural order of living beings. Pratt's remarks on the systematizing of Nature are in keeping with the concept conveyed by 'the descriptive apparatus of natural history'. In her analysis of the ways by which travel and exploration narratives employ natural history to legitimate territorial possession, however, Pratt is not speaking of 'the descriptive apparatus' as defined according to Michel Foucault's concept of '*mathesis*, understood as a universal science of measurement and order,'[3] but, rather, is speaking of description in the objective or scientific voice, which enables an observer to assume a position of authority when describing objects of observation.

Unlike the observer using the scientific voice to describe according to the system of Nature, the observer using only the scientific voice may speak from a position of authority but does not necessarily assume that authority to be natural. Thus, although Pratt's 'descriptive apparatus' has rhetorical force because it carries an Althusserian echo of an 'ideological apparatus' endlessly reproducing imperial ideology, description itself has the potential to proliferate disorder and, thereby, question the authority of 'imperial eyes'.[4] Those extremes of empiricism, illustrated in Hearne's and Mackenzie's narratives, are the contexts in which observing-Self and observed-Other are constituted. Aligned with natural history and cartography, respectively, the observational perspective of each narrative not only determines the nature and extent of first encounters between Self and Other but also the failure or success of each exploration. Producing contrasting human geographies through description, the narratives show that while Mackenzie's cartographic perspective sharpens distinctions between Self and Other, Hearne's natural history perspective blurs them.

The objective or scientific voice that enables an observer to assume a position of authority when describing objects of observation depends upon a detached style of description that presumes to deliver an accurate and unbiased eyewitness account. The style is predicated upon the separation of Self and Other into observer and observed, whereby Self constructs Other but disguises the construction by removing reference to the 'I' or eyes of the observer. The style relies on what Foucault explains as the 'almost exclusive privilege' that was accorded to 'sight'[5] or to 'observation'[6] in the eighteenth century. In Samuel Johnson's 1775 *Dictionary of the English Language*, 'observation' was defined as '[t]he act of observing, noting, or remarking', and the verb 'observe' was defined as '[t]o watch; to regard attentively'.[7] Here is observation at its most general. But in speaking of the 'almost exclusive privilege' that was accorded to 'sight', Foucault is characterizing the knowledge-structures of the period as depending upon the privilege accorded to sight working *with* the *mathesis*, or method of ordering. Although Foucault describes *mathesis* 'as a general science of order'[8] that involves measurement, it is not, he argues, the scientific enterprise as we understand it: '*mathesis* as a general science of order does not signify that knowledge is absorbed into mathematics' because 'it is always possible to reduce problems of measurement to problems of order'.[9]

Although Foucault subsumes mensuration within the ordering system, he does note that the 'attempt ... to mathematicize empirical knowledge' was 'constant and continuous in the case of astronomy'.[10] The note is significant because the relationship between mathematized astronomical empiricism and the geometry and trigonometry of navigation and cartography points to another site of privilege: mathematical theory. As early as William Cunningham's 1559 *The Cosmographical Glasse*, observation referred to navigation: 'Longitudes and Latitudes ... require longe and diligent observation'.[11] By the time that Daniel Defoe's 1719 *Life of Robinson Crusoe* was published, observation had become a synecdoche for the calculating of latitude and longitude: 'I ... learn'd how to ... take an Observation'.[12] When discussing 'the new privileges accorded to observation' in the eighteenth century, Foucault explains that '[t]he use of the microscope was based upon a non-instrumental relation between things and the human eye – a relation that defines natural history'.[13] The use of the quadrant or sextant, pieces of cartographic equipment, was, however, based upon an *instrumental* relation: that is, the quadrant or sextant calibrates the sense of sight. Because navigation and cartography are, in effect, applied astronomy, the observation of the instrumental eye is limited to the purpose of measurement necessary to the calculation of relations within a predetermined system.

For both Hearne and Mackenzie, the purpose of their explorations is cartographic. In the introductions to their narratives, neither disguises the imperial ambitions of his explorations but, rather, sets them firmly within the progress of territorial and trade expansion into regions unmapped. Hearne's title alludes to these two elements: '*for the Discovery of Copper Mines, a Northwest Passage*'. An employee of the Hudson's Bay Company, he is also ordered, in the course of his journey, to 'encourage' the Native peoples whom he encounters 'to exert themselves in procuring furrs and other articles for trade' and to determine whether the Coppermine River is 'navigable' and whether 'settlement can be made' at its mouth.[14] From Hearne's point of departure from Prince of Wales's Fort on the shore of Hudson's Bay, the *Journey* narrates his two unsuccessful attempts and his third and successful attempt to reach his destination at the mouth of the Coppermine River at the Arctic Ocean. Mackenzie is also invested in extending trade from east to west, '*through the Continent of North America*', but for the North West Company. A share holder in the Company, Mackenzie explains that he was 'led ... by commercial views' to determine 'the practicability of penetrating across the continent', and he concludes that his enterprise 'adds new countries to the realms of British commerce',[15] realms that 'may ... be considered as part of the British dominions'.[16] Mackenzie's *Voyages* narrates a general trip from Montreal to Fort Chipewyan, near the mouth of the Athabasca River. The fort then serves as the base from which he makes one failed and one successful voyage to the Pacific Ocean.

Although Hearne and Mackenzie both act in the capacity of cartographers, and although the reasons for their explorations are the same, they justify their narratives oppositely, and it is the justification for their narratives rather than the purpose of their explorations that forms the context in which Self and Other are constituted. Hearne's justification aligns his narrative with the non-instrumental observation of natural history, whereas Mackenzie's aligns his with the instrumental observation of cartography. In his preface, Hearne notes that he has produced his narrative,

> not so much for the information of those who are critics of geography, as for the amusement of candid and indulgent readers, who may perhaps feel themselves in some measure gratified, by having the face of a country brought to their view, which has hitherto been entirely unknown to every European except myself. Nor will, I flatter myself, a description of the modes of living, manners, and customs of the natives, (which though long known, have never been described), be less acceptable to the curious.[17]

As Chloe Chard explains, in the eighteenth century an appeal to readers' curiosity could be used to justify a travel narrative because concepts of curiosity created 'continuities between pleasure and [the] benefit' that might be derived from instruction.[18] Although Hearne's stated appeal is general, there is in the prefatory matter what might be read as a more specific appeal, to the Royal Society. In dedicating his work to 'SAMUEL WEGG, Esq. – Governor' of the Hudson's Bay Company,[19] Hearne covertly aligns his narrative with natural history: Wegg was '[e]lected to fellowship in the Royal Society in 1753', and 'fostered two-way co-operation between the Company and the Society' concerning the collection of natural history specimens.[20] Moreover, in his dedication Hearne describes his narrative as being written 'in a plain and unadorned Style',[21] a style in keeping with the style dictates put forth by the Royal Society. As Thomas Sprat explains in his 1667 *History of the Royal Society*, the Society exacts from its members 'a constant Resolution, to reject all amplifications, digressions, and swellings of style: to return back to the primitive purity, and shortness, when men deliver'd so many *things*, almost in an equal number of *words*'.[22] Although Hearne takes on the plain style advocated by the Royal Society, he notes that, in describing the animals of the north, he has 'not described [them] in a scientific manner':[23] that is, his descriptions are not ordered by the scientific apparatus used for the purpose of classification within the system of Nature. Thus, Hearne's empiricism is defined by individual experience operating inductively.

Mackenzie's remarks on style are also in keeping with the dictates of the Royal Society: 'I must beg to inform my readers, that they are not to expect the charms of embellished narrative, or animated description; the approbation due to simplicity and to truth is all I presume to claim'.[24] In his presumptuous self-deprecation, Mackenzie not only associates himself with the plain style advocated by the Royal Society but also makes a claim for the veracity and accuracy of his narrative, a claim that is essential given Mackenzie's conception of his audience. Mackenzie ends his preface with 'the hope that this volume, with all its imperfections, will not be thought unworthy the attention of the scientific geographer'.[25] '[T]he scientific geographer' is likely Alexander Dalrymple, a speculative geographer, 'elected a Fellow of the Royal Society [in] 1771',[26] and the man, 'Mr. Dalrymple',[27] against whom Hearne defends his narrative. Dalrymple compiled collections of exploration narratives for the purpose of promoting 'British commercial expansion'[28] and, in 1789, produced the *Plan for promoting the Fur-Trade* in which he speaks of the possibility of a northwest passage *through* the continent via 'the river that flowed out of Great Slave Lake',[29] the river that Mackenzie takes on his first voyage.

Not only does Mackenzie associate himself with scientific geography but he also actively dissociates himself from natural history. First, he explains that the environment through which he travelled is not conducive to description. He then remarks that 'small bands of wandering Indians are the only people'[30] that he can present to his reader. To impress upon his reader the seriousness of his venture, he makes the following dismissive disclaimer: 'I do not possess the science of the naturalist; and even if the qualifications of that character had been attained by me, its curious spirit would not have been gratified' because there was no time 'to dig into the earth'[31] or to 'collect the plants which nature might have scattered on the way'.[32] There was time, however, for cartographic observation, and Mackenzie notes that his work 'extends the boundaries of geographic science'.[33] In speaking of geographic science, he aligns himself with a method of observation depending upon measurements derived from mathematical theory. Thus, Mackenzie's empiricism operates deductively.

In justifying their narratives, Hearne and Mackenzie not only present the extremes of empirical knowledge to which they subscribe but also the observational perspectives that characterize Self and delimit the field of observation from which descriptions of Others are produced. Mackenzie sees with the calculating eye of the cartographer, whereas Hearne sees with the curious eye of the natural historian. When Mackenzie says that he 'had an *observation* of Jupiter and his satellites',[34] it is not an observation from which Mackenzie will produce a description of Jupiter and its moons but from which he calculates his position. The character of his astronomical observations is reflected in the way in which he narrates his progress and in the nature of his ethnographical descriptions of the Native peoples whom he encounters. His narrative abounds with 'courses and distances'[35] like those given on the nineteenth of August, '[o]ur course to-day was South-South-West three quarters of a mile, North half a mile, North-West by West three quarters of a mile, North by West half a mile',[36] which continue for more than a page of the narrative. The description of an abandoned Native encampment encountered on the day begins, 'there were eight ... lodges of last year',[37] and an inhabited encampment encountered later in the journey is similarly described: 'four elevated houses and seven built on the ground'.[38] The buildings are surveyed; habitation is quantified. People are also quantified, 'I counted sixty-five men',[39] and they are either instrumental to Mackenzie's goal or they are problems that he must solve.

Hearne's descriptive tendency speaks in the list of his narrative's contents. Hearne describes the practical matters of the journey, such as weather, location and the acquisition of food : '[w]eather very bad', '[a]rrive at the woods, where we kill some deer'.[40] He also describes elements of Native cultures: '[a]rrive at a tent of strangers, who are employed in snaring deer in a pound. – Description of a pound'.[41] Hearne details not simply the physical structure and operations of the pound but also the pound's significance to the people who employ it: '[t]his method of hunting ... is sometimes so successful, that many families subsist by it without having occasion to move their tents above once or twice during the course of a whole winter'.[42] His descriptive interest even extends beyond general cultural observations to specific human incidents that provide further insight into culture. When '[o]ne of [his guide's] wives elopes',[43] Hearne's narrative turns to a description of 'the custom' of the Chipewyan, 'for the men to wrestle for any woman to whom they are attached'.[44] While it may seem that Mackenzie's self shifts because it moves over terrain, its position is fixed as the origin of measurement; by contrast Hearne's self, as the origin of experience, shifts according to the changing cultural context that he encounters.

Although both Hearne's and Mackenzie's observational perspectives people the landscape, Mackenzie's materialist view not only positions people as objects but also limits interaction in encounters between Self and Other, whereas Hearne's observations, in presenting people as cultural beings, expand the possibilities for interaction. Encountering a tribe of Sekani for the first time, Mackenzie has this to say: 'They examined us, and every thing about us, with a minute and suspicious attention. They had heard, indeed, of white men, but this was the first time that they had ever seen an human being of a complexion different from their own'.[45] The limited description reflects limited interaction. By contrast, Hearne's description of his first encounter with a group of Chipewyan revels in detail:

> As I was the first [Englishman] whom they had ever seen, and in all probability might be the last, it was curious to see how they flocked about me and expressed as much desire to examine me from top to toe, as an European Naturalist would a non-descript animal. They, however, found and pronounced me to be a perfect human being, except in the colour of my hair and eyes: the former, they said, was like the stained hair of a buffaloe's tail, and the latter, being light were like those of a gull. The whiteness of my skin also was, in their opinion, no ornament.[46]

Here 'non-descript animal' refers to an animal that has not been scientifically described. In casting himself as such in the eyes of Native observers, positioned as 'an European Naturalist', Hearne inverts the observational perspective of his narrative and, through the humour elicited at his own expense, suggests that the authority of his observational perspective is a European construction. Thus, although Mackenzie's brief and superficial descriptions maintain a consistent or monologic narrative perspective, Hearne's detailed descriptions make his narrative dialogic because they include other voices hinting at other ways of perceiving the world.

Because Mackenzie's and Hearne's descriptions of first encounter reflect their perceptions of themselves in relation to the Others they meet, the function of the eye might serve as a metaphor for the outcome of encounters in which the presumed authority of the Self is called into question by the Other. The calculating eye reconfigures; the curious eye incorporates. In each narrative, the effect of the eye's perceptions reveals itself in the representation of Native speech. After enquiring of a Shuswap details of the river upon which he travels, Mackenzie remarks, 'I was very much surprised by the following question from one of the Indians: 'What', demanded he, 'can be the reason that you are so particular and anxious respecting a knowledge of this country: do not you white men know every thing in the world?'[47] Mackenzie notes that '[t]his interrogatory was so very unexpected, that it occasioned some hesitation before [he] could reply';[48] but reply he does and in doing creates a distinction so as to simultaneously assert white superiority and excuse the need for information. He says, 'we certainly [are] acquainted with the principal circumstances of every part of the world',[49] but notes that he is interested in the geographic particulars of the area. In saying so Mackenzie reconfigures the power dynamic that the challenging question presents. Because the success of his exploration depends upon the authority of the European Self, he suggests that European knowledge is of a higher order than Native knowledge.

Hearne's assumed authority is challenged after he observes the birthing procedures of the Chipewyan. Although not a moment of first encounter between himself and the Chipewyan, it is a moment of first encounter with the customs surrounding birth. Hearne notes to his reader that the women have no 'external help whatever'.[50] He then describes himself informing the band with whom he is travelling 'of the assistance which European women derive from the skill and attention of [their] midwives' and notes to his reader that the Chipewyan 'treated [the information] with the utmost contempt; ironically observing, "that the many hump-backs, bandy-legs, and other deformities, so frequent among the English, were undoubtedly owing to the great skill of the person who assisted in bringing them into the world, and to the extraordinary care of their nurses afterward"'.[51] In this instance, as in others, Hearne represents a translation of the Native speech and does not counter with his own remarks but, rather, ends the paragraph with the speech and, in allowing it to speak with its own wit, incorporates its perspective. While Mackenzie must enclose or control the challenging speech of the other, Hearne is open to other ways of seeing and does not have to have the last word.

Each explorer's representation of Native speech speaks of the value that he attributes to that speech and this attributed value bears upon the exploration that each narrates. After probing a group of Native people for geographic details, Mackenzie remarks that '[t]he Information they gave us respecting the River seems to me so very *fabulous* that I will not be particular in inserting' it.[52] He disregards their talk of 'many Monsters'[53] and also their mention of 'the other great River'[54] that goes to the west. On 10 July he realizes that he has been mistaken in rejecting the advice:

> At Noon I got an Observation which gave me 67° 47' North Lat ... I am much at a loss here how to act being certain that my going further in this Direction will not answer the Purpose of which the Voyage was intended, as it is evident these Waters must empty themselves into the Northern Ocean.[55]

As when his authority is questioned, Mackenzie finds himself at a loss, but instead of admitting failure, he turns the voyage into a success by reformulating its significance: 'I determined to go to the discharge of those Waters, as it would satisfy Peoples Curiosity tho' not their Intentions'.[56] It does not matter that Mackenzie could have made just one successful trip to the Pacific Ocean had he followed the advice of the Native-Other; what matters is the proof of his error in the observation that he takes, because the success of Mackenzie's exploration depends upon a theory of his own infallibility.

Conversely, Hearne accepts Native advice, a decision that leads to the success of his third attempt to journey to the Arctic Ocean. On the return from his second attempt, his second failure, Hearne meets the Chipewyan leader Matonabbee, who explains that part of the reason for the failure of the two expeditions was the result of 'the very plan ... pursued, by the desire of the Governor' of the fort.[57] Hearne not only credits and acts on Matonabbee's advice but, in defiance of the Governor of Fort Prince of Wales, he employs Matonabbee as his guide for his third journey. In speaking of Matonabbee's description of 'the plan he intended to pursue' in the journey, Hearne remarks that the plan 'did honour to [his guide's] penetration and judgement' and 'proved him to be a man of extensive *observation* with respect to the times, seasons, and places'.[58] For Hearne, the observation of the Native-Other produces knowledge much in the manner that the European natural historian might, and Hearne, therefore, credits the knowledge that is produced. The way in which each explorer articulates the failure or success of exploration points to where each places authority. For Hearne, authority resides in human experience whereas, for Mackenzie, authority resides in numerical proofs.

The contrasting forms of observation through which characterization of Self and description of Other are constructed are reflected in later critical readings of the narratives. Maurice Hodgson provides an aesthetic reading of the narratives, in which he remarks that Mackenzie's *Voyages* 'reflect the haste and superficial nature of [Mackenzie's] experience', whereas Hearne's *Journey* reflects 'Hearne's sensitive powers of observation'.[59] Hodgson pronounces that 'Mackenzie as a journal writer is a disappointment',[60] and calls Hearne a 'consummate story-teller',[61] arguing that because of his 'sensitive powers of observation' Hearne 'builds his narrative not only toward the goal of *his* explorations', but also parallels his quest with the goal of the Chipewyan – which is to massacre a group of Inuit living at the mouth of the Coppermine River.[62] In other words, Hodgson views Hearne's as the better narrative because Hearne tells not only his own story but also the Chipewyan's story.

Bruce Greenfield takes an opposite view of the achievements of Hearne's and Mackenzie's narratives but cites Hodgon's idea that Hearne tells two parallel stories as the weakness of Hearne's narrative. He argues that 'Mackenzie writes the purest kind of discovery narrative' because, '[a]ll actions and events signify in terms of the traveller's stated intentions'.[63] Moreover, 'these intentions are defined in relation to a global vision of European trade and power. Who Mackenzie is as a traveller and what happens to him are understood unambiguously in relation to the history of an expanding European-centred trade network'.[64] Greenfield believes that Hearne's narrative, instead, reveals a conflict between 'the imperial context' of his narrative and 'the specific demands of life and travel in the remoter regions of the eighteenth-century North America',[65] and he argues that, although 'Samuel Hearne's achievement seems to recent readers to have more to do with his personal adaptation to the Northern culture that sustained him on his travels, this very ability to change was what most threatened his success as the author of his own discovery narrative'.[66] Greenfield argues that because Hearne depended on the Chipewyan, he 'was obliged to tell two parallel versions of his trip'.[67]

While I agree with Hodgson's aesthetic sense and with Greenfield's reading of the narratives as *discovery narratives*, I disagree with the contention that Hearne tells 'two parallel versions of his trip'. What I intend to do is present a simple structural analysis of the successful expeditions related in the two narratives to suggest that, while Mackenzie's narrative *should* be read as a narrative of geographic discovery, Hearne's should be read as a natural history narrative, as the authors themselves indicate.

Discussing the structural arrangement of exploration narratives, MacLulich says that 'the explorer is engaged in imposing order on a set of events'[68] and argues 'that most accounts of exploration are emplotted in one of three ways, either as *quests*, *odysseys*, or as *ordeals*'.[69] In describing the distinguishing characteristics of these three forms, MacLulich explains that quests have heroes, ordeals *may* have survivors and odysseys have a 'digressive structure'.[70] Because Greenfield's definition of 'the purest kind of discovery narrative'[71] requires a hero, I shall use discovery and quest synonymously. If one considers a simple narrative structure with a rise in action, a climax, and a dénouement, as represented by travel from the point of departure, the destination, and travel to the point of return, and if one considers the action that takes place at the destination as the defining moment, Mackenzie's narrative is clearly intended to be a quest, or a narrative of discovery. The structure of Mackenzie's narrative positions the enunciator as the hero at the voyage's destination. Finally arrived on the Pacific coast, Mackenzie is 'taking a meridian'[72] when two canoes of Natives expressing hostile intent approach his party. While his party panics, asking if it is his 'determination to remain there to be sacrificed', Mackenzie continues his measurements: 'My altitude, by an artificial horizon, gave 52° 21' 33'; that by the natural horizon was 52° 20' 48' North latitude'.[73] Here is a tableau of heroism: hostile Natives approaching, panicking members of his party, and yet the collected and calculating Mackenzie continues taking his observations. Mackenzie follows his observations by a proud territorial assertion, writing on a rock in 'vermillion', 'Alexander Mackenzie, from Canada, by land, the twenty-second of July, one thousand seven hundred and ninety-three',[74] and thus takes possession of the land through which he has voyaged.

By contrast, when Hearne reaches his destination at the mouth of the Coppermine River at the Arctic Ocean, because it is cloudy and because he has recently taken latitude readings, he notes, 'I did not think it worth while to wait for fair weather to determine the latitude exactly by an observation ... For the sake of form, however, after having some consultation with the Indians, I erected a mark, and took possession of the coast, on behalf of the Hudson's Bay Company'.[75] While '[f]or the sake of form' might suggest that possession is a given, the moment of possession is not simply done '[f]or the sake of form' but in 'consultation with the Indians'. Furthermore, Hearne explains in a note in his introduction, because 'he was not provided with instruments for cutting on stone', so to indicate possession, he cut 'his name, date of the year, &c. on a piece of board that had been one of the Indians' targets'.[76] Here Hearne is referring to one of the shields that had been used by the Chipewyan during their recent massacre of a group of Inuit. The shield points to the climax of the narrative, which is not the stated goal of Hearne's journey, but the goal of the Chipewyan journey. What should be the climax of Hearne's *discovery* narrative is dénouement. Hearne writes neither a discovery narrative that disproves the possibility of the North West Passage nor two parallel narratives. Because the shield that he uses to stake his territorial claim is emblematic of shared experience, he writes a narrative acknowledging the dependency of the British upon the assistance of the Native peoples.

Pratt describes natural history metaphorically as a 'systematic surface mapping of the globe', one that 'maps out not the thin track of a route taken, nor the lines where land and water meet, but the internal 'contents' of those land and water masses'.[77] She says that, '[u]nlike navigational mapping ... natural history conceived of the world as a chaos out of which the scientist *produced* an order'.[78] It would seem that in the light of Hearne's and Mackenzie's narratives, the distinction that Pratt makes between natural history and 'navigational mapping' is somewhat artificial. The cartographer is still producing order – but that order is being produced mathematically rather than linguistically. While the system of Nature may offer the late eighteenth century a new means for justifying imperial expansion, describing elements of natural history offers a way by which to upset the order that is assumed natural to the system of Nature. In aligning their exploration narratives with what I have called such extremes of empiricism, Hearne and Mackenzie show that they are aware of the observational perspectives available to the late eighteenth-century explorer and of the scope that these perspectives offer for defining relations between Self and Other. In aligning his observations with cartography, Mackenzie is able to map the goals of his exploration onto the Others that he encounters, while, in aligning his observations with natural history, Hearne describes Others into his narrative. Moreover, by highlighting conflict at the moment of territorial possession, Mackenzie insists upon the opposition of Self and Other, whereas, by highlighting a moment of cooperation and sharing, Hearne collapses the opposition.

10 JOHN FRANKLIN AND THE IDEA OF NORTH: *NARRATIVE OF A JOURNEY TO THE SHORES OF THE POLAR SEA IN THE YEARS 1819-1822*

Catherine Lanone

In *Geography and Some Explorers*, Joseph Conrad mapped the three phases of colonial history, beginning with '*Geography Fabulous*', the extravagant speculations concerning distant lands, the mythical visions with their strange pageants of uncanny beings, trees and beasts; the second phase, '*Geography Militant*', referred to the eighteenth- and nineteenth-century scientific voyages of exploration, leading to the third phase, '*Geography Triumphant*', or modern geography. Conrad's 1924 essay draws our attention to the construction of geography, and to the revisioning of scenes of first encounters as we switch from '*Geography Fabulous*' to '*Geography Militant*'. A case in point may be the quest for the Arctic Grail (to borrow Pierre Berton's title), the attempt to conquer the Arctic where the Other turns out to be not so much the native inhabitants of the wilderness – be they the Indians or the Inuit – as *the icy wilderness itself*, Mary Shelley's unpredictable 'everlasting ices of the North'.[1] Although the first Franklin expedition does meet an old Inuk who has only heard stories about white people, most encounters are not strictly speaking scenes of first encounters, since most Indians have come across white traders before. My purpose in this essay is to pay attention to the groundbreaking expeditions of the 1820s, and more particularly to John Franklin's journal of the first land expedition, to see how the scenes of first encounter with the *Arctic shores* become a rhetorical construct both disguising and revealing a cultural clash and a cultural betrayal.

Let us begin with two illustrations, in order to sketch a brief survey of the history of exploration in the 1820s. Early attempts to find the fabled Northwest Passage date back to Martin Frobisher and the sixteenth century, but little progress had been made by the time the old dream was revived after the Napoleonic Wars. Suddenly, the exploration of the Arctic was once more promoted by the Navy as a great scientific and geographical venture, turning into little less than a national obsession. The quest was adamantly pursued, even when it proved less and less likely that the mythical Passage might be found. The first illustration, 'First Communication with the Natives at Prince Regents Bay, As Drawn by John Sacheuse and Presented to Captain Ross, August 10 1818', was included in John Ross's account of his 1818 journey and depicts a scene of first encounter between two English officers and a band of Eskimos.[2] The Inuit, who have never seen white men before, ask them whether they come from the sun or the moon. The two officers are John Ross and William Parry, officers who had only met one Inuk so far, their Anglicized interpreter Sacheuse, who actually drew that picture himself. Pierre Berton draws attention to the contrast between the Inuit's furred jackets and boots and the two Englishmen's pose, 'resplendent in cocked hats, tailcoats and white gloves',[3] with shoes better fitted for a dance floor than for snow drifts: 'Officers and natives are equally startled by this unexpected encounter. The two peoples view the world in ways as different as their appearance'.[4] The second example is an 1824 engraving of John Franklin celebrating his first land expedition: 'Captn. Franklin, R. N. F. R. S. Commander of the Land Arctic Expedition with Fort Enterprise in the background', drawn by G. B. Lewis and engraved by F. C. Lewis.[5] After the failure of Ross's sea expedition, the Admiralty had determined on a joint venture by sea and land which might ease the survey of blank territory. The expedition by sea was entrusted to William Parry, Ross's second in command, and the land expedition to John Franklin, who had just returned from Buchan's failed attempt to reach the North Pole. Hopefully, Franklin and Parry were to meet by the Arctic shores, share information and solve the mystery of the Northwest Passage together. The fact that Franklin was a Navy officer, ill-equipped to face the challenge of land survey, crossed no one's mind. Franklin was to survey about 5,500 miles during his round trip, but the expedition also caused appalling suffering among the 'misery of cold and frost'.[6]

A glance at the engraved portrait of Franklin sets the tone of our tale; it depicts a heroic explorer, confident, quiet and calm, a gentle smile hovering on his lips, with picturesque clouds and trees in the background, but also with, in the foreground, the modern instruments which imply that order is being imposed on that wild, primitive space. The sturdy stability of the posture suggests that the encounter with the Other has left no scars. From the start, the portrait reveals that the account mingles testimony and propaganda, in an attempt to save face after a somewhat misguided attempt to rule the North. The portrait fits in with the Admiralty's ideological construct. Much of the Northern dream was derived from the delusions of John Barrow, second secretary to the Admiralty, a rather formidable figure who thought that now that the war with Napoleon was over, the fine officers who were no longer of use could be sent to solve the mysteries of the unknown, especially of the Arctic. Barrow believed that a warm sea lay behind the barrier of ice; he was obsessed with the idea that Britain should find the Northwest Passage before Russia in order to maintain its economic and political supremacy. Giving up was – in his own words – a kind of national suicide.

The voyage of discovery was thus subverted from the start. The point was not to explore, to face the unknown, but to impose upon the smooth slippery surface of Arctic ice a cultural and commercial construct. Since the Passage was deemed necessary for trade, it must exist, and it must be found. The explorer was sent to fulfil the fantasies of armchair adventurers, to obey a model, or, in Deleuze's terms, a 'tracing', 'on the basis of an overcoding structure or supporting axis, something that comes ready-made'.[7] The fairy tale, however, was highly disguised by scientific precision. Technology was at hand, to prove that modern science could take the modern man exactly where he wanted to go, where he could not possibly have ventured before. Franklin's *Narrative of a Journey to the Shores of the Polar Sea* begins by recalling the official instructions given to the head of the expedition: he was to determine the latitude and the longitude of every remarkable spot, trace the coast from the mouth of the Coppermine River, register the temperature of the air at least three times a day, describe the weather and the aurora borealis and note down 'the dip and variation of the magnetic needle, and the intensity of the magnetic force'.[8] He was also to study minerals and vegetation, the land and the natives. As a consequence, Franklin's entries offer endless lists of figures, details of degrees, temperatures, magnetic variations and positions compared with previous measurements. Like Samuel Hearne or Alexander Mackenzie, Franklin clearly relishes the technical aspect of the job, leaving more insightful encounters with the land and the natives to his midshipmen, George Back and Robert Hood, or to the doctor of the expedition, John Richardson, who was also a fine naturalist by training.

The scientific idiolect runs counter to the travellers' acute sense of disorientation. The landscape must be 'traced', measured, chartered, conquered by deed, word and image. Franklin apologizes for the stiffness of his own narrative, but as Richard Davis points out, it was no easy task to provide the lenses 'through which Europeans constructed an image of the New World' for a man who had been trained on the job and had very little education to speak of:

> Even to the highly educated humanist, the prospect of writing a book that accounts for the past two years of one's life might well seem daunting. Imagine, then, how such a prospect might have appeared to men whose formal schooling ended before they were fourteen years old.[9]

Reading and writing appear as obsessional activities during the journey. All the officers keep a journal of the expedition, and no matter how tired or hungry they are, they trace their slow progress on paper or, in the case of Back and Hood, draw and paint watercolours. When ink freezes, they write in pencil. In fact,

Franklin's published account pieces together texts written by himself, Hood, Back and Richardson, whenever the expedition splits into separate groups. And the story of the return from the Arctic shore is reconstructed, since Franklin lost his own journal in the rapids blocking their way. Like figures, words may therefore be seen as performative talismans. Each step is marked by an obsessional attempt to leave a significant trace: letters and accounts are handed to traders or dismissed *voyageurs* to be forwarded to England; when they reach the Arctic sea, Franklin buries a letter for Parry at the mouth of Hood's River, with a flag upon it to draw attention, and sets papers adrift in a buoyant box on the odd chance that it may be found by Parry's boat sailing on the Arctic sea. Naming is of course the ultimate way of writing one's position on – or possession of – the land. Words are used to inscribe a logic upon the smooth Arctic space, paying a tribute to the world of the explorers, including various Lords of the Admiralty or heroic figures engaged in the same pursuit: Cape Hearne, Buchan's Bay, Parry's Bay, Banks's Peninsula named 'in honour of the late Right Honourable Sir Joseph Banks, President of the Royal Society',[10] not to mention Cape Barrow, named 'after Mr. Barrow of the Admiralty, to whose exertions are mainly owing the discoveries recently made in Arctic geography',[11] or the more striking 'George IV'.s Coronation Gulf, in honour of His Most Gracious Majesty',[12] with of course the inevitable homage paid to Hood, Back, Richardson or Hepburn – a far cry from Indian or Inuit names indeed.

But, again, such a map is just a 'tracing'. For Arctic space, in reality, is susceptible to constant modifications, and is therefore unstable, challenging, reversible, in the Deleuzean parlance: 'smooth'. The 'tracing' is thus dangerous, and should always be put back on the 'map', a term I use in its Deleuzean sense, too, in order to describe an unpredictable, random space, open to nomadic lines of flight rather than amenable to rigid appropriation. In Franklin's journal, the difference between 'tracing' and 'mapping' may thus be measured in terms of suffering. Danger and uncertainty loomed from the start; even the voyage out was perilous, as long before reaching York Factory, the starting point of the land expedition, the *Prince of Wales* had hit an iceberg in the fog. Throughout the rest of the voyage, the men seem to be constantly aching from fatigue, cold and hunger. There is a gradation in pain, however, due to the weather conditions and the effort exacted from all the men involved in the expedition. Early on, Franklin repeatedly recalls that snow-shoes hurt the feet of those who, like himself, are not familiar with them. When the cold is not too intense, the landscape swarms with bloodthirsty mosquitoes, 'goring us with their envenomed trunks, and steeping ou clothes in blood', says Hood.[13] The only remedy to this plague is smoke, but the tent may catch fire. The other remedy, of course, is cold, but that too entails excruciating pain. The temperatures (around −45°C in winter) cause bad frost burns. During the winter, even Fort Enterprise, the wooden fort built by Franklin's men, offers no fitting protection against the cold, as the mixture of mud and snow used to fill the cracks soon freezes and breaks. Things, of course, are worse when walking outside. Clothes freeze, as do tea and measuring instruments; so do the tents, which have to be somehow folded and carried. Boots also freeze, when the men fall into cold water, sometimes through the ice, or when they lie in a leaking canoe. As the expedition progresses they sleep in their shoes lest they be unable to put them back on again. The men keep rubbing their faces, to prevent them from freezing. They are also burdened by heavy loads, especially the Canadian *voyageurs*, who carry at least eighty pounds per person, besides the canoes, as the expedition ventures along the Arctic sea. The English, doing things by the book, hardly ever use dogs to pull sledges. All men therefore walk tremendous distances through ice and snow. From October 1820 to March 1821, for instance, Back makes an extra round trip of a thousand miles on foot, to walk back to a fort and try to secure more food before the whole expedition leaves Fort Enterprise and ventures along the unchartered Arctic coast.

For food is a constant problem. The officers have brought some chocolate, flour and portable soup from England, with official letters requiring the trade companies to give them whatever provisions the expedition may deem necessary, as well as presents for the Indians. But the expedition took place at a time of utmost rivalry between the Hudson's Bay Company and the North West Company, and the promised supplies were only partially granted. Throughout the trip Back, Hepburn (the gifted English seaman) or the *voyageurs* hunt for meat, and Franklin, who is no hunter – a severe setback for the leader of a land expedition – records every deer, bird or bear shot. Before straying from known tracks, the expedition relies mostly on Indians to provide enough meat and pemmican – a mixture of pounded meat and fat, supposed to last for two years. But badly cured pemmican often turns out to be mouldy and unedible. Supplies run very low as the officers attempt to trace the Arctic coast, unaccompanied by the Indians who refuse to go so far, and are convinced that no one would survive the expedition. Along the Arctic coast driftwood and animals become scarce; progress is exhausting, sometimes uselessly so, as when the expedition loses nine days following the coast in fog, rain and a severe gale, only to realize that they have mapped a pointless estuary, and have to retrace their steps, thus covering 'one hundred and seventy-four geographical miles',[14] in vain. Franklin glosses over the 'mortification' of the incident, borrowing Richardson's term but not his description of the useless 'broad but shallow and unnavigable river',[15] whereas Back's journal gives a clearer hint of bitter disppointment: 'to our unspeakable chagrin we found the water getting fresh and saw the termination of the inlet'.[16] Stung by this mistake, Franklin decides to carry on, not till Repulse Bay (where Parry's boat actually is, so that they miss each other by five hundred miles, as

Franklin recalls in a footnote, as if this counts as success, which in a way it almost was), but at least to a significant turning point on the coast.

In spite of the *voyageurs'* desperate pleas to go back, and of the obvious change of weather, Franklin had qualms about giving up. When they finally reached what might be considered as a significant point where the coast curved, a spot which was aptly named Point Turnagain, they had only half a bag of pemmican left, perhaps two meals. Franklin is confident that the Inuit are going to help them, and has copper kettles and trinkets to give them; but they meet noone. After hastily following part of the coast in fragile canoes, regardless of severe gales, the expedition opts for a shortcut instead of returning all the way to the Coppermine river, where meat has presumably been left *en cache* by the Indians. They find, however, that the shorter route means crossing what they come to call 'Starvation Barrens'. Gradually, they give up what they are carrying, kettles, Richardson's cherished specimens of plants and rocks, books (though they retain a couple of religious books), and the *voyageurs* break the canoes they are carrying on purpose, weary of endlessly falling and wading through snow – a tragic mistake, as it turns out. As hunting failed and portable soup and pemmican were gone, the men assuage gnawing hunger by relying on fried friable bones when found – including rotting marrow, almost a delicacy at that point – and *'tripe de roche'*,[17] a lichen which burns the mouth and causes severe bowel problems. Cutting and boiling strips of leather, the men eat a leather holster, trousers, shoes ('Every little scrap of shoe leather, is now highly prized').[18] When the survivors reach Fort Enterprise, where they hope to find supplies left by the Indians, the fort is empty. They dig out the bones and skins left from the previous winter, but soup made with crushed bones excoriates the mouth. Hollow ghosts, with legs bloated by fluids, they are hardly able to walk or crawl to collect the last strips of skin or wood to make a fire.

Franklin's narrative thus gradually turns into an epic of pain and estrangement. Tapping into the Romantic myth of sublime ice, Arctic exploration was deemed an example of British civilization at its best, the responsibility and pride of the British Navy, especially since the whiteness of Arctic snow was taken as an emblem of moral purity, representing not simply a physical but an ethical test. For Sherrill Grace, it is 'a response that persists in constructing North as a grail, a test... and as a place to find not the Other but the self'.[19] In a cheerful letter – not included, of course, in the selection of documents composing Franklin's published journals – which Richardson wrote to the pragmatic Back from an advance party in June 1821, he compares their 'motley crew' to 'Chaucer's Pilgrims',[20] a hint that ultimately the journey was perceived as a sacred pilgrimage (but Chaucer's pilgrims told very prosaic tales, too). England expected her men to do their duty quietly, and Franklin's officers had backbone. Hood does not mention the fact that he was the first to jump in a canoe in order to descend rapids to hopelessly try and save a drowning man; Richardson may describe his attempt to swim across a freezing, impassable stream, but not the fact that when he entered the water he stepped on a knife and cut his foot to the bone. The rhetoric of duty prevails, even in dire straits; Richardson recalls reading the scriptures with emaciated, starving Hood, 'and we conversed, not only with calmness, but with cheerfulness',[21] as if the two men were trying to live up to the ideal of British exploration.

But fate grants Franklin's tale an additional epic dimension. From the start, he says that he regrets nothing but the untimely death of the late Mr Hood, turning the journals into the chronicle of a death foretold. Richard Davis draws attention to the significant distinction between the terms 'journal' and 'narrative', though both terms seemed almost interchangeable at the time. 'Narrative' implies that a coherent whole is constructed out of a day-to-day recording of facts: 'This process occured not only as these men struggled to convert real-world experiences into verbally constructed written ones in their daily journals, but also as they subsequently transformed those journals into book-length public narratives for lay audiences'.[22] In Franklin's case, the travel narrative is implicitly shaped into a tragedy. Utterly unable to walk on towards Fort Enterprise after Obstruction Rapids, the debilitated twenty-two-year-old Hood is left behind with Richardson, Hepburn and a métis *voyageur*, Michel. Michel feeds the men some wolf meat he has miraculously found, before shooting Hood (claiming of course that Hood has committed suicide). Richardson, guessing that Michel has fed them the flesh of a dead *voyageur*, decides to execute Michel. The tale presented in 'Dr Richardson's Narrative' is thus spiced up with the sensational flavour of cannibalism.[23] But cannibalism can be safely blamed upon the métis, the monstrous mongrel, traitor, murderer and scapegoat. This tragic resolution allows Franklin to conceal the real disaster of the expedition, dramatizing instead the sudden encounter of highly civilized men with an absolute in savagery and otherness.

Casting the other as villain is a thread that discreetly runs through Franklin's narrative. Franklin's rhetoric makes a clear distinction between Englishmen and the Other in all its guises, beginning with the Scottish inhabitants of the Orkney islands, who ponder and hesitate before joining the happy crew. Franklin mocks their hesitations, preferring the sturdy enthusiasm and discipline of English sailors. *Voyageurs*, the Catholic French or Métis Canadians, are even more problematic. Not only do they dare moan before their officers; they are also accused of being improvident, gobbling down all the food they can lay their hands on, regardless of the morrow. Franklin never seems to equate the incredible effort demanded from those men with their need for food. He also often blames the interpreters for stirring up trouble, first with the Indians, then among the *voyageurs*. On 13 August 1820, the situation verges on mutiny; even though a messenger from the Indians has promised nearby food, the *voyageurs* refuse to

go on on their scanty rations. Franklin belittles their complaint: 'they invariably
try how far they can impose upon every new master',[24] and speaks out: 'I, therefore, felt the duty incumbent on me to address them in the strongest manner
on the danger of insubordination'.[25] Back's journal strips Franklin's circumlocu-
tions of their mundane surface: it appears Franklin actually threatened to blow
out the brains of the first man who stepped forward to pilfer food. Things get
worse along the Arctic coast, as the *voyageurs* try to compel their leader to go
back. When they successfully venture on the Arctic sea in frail birch bark canoes
in spite of drifting ice, storm and gale, Franklin comments on their remarkable
achievement,[26] but insists mostly on their constant fear for their safety. Later, he
recalls how they broke the remaining canoe on purpose out of sheer exhaustion
– a disastrous move which was to block them all hopelessly at Obstruction Rapids and lead to the death of several more *voyageurs*. But Franklin never blames
himself for not having turned around sooner; indeed, he apologizes to his reader
when he does so eventually. The figure of the Arctic leader carved out by Franklin's narrative is indeed a stiff rhetorical construct.

The first encounter with the Indians also plays on cultural stereotypes. The
English flourish the Union Jack, dress up and wear medals, but only because they
have been 'informed that external appearances made lasting impressions on the
Indians'. The Indian chief, on the other hand, is said to have 'assumed a very great
aspect',[27] the repetition of the verb 'assume' ('the dignity which Indians assume
during a conference') suggesting that his composure is not natural. The expedition is thus cast in a patronizing colonial light, as the 'Great Father Across the
Sea' is supposed to seek the Passage to bring goods to the Indians and to end all
wars between Indians and Inuit. The tale is then moralizing, for the Indians are
blamed for being naturally lazy, for failing to provide enough food for the expedition, for being always sick, or in mourning:

> but it was generally feared that their spirits had been so much depressed by the loss of
> their children and relatives that the season would be far advanced before they could
> be roused to any exertion in searching for animals beyond what might be necessary
> for their own support. It is much to be regretted that these poor men, during their
> long intercourse with Europeans, have not been taught how pernicious is the grief
> which produces total inactivity, and that they have not been furnished with any of the
> consolations which the Christian religion never fails to afford.[28]

Franklin mocks the Indian prayer-houses, offering steam as a cure for all diseases,
never pausing to reflect that white men may well be responsible for the epidemics
decimating the Indian tribes. He does regret the devastating effects of alcohol-
ism, but gives the Indians rum. Although Franklin disallows Indians a central
place in the narrative, choosing to mention few Indian names for instance, fric-
tions are obvious. First, the Indians desperately seek to convince Franklin to stay

at Fort Enterprise during the winter of 1821. Relying on his instruments, calculating and reckoning, Franklin patronizingly admonishes them that winter is still far away. He complains that he is subjected to the Indians' capricious moods and never acknowledges that they may be right. Secondly, the Indians doubt that anything may be found by the Arctic sea. They draw fairly accurate maps on the ground for Franklin, and warn him against persisting in his attempt, lest he and his men should perish. They ask him 'why a passage had not been discovered long ago, if one existed'.[29] All such objections are nevertheless written off as naive reluctance and selfish fickleness:

> I have deemed it my duty to give the details of these tedious conversations, to point out to future travellers, the art with which these Indians pursue their objects, their avaricious nature, and the little reliance that can be placed upon them when their interests jar with their promises.[30]

Franklin's blindness may be opposed to the more sensitive approach of his three officers, Richardson, Hood or even the sturdy, ambitious Back. In fact, Hood's watercolours may be seen as a way of negotiating otherness from an altogether different perspective. There is even a wistful delicacy in such watercolours, as Hood superbly observes his surroundings. In his journal, he praises certain aspects of the Indian way of life, like the perfection of snowshoes: 'All the superiority of European art has been unable to improve the native contrivance of this useful machine'.[31] He paints Indians, like Keskarrah and his daughter Greenstockings, in a way which reaches beyond taxonomy.[32] The casual, slightly diffident Indian girl is not simply a stereotype (although it does not appear in any of the officers' journals, Hood actually had a relationship with her). Hood's watercolour depicting the interior of a Cree tent also vibrates with warmth, this warmth which was so cruelly absent from Fort Enterprise and all the British settlements.[33] The seams of the skins vaguely recall lines on a map, as if secretly contrasting pointless exploration and nomadic logic. Meat is hanging from the beam, again a hint which recalls the indigenous hunters' ability to find food, eat a lot when there is plenty, and fast when there is none. Far from the stiffness of English manners, the scene is casual and relaxed. The men are smoking, a ritual gesture of friendship, a woman is holding her baby (Hood was very much struck by the little portable cot used to carry babies around) and the man in the foreground is simply lying and eating. There are no tensions in the scene, the knife lies on the ground, the spectator shares the warmth of the womblike tent.

The watercolours, which may now be seen in the National Archives of Canada, Ottawa, give us glimpses of the true story. Whereas Franklin simply uses the password 'picturesque' to define the landscapes he sees – a classic, Romantic topos of landscape painting since the eighteenth century – Hood and Back actually venture beyond the expected picturesque compositions. Interestingly enough, however, the engravings which were included in Franklin's *Narrative* tend to remove all hints of otherness (most of the illustrations in Franklin's published account were drawn by Back). 'Setting out on Point Lake', for instance, refers to what Back describes as 'a most interesting and novel scene', the art of transporting canoes over ice: 'the deep contrast between the perpetual silence of the place, and the animation of the party – afforded a most perfect view of a voyage of discovery'.[34] The engraving by Edward Finden, published in Murray's first edition of Franklin's *Narrative*, reproduces Back's original watercolour faithfully, but touches it up slightly. The two officers now stand on a vantage point on the right, while a few primitive Indians are added on the left, for greater local colour. Similarly, the watercolour depicting the first 'View of the Arctic Sea' creates a sense of loss which is gently corrected, as MacLaren points out, by the engraving's cropped tundra, the smooth sea, the two tents (instead of a single tent) with their Union Jacks creating a sense of perfect control and stability.[35] The sublime setting of 'The Falls of Wilberforce' is tamed by the staging of the travellers on the left-hand side, pointing towards the foaming water, controlling the picturesque perspective.[36] In 'Expedition Landing in a Storm',[37] the sea is smoothed, the men reorganized in a semicircle leading to the two officers; the coat of the officer on the left-hand side is blown by the wind, as he gazes at the sea, in the manner of a Romantic Caspar David Friedrich painting.

If by 'de-othering' the Other the engravings stress the sense of English poise and control, the boundaries between the primitive Other and the civilized Englishman nevertheless become dangerously blurred towards the end of Franklin's narrative. For the English are saved by the Indians, although the pieces of paper the white people give are quite useless and the companies do not abide by them, so that the Indians expect very little reward for their help. Richardson stresses the chief's sense of humour:

> 'The world goes badly', he said. 'All are poor. You are poor, the traders appear to be poor, and I and my party are poor likewise, and since the goods have not come in, we cannot have them'. 'I do not regret having supplied you with provisions, for a Red Knife can never permit a white man to suffer from want on his lands without flying to his aid'. 'I trust, however, that we shall receive all that is due to us, next autumn, and at all events' he added in a tone of good humour 'it is the first time that the white people have been indebted to the Red Knife Indians'.[38]

On 15 December 1821, Richardson underlines Akaitcho's disinterested kindness:

> Previous to our conference we had another short conference with Akaitcho who bid us farewell with a kindness of manner, rarely seen in an Indian. We felt a deep sense of humiliation at being compelled to quit men of such liberal sentiments and humane feelings, in the beggarly manner in which we did.[39]

In *Playing Dead*, Rudy Wiebe points out that in his published journals, Franklin uses Richardson's account, but cuts out the phrase 'we felt a deep sense of humiliation' to insist rather upon the Indians' warmth: '[Akaitcho] bade us farewell, with a warmth of manner rare among the Indians'.[40] He thus subtly subverts the sudden sense of inferiority which blurs the boundary between natives and explorers. We move here from the heroic myth of men attempting to achieve the impossible to Barthes's sense of the word, i.e. a fictitious belief, a construct which freezes the truth, displaces it slightly, and circulates it in everyday life.[41] Franklin must hide the fact that the Other, at this point, may well be the dirty, gaunt, starving Englishmen and remaining *voyageurs*, rather than the food-providers, the Indians, as may be gathered from Richardson's dismay:

> Upon entering the now desolate building, we had the satisfaction of embracing Captain Franklin, but no words can convey an idea of the filth and wretchedness that met our eyes on looking around. Our own misery had stolen upon us by degrees, and we were accustomed to the contemplation of each others [*sic*] emaciated figures, but the ghastly countenance, dilated eye-balls, and sepulchral voices of Captain Franklin and those with him were more than we could at first bear.[42]

On the other hand, the Indians appear more than humane, insisting on removing corpses from the log cabin, on cutting dirty hair and beards, paying a respectful tribute to the wretched whites, as when Akaitcho insists on cooking for Franklin, though a chief never cooks for himself. Richardson underlines the blurring of boundaries between savage and civilized: 'The Indians cooked for us and fed us as if we had been children evincing a degree of humanity that would have done honour to the most civilized nation'.[43]

It is easy, today, to read against the grain and locate hegemonic discourse, balancing the shreds of an Indian viewpoint against the missionary blindness of Franklin's narrative. At the time, the tale met with great success, as it addressed, in Davis's words, 'a surprisingly avid public readership'.[44] The ordeal turned Franklin into a hero; he came to be known as 'the man who ate his boots'. Regardless of casualties, Franklin claimed towards the end of his *Narrative* that the quest for the Northwest Passage could only be rewarded by success:

> Our researches, as far as they have gone, favour the opinion of those who contend for the practicability of the North-West Passage.... I entertain, indeed, sanguine hope that the skill and exertions of my friend Captain Parry will soon render this question no longer problematical.[45]

This led to a second, more successful land expedition, then to the disastrous 1845 venture aboard the ominous ultra-modern HMS *Erebus* and HMS *Terror*, which were to vanish in the Arctic without a trace. Countless rescue expeditions were launched to attempt to solve the national mystery. In 1854, a Scottish explorer for the Hudson's Bay Company, Dr John Rae, was given relics of the lost expedition as some Inuit told him a gruesome tale of white men having abandoned ship, walked across the ice and yielded to the last extremity – cannibalism. This sensational tale shattered England's self-confidence, and Lady Franklin was adamant on restoring her husband's good name; she commissioned Leopold M'Clintock, also of Scottish origins, who in 1859 discovered a cairn containing a lone sheet of paper establishing that Franklin had actually died before the ship was abandoned. According to Lady Franklin's wish, a statue was erected at Waterloo Place in 1866 to honour the national hero, or, to quote the memorial inscription, 'the great Navigator / and his brave companions / Who sacrificed their lives / Completing the discovery of the North-West Passage', adding that the statue had been erected by the unanimous vote of Parliament. A firm mythic construct was thus re-established in order to erase the mystery and hints of shame; considering that the last survivors had potentially completed the trip after leaving the ice-locked ships, the doomed trip was hailed as a success, since (to quote John Richardson's famous words which were added to the inscription) they had 'forged the last link with their lives' – and imperial England had forged the story of 'tedious toil and horrible pilgrimage' uncannily foreseen, among other things, by Mary Shelley's prescient 1818 novel, *Frankenstein*.[46]

11 'CULTIVATING THAT MUTUAL FRIENDSHIP': COMMERCE, DIPLOMACY AND SELF-REPRESENTATION IN HUGH CLAPPERTON'S *JOURNAL OF A SECOND EXPEDITION INTO THE INTERIOR OF AFRICA FROM THE BIGHT OF BENIN TO SOCCATOO* (1829)

Anne-Pascale Bruneau

Hugh Clapperton's *Journal of a Second Expedition into the Interior of Africa* (1829) is the posthumously published account of the Scottish explorer's mission to the Sokoto Caliphate, in the central part of the region then known as the Sudan. The volume presents a slightly abridged version of the diaries and notebooks to which the editor, John Barrow, had had access, leaving out the pages recording the voyage and the initial stages of the journey, from the Coast of Sierra Leone to Badagry. The journal thus covers the period from December 1825, when Clapperton, then a Royal Navy commander, arrived in Badagry, in the Bight of Benin, to March 1827, when he arrived in Sokoto, where he was to die of dysentery a month later. The entire region is now part of Nigeria. This 'second' expedition was the immediate continuation of one undertaken from 1822 to 1825, in which Clapperton, together with two companions, Dixon Denham and Walter Oudney, had travelled across the Sahara, from Tripoli to Borno and Sokoto; it shared, then, the destination of that earlier expedition, but differed in its use of a different, southern route that started on the Guinea coast.

Published in logbook form, without the subsequent elaboration of a narrative, the text offers no kind of explanation as to the objectives of the mission, contenting itself with recording the explorer's progress from the coast through Yorubaland, Borgu, Nupe and Hausaland to Sokoto, and his contacts with the populations of these small kingdoms. Some of these objectives may nonetheless be inferred from a variety of elements in the journal, in particular the subjects of Clapperton's observations, which are frequently geographical and economic, and the presence of reported conversations in which summary explanations of the mission's objectives are offered to the explorer's African interlocutors. Clapperton's concerns seem to have been the charting of previously unknown regions – in particular, he was seeking to gain knowledge of the course of the Niger – as well as the promotion of the development of Anglo–African commerce. That the aims of his expedition are not more explicitly set out can in part be explained with reference to the status of the text, which although almost certainly intended to serve as a basis for a published account of the expedition – as was customary with nineteenth-century explorers' journals – was not meant to be read by the public in its rough state. Recent research, carried out by Jamie Bruce Lockhart and Paul Lovejoy, has unearthed certain documents relating to the mission, including Clapperton's letter of instructions from Earl Bathurst, the Colonial Secretary, dated 30 July 1825, demonstrating that the journal was intended, in the first place, for the attention of the Colonial Office.[1]

Bruce Lockhart and Lovejoy have also brought to light more details of the geographical, commercial, and diplomatic aspects of Clapperton's brief than were available to his original readers. His return to Sokoto and, as originally envisaged, to Borno, was intended to permit the establishment of a trade route between Britain and those regions, which themselves were connected, through other trade routes, to Eastern and Western Africa as well as to the Mediterranean. It was anticipated that the Niger, whose course was yet to be ascertained, would play a crucial part in the development of commerce with Africa. Finally, Clapperton was expected to press for an end to the slave trade, banned by British law since 1807, but which, with keen transatlantic demand, was still rife in West Africa, and in which Sultan Bello, the Sokoto ruler, was implicated. This was evidently part of the unfinished business from Clapperton's first expedition, for an agreement had been reached, during his first stay in the caliphate, that Bello would help end the trade in return for British arms supplies, an agreement set out in a letter from Bello to George IV which Clapperton had brought back to London.[2] A British consul and a doctor were to be installed in Sokoto by the second mission, headed by Clapperton, which included another Royal Navy commander, two doctors, their four servants, and two guides and interpreters. However, with the exception of Richard Lander, his servant, and of one of the interpreters, all of Clapperton's companions died shortly after arriving in Africa, leaving him to discharge the duties intended for a team. He himself suffered frequent attacks of malaria and dysentery, but despite this had walked, by the time he reached the Sokoto Caliphate, approximately 800 miles.

Leaving aside the account of Clapperton's second stay with Sultan Bello, this study focuses on that part of Clapperton's journal which recounts first encounters, that is to say the pages covering the eighteen months during which the explorer pressed in a northeastern direction from the coast to Kano. Two aspects can be addressed here. The first pertains to the fact that Clapperton's account of his contacts with West Africans was intended to serve as an introduction for a British readership to little-known parts of the continent and their inhabitants, and it is thus rich in descriptions of the individuals and the societies encountered. These portraits are marked by a broadly sympathetic and universalizing outlook, an outlook which, as I shall argue, was also entirely congruent with the commercial interests underpinning the exploration of Africa. Having established this continuum of sympathy and self-interest as the ideological basis for the narrative, I will then go on to explore the specificities through which the negotiation of these two terms takes place in the events the journal describes: via the codes of gift-offering which govern many of Clapperton's transactions with his hosts, and via the manipulation of diplomatic discourse, as well as of wonder, which enables Clapperton to acquire status in the course of these transactions.

Although Clapperton's notebooks were not intended for publication in their rough state, they were, from the outset, very much inscribed in the public sphere. Earl Bathurst's letter instructed him clearly that he was to 'avail [himself] of every possible opportunity of transmitting to [him] an account of [his] proceedings & at the same time to send home Copies of the journals and remarks kept by [himself and his three companions] respectively'.[3] The text thus has a hybrid identity: it is both a log of the mission, charting its progress from one locality to another, and a compilation of observations on the regions travelled through, as well as on the customs and moral characteristics of their inhabitants. The length and level of detail of these observations is evidence of a more writerly concern.

The notebooks list the natural resources and describe the economic activities (agriculture, trade, industry) of the regions traversed, as requested by Earl Bathurst,[4] while also paying attention to the social structures and cultural pratices of the indigenous populations encountered. Some of the observations are clearly made with a view to the establishment of future commercial links:

> Oxen are in great plenty, principally in the hands of the Fellatas; sheep and goats are also plentiful; domestic fowls plenty and cheap, honey and bees' wax abundant; ivory and ostrich feathers they say are to be procured in great plenty, but they can get no sale for them... The people of Wawa would take beads in exchange for any articles their country might produce; also brass bracelets for the arms and legs; brass, copper, pewter and earthenware dishes; Manchester cottons of gaudy colours, and calicoes.[5]

Yet economic considerations are only one of the prisms through which Clapperton's observations are made. Sympathy is another. The explorer seems possessed of genuine sociological curiosity and a strong interest in the human detail of African existence, as is perceptible in his notes on the daily routine of family life in the city of Kulfo (ten to twelve thousand inhabitants):

At daylight the whole household arise: the women begin to clean the house, the men to wash from head to foot; the women and children are then washed in water, in which the leaf of a bush has been boiled called Bambarnia: when this is done, breakfast of cocoa is served out, every one having their separate dish, the women and children eating together. After breakfast the women and children rub themselves over with the pounded red wood and a little grease, which lightens the darkness of the black skin. A score or patch of the red powder is put on some place where it will show to the best advantage. The eyes are blacked with khol... Then the women who attend the market prepare their wares for sale, and when ready go... The master of the house generally takes a walk to the market, or sits in the shade at the door of his house, hearing the news, or speaking of the price of natron or other goods. The weavers are daily employed at their trade; some are sent to cut wood, and bring it to market; others to bring grass for the horses that may belong to the house ... About noon they return home, when all have a mess of the pudding called waki, or boiled beans ... The mistress of the house, when she goes to rest, has her feet put into a cold poultice of the pounded henna leaves. The young then go to dance and play, if it is moonlight, and the old to lounge and converse in the open square of the house, or in the outer coozie, where they remain until the cold of the night, or till the approach of morning drives them into shelters.[6]

The life of rural simplicity and domesticity which is described here is a far cry from representations of Africans as savages or children; were it not for the few exotic references to bambarnia, natron or waki, Clapperton's depiction might be set in Britain, the embodiment of the pastoral idylls of a Goldsmith or a Gray. Indeed, in his depiction of the various communities encountered, Clapperton is often at pains to lay stress on sameness rather than emphasize otherness. He relies on familiar referents in order to provide a way of understanding local habits – such referents, for instance, as the Scottish 'sowens' (porridge) to which a type of ground millet is likened, or as the apparently readily exportable concept of the 'spoiled child'.[7] The attention paid to the particulars of existence in West Africa is not only a sign of the more general attentiveness which seems to characterize Clapperton's approach to other cultures. It bespeaks, too, an unspoken universalizing agenda in the journal, that of presenting Africans as possessed of the same human makeup as Europeans, albeit modulated by local idiosyncrasies.

Clapperton is particularly keen to point out markers of civility, of polity, and thus of 'civilization'. Remarking at the beginning of his journal upon the preparations made by the inhabitants of Badagry to 'go on a slaving expedition' owing to the arrival of a Brazilian slave ship, he insists that nevertheless they are not to be viewed as savages, and points to the existence among them of 'a degree of subordination and regular government which could not have been supposed to exist amongst a people hitherto considered barbarians'.[8]

This does not mean, however, that his narrative seeks to present an idealized view of the populations with which he comes into contact – especially in the context of a slaving expedition – nor that it recoils from depicting unpalatable realities. Allusions are made, for example, to the practice of human sacrifice in Dahomey, moral condemnation of which is significantly expressed through an African voice, that of the King of Yoruba, whose reaction Clapperton faithfully transcribes.[9] Likewise, the journal contains affecting eyewitness accounts of the poor treatment of women, and of the slave trade as carried out by African dealers:

> When on their march, they [the captured slaves] are fastened night and day by the neck with leather thongs or a chain, and in general carry loads; the refractory are put in irons, in addition to the other fastening, during the night. They are much afraid of being sold to the sea coast, as it is the universal belief that all those who are sold to the whites are eaten; retorting back on us the accusation of cannibalism, of which they have perhaps the greatest right to blame us.[10]

This last remark, placing Africans and Europeans face to face, is again characteristic of Clapperton's universalizing tendencies, his willingness to remove some of the clarity from easy distinctions between Self and Other; not only is the Europeans' share of responsibility in the slave trade recalled, but the categorizing association of Africans with cannibalism is turned on its head. Time and again, Clapperton's remarks in his journal argue for a reconsideration of the conceptual grids through which the 'other' is apprehended. At one point, he approaches a form of moral relativism, noting that notions of humanity and inhumanity are relative to context:

> My servant with a load on his head, was obliged to lead on the fatigued bullock, and I, with another servant, managed to drive it along at a quick pace, but not without incessant beating, which, in a country like ours, famed for its humanity, would have appeared extreme cruelty; but a man will do many things here in Africa, that his humanity would revolt at in our more happy country.[11]

At another, he offers a nuanced account of the kinds of deceit that his African interlocutors will and will not envisage:

> In all my dealings with them they tried and succeeded in cheating me, but they had an idea that I was possessed of inexhaustible riches; and besides, I differed with them in colour, in dress, in religion, and in my manner of living. I was considered therefore as a pigeon for them to pluck. Had they been rogues, indeed, they might have taken all I had; but, on the contrary, I never had an article stolen, and was even treated with the most perfect respect and civility they were masters of.[12]

Clapperton's text offers a varied and measured assessment of the behaviour of the Africans with whom he comes into contact. Remarks, such as this one, to the effect that he is perpetually being cheated, are balanced with his careful recording of numerous acts of disinterested generosity.[13] The journal thus presents the inhabitants of those hitherto little-explored West African regions as people who share a common ground of humanity and decency with the British. It becomes therefore possible to make merry – as the entries repeatedly exemplify – with fellow human beings who are animated by motives which are universals of human nature. Significantly, such motives include the aspirations to economic prosperity which Clapperton reports as having been expressed by some of his West African interlocutors, and to which he replies by representing to them the advantages of trading with Britain.

The sympathetic approach to the 'Other' which is such a distinctive characteristic of Clapperton's journal may thus be seen as compatible with, and indeed perhaps one of the mainstays for, British efforts to penetrate the interior of Africa in order to establish secure trade routes. It is worth noting here that Lord Bathurst's letter of instructions makes specific mention of the desirability of 'open[ing] an amicable intercourse' between Britain and the Sudan and 'cultivat[ing] that mutual friendship, which cannot fail, in due time, to produce mutual benefit'.[14] Clapperton's presentation of this common commercial ambition might also vindicate the British belief that the development of commerce would naturally contribute to a halt in the slave trade, the benefits derived from the sale of other commodities outweighing those of that trade.

The basis upon which African rulers might be persuaded to support Clapperton's enterprise is thus one of the questions on which his encounters with them turn. More generally, Clapperton's journal provides an instructive record of the manner in which transactions are performed within the context of a first encounter: their construction around pre-existing codes, and the negotiation by each party of an advantageous role within this codified relation.

Since Clapperton's progress through the territories that lie between the coast and Hausaland is dependent on the help of the native populations, it is not surprising that a large proportion of the journal should be devoted to scenes of first encounters, essentially with the chiefs, and, sometimes, the rulers, of these places. The explorer rides or walks from one village or town to the next, escorted by luggage bearers hired locally, and by messengers who announce his arrival at the next place and subsequently act as interpreters. Typically, he will be greeted by the chief who appears in state, surrounded by his headmen, a number of wives (as many as 200), and the whole assembled population; housed in one of the best compounds, the explorer will receive food supplies, and logistical help for the next leg of his journey. Most of the people he meets have never seen white men before, and Clapperton expands on the great curiosity that he excites:

> The road was now very difficult and dangerous, over broken rocks, and through rugged passes, where the inhabitants were perched in groups to look at us as we passed by … The caboceer, on coming to bid us good morning, said that our guide had not told him that we wished to go away to-day, a manœuvre of the caboceer and the guide to detain us, so that all the people might have an opportunity of seeing us.[15]

The large court, about two hundred yards square, in which we are lodged, is constantly filled with some thousands of people, who will not be driven away, party succeeding party in their curiosity to see us; and 'wide-mouthed wonder stares apace'.[16]

Such curiosity signals the novelty, for most of the Africans involved, of encounters with Europeans. Yet even if no direct face-to-face contact between Africans and Europeans has been experienced previously, there is evidence in Clapperton's account of how relations have already been established through trade. This is visible in the European manufactured goods which Clapperton notices in many places of the interior, used either in the apparel of dignitaries or as household commodities. Typically, these goods will include Manchester cotton fabrics, pewter, copper and brass objects, as well as earthenware. European merchants had long been settled on the coast, and Clapperton is indeed for some time accompanied by one of them, John Houtson, who acts as a guide while conducting his own business – a palpable reminder of the intimate connection between exploration and commerce. The regions may have remained unmapped by British cartography, but as Clapperton makes clear, the terrain on which the two parties meet is not an untrodden one.

In this context, first encounters are frequently structured by pre-existing codes of exchange. The existence of such codes is particularly obvious in exchanges of goods and services – one of the main modes of interaction between the members of the expedition and the local population. For the hospitality extended to the travellers is not entirely gratuitous. It is caught in a system of trade, but also in a system of communication whereby power relationships are subtly established or reestablished. Clapperton provides a precise account of the victuals which are brought to him, and of his repayment of his hosts in items that he has brought from England or bought from John Houtson in Badagry – mostly cloth and rum, salt and cowries (seashells used as currency), more rarely, coral beads. Interestingly, although the journal depicts the commodities received or tendered by Clapperton as 'presents' or 'gifts', his letters of accounts to Houtson refer to what he gives to the local chiefs as 'payments'. The amounts of the payments often seem to be left to his judgement, but he reports several instances of being made to increase them. It is quite clear, too, that many of the gifts he receives are made by local chiefs in part out of a sense of obligation, not to him, but to the rulers whose vassals they are. If Clapperton should consider himself badly treated at their hands, the threat of reporting them to their monarch, which he extends twice, is enough to effect a change of manners.[17] Such episodes remind Clapperton's potential readers of the explorer's status in these encounters, a status which it is sometimes possible to forget in Clapperton's anecdotal accounts of easygoing intercourse with his hosts. For his real interlocutors, as the chiefs well know, are these monarchs, to whom Clapperton, presenting himself as the King of England's 'servant' or 'messenger', has come on a mission of diplomacy.

In encounters with the rulers of the small kingdoms through which Clapperton travels, the different roles attendant on the explorer are apparent. He is
an ambassador for his country seeking to impress African rulers with the might
of England and the desirability of forming an alliance with her. But he is also a
traveller seeking to obtain information on the Niger, and a stranger in need of
their protection; the progress of the expedition, in these times of extreme unrest,
is entirely dependent on such protection, which of course complicates Clapperton's representation of himself. Unsurprisingly in such conditions, the unfolding
of encounters entails the deployment of specific strategies on both sides. This
begins with the chosen mode of salutation, with Clapperton ruling out all possibility of prostration in front of an African sovereign:

> I told them if any such thing was proposed, I should instantly go back; that all the
> ceremony I would submit to should be to take off may hat, make a bow, and shake
> hands with his majesty, if he pleased. They went and informed the king, and came
> back and said I should make only the ceremony I had proposed.[18]

Coming next, the presentation of gifts is the *pièce de résistance* in the explorer's
strategy.[19] It is implemented with a view to maximum effect, and at carefully
chosen moments – for instance just after delivering a speech on England's might
and readiness to help her allies, and in lieu of an answer to the request for help
against the sovereign's enemies that follows. The presents intended for sovereigns consist essentially of manufactured commodities, brought from England
under the auspices of the Colonial Office, which might confer prestige upon
their possessor. They include clocks, swords, guns and powder, as well as gold
and coral, and portraits of the royal couple. Functioning in Africa as objects of
conspicuous consumption, they are calculated to arouse wonder, which effect
is indeed observed by Clapperton in one of the sovereigns on whom he attends:

> On seeing the sword he could not restrain his delight, and drawing it, and brandish-
> ing it around his head, he called out, '*Ya baturi ! Ya baturi* !', 'Oh, my white lord! Oh,
> my white lord!' He was certainly more pleased than any man I ever saw with a present;
> his eyes sparkled with joy, and he shook me about a dozen times by the hand.[20]

The power of the explorer within such transactions depends in part on his interlocutor's acceptance of his diplomatic role. In general, Clapperton's journal
points to an acceptance of the discourse of diplomacy – based on the necessity
of friendship for the sake of commercial and political complementarity. But it
also happens that this discourse is appropriated by some Africans, with a view
to subverting its implicit structuring of power. For example, the King of Yoruba
repeatedly delays Clapperton's departure, arguing that exposing the King of
England's servant to the dangers of the road in times of unrest would be to incur
the wrath of that sovereign – thereby exposing him to the no less real dangers of

the rainy season. A desire to resist the manifest power imbalance appears to be at work also in a general reluctance to provide information about the course of the Niger, and thus to facilitate British access to the territory:

> they either could not, or were afraid to give any the least account of the river Quorra [Niger], and I therefore sent them off, after asking a few questions. Indeed there seems a great unwillingness in both the king and the people of this place to say any thing at all about the subject, for what reason I cannot yet conjecture.[21]

Likewise, some hints seem to be passed to Clapperton that British or European presence in the region may be undesirable, notably through questions put to him as to whether 'Englishmen [will] come into the country', and through warnings of planned attempts on the explorer's life as he approaches Bussa, the place of Mungo Park's death.[22] Clapperton does not linger on these. Finally, and most memorably, the journal hints at a certain resistance to the terms imposed by Europeans in their relations to Africa, in the form of a pantomime performed by actors for the benefit of their king during festivities attended by Clapperton and his companions.[23] Entitled 'The White Devil', the act offers a caricature of white men in Africa as evil, rapacious weaklings, and Clapperton recounts that he and his companions were strongly invited to mark their approval of this 'admira[ble]' burlesque.[24] Encounters are thus presented by the journal as real interactional events, taking place on a coded stage, but the outcome of which may be unpredictable, especially in terms of self-representation. Clapperton's decision to give an account of the pantomime may be taken as revealing, once more, a willingness to present potential readers with a reversal of perspective – an African vision of Europeans.

Clapperton's text furnishes its readers with several such points of access to a picture of a less readily amenable, more intractable Africa. Among the explorer's observations, those made outside the framework of the diplomatic and commercial transactions that structure his account carry particular weight. For, on a few occasions, rare enough to stand out, Clapperton appears to be under the spell of figures that impress on him an image of their dignity, freedom and power. One of these meetings involves, paradoxically, a group of six female slaves, observed by the explorer as they escort their master – Yarro, the ruler of Kiama – running alongside his horse, light spears in hand, wearing nothing but a piece of ribbon tied round their heads. Yarro himself, the embodiment of lawless swagger, forces Clapperton's admiration, and the depiction of his female slaves is notable as a rare occasion for lyrical profusion on the part of the explorer, who presents them as transcending their condition:

> Their light form, the vivacity of their eyes, and the ease with which they appeared to fly over the ground, made them appear something more than mortal as they flew alongside of his horse, when he was galloping, and making his horse curvet and bound.[25]

A briefly glimpsed hunter returning from his chase is another such embodiment of freedom and independence:

> He had a leopard's skin over his shoulder, a light spear in his hand, and his bow and arrows slung over his shoulder. He was followed by three cream-coloured dogs, a breed as if between the greyhound and cur: they were adorned with round collars of different coloured leather. The hunter and his dogs marched through the village as independently as ever I saw a man, without taking the least notice of us, or even looking at us. He was followed by a slave carrying a dead antelope that he had killed this morning.[26]

A musician who 'when he sang ... sometimes looked sublime' would be another such memorable figure.[27] Such visions of power, independence and spirituality – ambiguously articulated as they may be on an exoticized vision of master–slave relationships – depart from the usual register of Clapperton's observations in their constitution of a fleeting admission of awe and wonder on his own part. They imply a relaxing of the sense of public mission which informs the journal throughout and provide evidence of Clapperton's capacity to construct a certain distance from the more commercial framing of his habitual representations of Africans and of himself as a representative of British power.

Clapperton's *Journal* is best viewed, therefore, as a locus for the promotion of contact between Europeans and Africans. The construction of Self and Other in this more global political context is achieved through a sympathetic, universalizing outlook in which differences are for the most part minimized, with the British explorer espousing the public cause of commerce as beneficial to both sides. As a consequence, Clapperton's representation of Africans is characterized by benevolent curiosity, a stance informed by this 'public' perspective which may, on occasions, however, become destabilized by the journal's admission of a more private one. That occasions for the expression of wonder or surprise on Clapperton's part are few is to be related to the position of the explorer on a mission to map out new territory, a position in which otherness is apprehended as capable of lending itself to assimilation. But their rarity must also be related to Clapperton's universalizing outlook, which precludes an apprehension of the not-self as totally other. This outlook undoubtedly provides a bulwark against representations of Africans as inhuman or savage, and against the legitimizing of violence that such representations entail. Such violence as is present in Clapperton's accounts of 'first' encounters finds expression through allusions to subtle forms of indigenous recalcitrance to assimilation, such as pantomime, which further contribute to producing Clapperton's interlocutors as alter egos. As they punctuate the predominantly commercial context of Clapperton's text, these textual constructions of critique and awe constitute atypical challenges to British self-representation.

12 TRYING TO UNDERSTAND: JAMES TOD AMONG THE RAJPUTS (1829, 1832)

Florence D'Souza

The Rajputs are a group of non-Brahmin Hindu warrior clans who established their domination over several kingdoms in Northwest India from AD 720 onwards, after warring with Arab invaders from Sindh. The main Rajput dynasties have their seats at Udaipur (kingdom of Mewar), Jodhpur (kingdom of Marwar), Jaisalmer, Bundi and Kotah. The British waged several wars on the Rajputs under the Governor-Generalship of the Marquess of Hastings (1813–23), who imposed British supremacy on Rajputana (the pre-1949 name of the present-day Rajasthan) in 1818, through a protective British alliance that allowed the Rajput rajas to continue to rule their kingdoms under the strict supervision of British Residents, aided by British troops. Of Scottish descent, James Tod was the first political agent of the British Governor-General in the western Rajput states, from 1818 to 1822. Tod was also among the many British officers of the East India Company who in the course of the nineteenth century carried out land surveys in India with the help of Indian teams, and took advantage of the situation to gather information about the local ruling families, while collecting artefacts as well as ethnographic data. His *Annals and Antiquities of Rajasthan*, published in two volumes in 1829 and 1832, thus constitutes a major contribution to a European history and ethnographic description of Rajputana.

That Tod was a complete pioneer among Europeans ever to set foot among the Rajputs is evident from his own declarations about the unprecedented nature of his experiences there. For example, before setting out on his trip to Bundi and Kotah in January 1820, he underlines the unique opportunity that this provided him with:

> Oodipoor, Jan.29, 1820: The Personal Narrative attached to the first volume of this work terminated with the author's return to Oodipoor, after a complete circuit of Marwar and Ajmer. He remained at his headquarters at Oodipoor until the 29th January 1820, when circumstances rendering it expedient that he should visit the principalities of Boondi and Kotah (which were placed under his political superintendence), he determined not to neglect the opportunity it afforded of adding to his

portfolio remarks on men and manners, in a country hitherto untrodden by Europeans.[1]

Later, while recounting his travels in the valley of the river Chambal in February 1820, Tod again points out that with considerable discomfort he was treading territory that had never yet been traversed by Europeans:

> The road was execrable, if road it could be termed, which for many miles was formed for me by the kindness of the pundit, who cut a path through the otherwise impenetrable jungle, the abode of elks and tigers, sufficient to pass my baggage. This route is never passed by troops. But I had curiosity to indulge, not comfort.[2]

It should be added to this that Tod did not know Sanskrit and only learned the locally-spoken Urdu language *in the field*, i.e. through his contact with Indians, so that his published texts on Rajputana show his regular recourse to various Indian interpreters. What most particularly distinguishes Tod's travel accounts, however, is their marked tendency to record a material which is presented as irreducibly elusive, piecing together only fragments of historical evidence, or paying puzzled attention to extremely complex social relationships, be they between Indians of the same ethnic origin, or of different ethnic origins.

'Anthropology' was then only in its infancy. According to Michèle Duchet, it was the Swiss philosopher Albert de Chavannes who first used the term in 1788.[3] Under the influence of the Scottish and French Enlightenment philosophers, the term had then come to include a comparative analysis of genealogies, systems of kinship and social customs, placing specific societies on a universal scale which specified a series of progressive stages, from savage to civilized organization.[4] According to Duchet, this system of knowledge barely concealed the racialist paternalism of a colonialist ideology which subsequently crystallized into a rigid division between 'civilized societies', characterized by their awareness of their historical past, and 'uncivilized societies', characterized by an absence of such awareness, due to their ignorance of writing and other recording devices.[5] It would appear that this firm hierarchization of cultures only consolidated the 'comfortable assumptions of superiority' with which European travellers had begun filling in 'the great map of mankind' from the sixteenth century onward.[6] In relation to India, the general assumption has been that Edward Saïd was right in claiming that early Western scholars of Asian history and culture had more or less intentionally constructed an 'imaginary Orient' in order to prove the superiority of the West.[7]

I argue that such a notion of early 'anthropology' pays no attention to the process of two-way negotiation involved in the discursive construction of difference. The point I wish to make is that Tod did not have a preconceived grid of interpretation when he set out to describe the genealogies and social practices of the hitherto relatively unknown Rajputs. Instead, it seems from his texts that, due to the scarcity of information the British could rely upon concerning the Rajputs, Tod was simply doing his best to put together *disparate* pieces of information available from *varied* sources – his Jain guru, the chronicles of local bards, the various persons he encountered, the translations of inscriptions he found in the course of his travels. Tod's ambition seems to have been to arrive at as coherent an interpretation as possible of the manners and customs of the Rajputs of his time, as well as of their political organization in connection with land ownership. No inferiorizing agenda is observable in his gropings to make sense of the different clans and social groups, their degrees of cultured literacy, the social and political role of women, the system of land ownership and trans-missibility, the epic or tragic dimension of Rajput history, ancient and modern. Tod's gathering and interpretation of anthropological data can be seen rather as an illustration of the eminently unstable zones in which colonial officials often found themselves. As a matter of fact, Tod's experience in Rajasthan seems to suggest that the meaning to be attributed to the information collected was not fixed in advance, and had to be improvised along the way, in specific contexts.

At the beginning of the first volume of his *Annals*, Tod mentions a highly cultured nephew of his host the Rana of Mewar, the prince of Marwar, Zalim Singh:

> We passed Deopoor, once a township of some consequence, and forming part of the domain of the *Bhanaij*, Zalim Singh, the heir of Marwar, whose history, if it could be given here would redeem the nobles of Rajpootana from the charge of being of uncultivated intellect. In listening to his biography, both time and place were unheeded; the narrator, my own venerable *guru*,* had imbibed much of his varied knowledge from this accomplished chieftain, to whom arms and letters were alike familiar [*note: My guide or instructor, Yati Gyan Chandra, a priest of the Jain sect, who had been with me ten years (1809–19). To him I owe much, for he entered into all my antiquarian pursuits with zeal].[8]

Here, Tod is pointing out that certain Rajputs, despite the general belief that they were uneducated, unrefined warriors, could, in fact, be highly cultured and knowledgeable. He thus deliberately shatters, through an example of his own – a personal acquaintance – the frequently repeated stereotype of literacy being the undisputed reserve of the Brahmins. On his return journey from Kotah and Bundi to Udaipur in February 1822, Tod halted at Beejoliya Kalan, where there were ruins of a castle and five Jain temples. He then reports the sketching and copying of inscriptions carried out by his Indian assistants:

> One of my scribes, who has a talent for design, is delineating with his reed (*culm*) these stupendous piles, while my old Jain Guru is hard at work copying what is not the least curious part of the antiquities of *Bijolli*, two inscriptions cut in the rock; one

of the Chohan race, the other of the *Sankh Puran*, appertaining to his own creed, the Jain.[9]

Here again, Tod underlines the fact that his Indian preceptor was not a Brahmin, but a Jain, yet fully competent in transcribing ancient inscriptions in the learned languages of India. In addition, we can notice that Tod resorted to the artistic talents of his Indian companions to obtain sketches of various sites he visited. The Indians of Tod's acquaintance were therefore neither illiterate nor ungifted, according to European standards. If we are to believe Jack Goody and Ian Watt that great weight should be attached to the technologies of communication as instruments of psychological and social development,[10] then what Tod suggests is that his indigenous interlocutors and companions were indeed the representatives of a highly advanced culture.

Among his observations on Rajput manners and customs, Tod also notes the political intervention of women in matters of state, a sure sign of cultural development for his readers at home. Tod is more particularly interested in the traditional Hindu offering of a 'sisterly bracelet' to a potential male ally, a bracelet presented on the occasion of the Hindu coconut festival held in August each year. Tod focuses on one such occasion in great detail, explaining how in the sixteenth century the widow queen Kurnavati of Rana Sanga had once offered one such 'sisterly bracelet' to the emperor Humayun. He comments that the gift had 'invested [Humayun] with the title of brother, and uncle and protector to Kurnavati's infant son Oody Sing', and that although Kurnavati herself, as well as 32,000 other Rajputs had been slain during the attack on Chittore in 1535 by Bahadur Shah, the Sultan of Gujarat, Uday Singh had been protected by the Raja of Bundi, and that Humayun had honoured his pledge of protection to Queen Kurnavati, even after her death, by expelling Bahadur Shah from Chittore.[11] A tale of loyalty and ethical principles meant to invite his readers to speculate whether European history, despite its tradition of written treaties, could offer similar examples.

What is more, Tod, speaking of himself in the third person, adds in a note at this point, his own, *personal* experience of the *Rakhi*, or 'sisterly bracelet':

> [He, i.e. Tod himself] was the *Rakhi-bund bhaé* of, and received 'the bracelet' from three queens of Oodipoor, Boondi and Kotah, besides Chund-Bae, the maiden sister, of the Rana; as well as many ladies of the chieftains of rank, with whom he interchanged letters. The sole articles of barbaric pearl and gold which he conveyed from a country where he was six years supreme, are these testimonies of friendly regard.[12]

We can see here Tod's awareness of the perpetuation of traditional Indian customs by Rajput queens and other women of importance, under recontextualized political circumstances. But Tod, a male representative of the British empire whose official status should have been sufficient in itself and led him to dismiss the importance of such 'barbaric articles', also seems to be personally proud of the honour made to him, as if the officer of the East India Company did not hesitate here to consider himself a Rajput among the Rajputs. That these sisterly bracelets were the only ornaments he carried back to England from India shows the importance he attached to this token of trust and emotional intimacy.

After the sudden death from cholera in July 1821 of the Bundi Raja, Rao Raja Bishen Singh, Tod was summoned to the Bundi court to sort out the succession proceedings of the eleven-year-old prince Lalji Ram Singh. Here is, according to Tod, how the Bundi queen mother enlisted Tod's protection over her princely son:

> Although the festival of the *rakhi* was not until the end of the month, the mother of the young prince sent me by the hands of the *Bhut*, or family priest, the bracelet of adoption as her brother, which made my young ward henceforth my *Bhanaij* or nephew. With this mark of regard, she also expressed, through the ministers, a wish that I would pay her a visit at the palace as she had many points to discuss regarding Lalji's welfare, which could only be satisfactorily argued *viva voce*. Of course, I assented; and, accompanied the *Bohora* [chief minister of Bundi] and the confidential eunuchs of the *Rawula* [palace], I had a conversation of about three hours with my adopted sister, a curtain being between us. Her language was sensible and forcible, and she evinced a thorough knowledge of all the routine of government and the view of parties, which she described with great clearness and precision... During a great part of this conversation, the *Bohora* had retired, so that her tongue was unrestrained. With *Utr-Pan* and her blessing (*asees*) sent by one of her damsels, she dismissed me with the oft-repeated remark, 'Forget not that Lalji is now in your lap'.[13]

From this, we can sense that, far from being perceived as an untrustworthy colonizer, Tod was accepted as part of the family at several Rajput courts.

This does not mean that Tod shirks the more controversial issues concerning the status of women in Rajput society. What particularly shocked all Europeans at the time was a practice all travellers' accounts made ample use of for denigrating a lower, barbaric form of culture – *sati*, a custom according to which widows choose to be burnt alive on the funeral pyres of their deceased husbands. Quite surprisingly, Tod simply refuses to align himself with unanimous Western condemnation and argues rather for a form of cultural relativism, based on fieldwork:

> The superficial observer, who applies his own standard to the customs of all nations, laments with an affected philanthropy, the degraded condition of the Hindu female, in which sentiment he would find her little disposed to join. He particularly laments her want of liberty and calls her seclusion imprisonment. Although I cordially unite with Ségur [who opposed all restraints on women] who is at issue with his compatriot Montesquieu [who favoured the seclusion of women] on this part of discipline, yet from the knowledge I do possess of the freedom, the respect, the happiness which

Rajpoot women enjoy, I am by no means inclined to deplore their state as one of captivity.[14]

Tod thus advances his field experience as a sound basis for his verdict that Rajput women should not be considered as captives, or victims of an infamous system of segregation. European 'philanthropy', although unfeigned, is here dismissed as armchair anthropology. Once again, it is preconceived ideas which seem to constitute the most serious obstacle to understanding the Other.

Of course, Tod's reports constantly justify the presence of British troops as a civilizing presence. This may take the form of humorous anecdotal details, as when he remembers the British takeover of the Rajputana states in February 1818:

> The author had passed through Bhilwara in May 1805, when it was comparatively flourishing. On this occasion (Feb. 1818), it was entirely deserted; it excited a smile in the midst of regrets, to observe the practical wit of some of the soldiers, who had supplied the naked representative of *Ad-Nath* [the Jain deity] with an apron – not of leaves, but scarlet cloth.[15]

More seriously, Tod applauds the 'progress' brought about by British occupation in terms of a passage from a savage state of marauding and plundering to a more civilized state of subordination and regular tax payment to the Rajput suzerain by the unruly tribe of the Mairs. However, he also makes clear his awareness of internal differences in degrees of settled law-abiding existence between specific groups of Rajputs:

> A corps of these mountaineers (Mairs), commanded by English officers, has since been formed, and I have no doubt may become useful. Notwithstanding their lawless habits, they did not neglect agriculture and embanking, as described in the valley of Shero Nullah, Mairwarra, which in time may yield a lakh of rupees annually to the State. . . Colonies of the Mairs or Meras will be found as far north as the Chumbul, and even in the peninsula of Saurashtra. Mairwarra is now in subjection to the Rana of Mewar, who has erected small forts amidst the most influential communities to overawe them. The whole tract has been assessed; the chiefs of the districts being brought to the Rana's presence, presented *nuzzerana* [tribute], swore fidelity, and received according to their rank, gold bracelets or turbans. It was an era in the annals of Mewar to see the accumulated arms of Mairwarra piled upon the terrace of the palace at the capital [Udaipur].[16]

Tod clearly considers it an achievement of the introduction of Pax Britannica in Rajputana that tribes of formerly nomadic plunderers could be gradually brought round to practising settled agriculture, paying regular tributes to the local landlords and even surrendering their arms, to the advantage of the entire local community. Tod thus apparently does not wish to write any group of persons off from the possibility of improvement and consensual inclusion in the civilized activities of the region. His intimate knowledge of the various tribes and cultural traditions of Rajasthan simply induces him to consider the most recalcitrant populations of the region not as hopeless barbarians to be tamed, or eliminated, but as potential members of a future, peaceful community.

In October 1820, while returning from Kotah to Udaipur, Tod observes settled groups in the urban centres of Jehazpoor and Kachola (Kujoori) of formerly semi-barbarous tribals known as Meenas. Traditionally, Meenas were nomadic *kumptas* or 'bowmen'.[17] In 1820, their chief or *tynati* at Jehazpoor maintained 'a very respectable troop of cavalry', superior in Tod's opinion even to the Rana of Mewar's own cavalry, at the time of the British takeover in 1818. Tod here notes with approval a very positive response to European benevolence, among 'semi-barbarians':

> At present [October 1820], I could by signal have collected 4000 bowmen around me, to protect or to plunder; though the Meenas, finding that their rights are respected, are subsiding into regular tax-paying subjects, and call out with their betters '*Utul Raj*'! ('May your sway be everlasting!') We had a grand convocation of the Meena *Naiques* and, in the Rana's name, I distributed crimson turbans and scarfs; for as through our mediation the Rana had just recovered the district of Jehajgurh, he charged me with its settlement. I found these Meenas *true children of Nature*, who for the first time seemed to feel they were received within the pale of society, instead of being considered as outcasts.[18]

Far from being discriminatory or deprecatory about the potential capacities of the Meenas – considered here as 'children of Nature', not as primitive, unruly warriors[19] – Tod's benevolent perspective appears to be conscious of the need to reduce the traditional inequalities between different social groups in the Rajput territories, convinced that this will ensure greater social cohesion and economic productivity in the area.

Tod's attempts to observe the political organization of the Rajputs through comparisons with similar phenomena in Europe is observable in his notes on Rajput feudalism, about which much has already been written.[20] In his chapter on 'Divine Kingship' in India, Ronald Inden opposes two early nineteenth-century British interpretations of Indian kingship: (a) James Mill's presentation of Hindu kings, in his 1818 *History of British India*, as theocratic despots who exercised their absolute power over their subjects with no other legitimation than that they were divinely elected to do so; (b) James Tod's views on Rajput kingship as a parallel (and perhaps earlier version) of medieval German feudalism, when the vassals were bound to their local lord either by the blood ties of a clan brotherhood, or by free association in a mutually beneficial defence alliance contract.[21] In both cases, however, that of Oriental 'despotism' and that of Oriental 'feudalism', Inden underlines the absence in India of sovereignty in the European sense of a nation-state, attributing the introduction of the concept of national sovereignty in the administration of Indian territories to what he calls 'Imperial Monarchy', under which the British colonizers entered into 'subsidiary alliances' with existing Indian monarchs and fixed the limits of their now-sovereign territories against specific land revenue dues.[22]

It seems to me, however, that one of the specificities of Tod's description of the Rajput system of land ownership and transmissibility is his awareness of the overlapping of *several* land tenure systems in the Rajputana of his time, and his cross-referencing of various Indian and European texts in his efforts to understand the nature of the Rajputs' attachment to their land. That Tod was not solely occupied with extorting the maximum amount of revenue from Rajput lands for the British colonial government can be seen at the very beginning of his first volume, in his dedication to King George IV, whom he invites to consider 'the restoration of their former independance' to the Rajput princes.[23] Tod's argument is clearly that of an astute anthropologist, who uses his fieldwork experience and insider's knowledge to avoid colonial misrepresentation – and therefore political misjudgement.

In particular, Tod gives foremost importance to the oldest form of Rajput attachment to the land: the hereditary right of the tiller-cultivator to the land tilled by his forefathers, or '*Bap*', known therefore as '*Bapota*', or 'belonging to the father'.[24] Tod compares Rajput *Bapota* with medieval Europe's 'allodial property', or 'land descended by inheritance subject to no burthen but public defence', as exposed by the Whig historian Henry Hallam.[25] Tod then analyses the nature of Rajputana's feudal fiefs as top-down grants from the local monarch to loyal military chieftains, implying links of loyalty between the feudal lord and the vassal as the result of 'long gradations and mutual duties'.[26] Tod concludes that the Rajput system meets four of Hallam's six criteria of feodality: relief or military assistance, escheats or forfeiture of land for want of an heir or by confiscation, aids or taxes levied, and wardships of infant successors, while excluding marriage and alienation as they were practised in Europe in relation to feudal land ownership.[27]

Thus, according to Tod, the blend of allodial tenantry and feudal militia in Rajputana meant paying a quit-rent to the crown, performing local but limited service, and being available to the prince for defence in exchange for daily rations only in case of invasion.[28] While detailing the links and disputes over sub-infeudation between holders of great 'puttas' or patents of estates,[29] and minor vassals, Tod quotes the Anglo-Saxon division of land into 'ploughs' and 'hides' referring this time to Scottish historians.[30]

He thus seeks to distinguish between the bonds of solidarity and 'devotion to the *Solum Natale*' of Rajput feudalism,[31] as distinct from the more arbitrary or despotic land grants (*jagirs*, *wuttuns*, and *meeras*) of the Muslim invaders,[32] and the predatory extortions of the Maratha plunderers in Rajasthan.[33] Tod also juxtaposes quotations from the ancient Sanskrit text *ManavaDhermashastra* with popular Rajput proverbs, like 'Bhog Ra Dhanni Raj Ho: Bhom ra Dhanni Ma Cho' ('the government is the owner of the rent [or tax], but I [the tiller] am the master of the land'), to illustrate how ancient statutes and evolving customary laws combined to consecrate the Rajput notion of *Bapota* or patrimonial land inheritance.[34]

Tod further develops his theory of the extremely complex issue of Rajput land ownership in his allusions to his own arbitrations of land disputes. What emerges from such examples is that Tod had to weigh the import of British self-interest against the local dictates of reason and justice. Such was the case according to him when settling the claims of the Rana of Mewar's vassal from Bheendir in February 1818.[35] British strategic interests also came into play when Tod alienated the Mewar fief of Neembaira in favour of the henchman of a Muslim ally of the British, the Pathan Khan of Tonk in February 1820.[36] But Tod also declares he upheld the sacred right of *Bapota* of a Mewar vassal at Nuddowaé, over the usurpations of the Maratha chief Holkar of Indore in February 1820.[37] Depending on the circumstances, Tod could therefore vary in his settlements of land disputes in Rajputana: giving priority either to the traditional Rajput attachment to their lands, or to British political concerns, or again to the contradictory claims of the various parties involved in such land disputes.

He seems thus to have paid uncommonly careful attention to the cultural complexities of land ownership in Rajputana, steering an uncertain course between his status as an outsider and his anthropologist's positioning as an insider. He certainly seems to have sought to avoid binary oppositions between cultivators and revenue collectors, or between recently acquired military claims and older ancestral land rights. That Tod traced the aristocratic pride of the Rajputs to their ancestral rights to land ownership (*Bhomia Raj* or land titles, as opposed to *Bania Raj* or commercial wealth,[38] never losing sight of the British need to restore order in the region, or of the political cost of ceding lands to adversaries of the Rajputs, while being fully aware of the competing claims of direct blood descendants as opposed to those of adopted heirs, shows that far from imposing pre-conceived British solutions on Rajput land disputes, Tod was acutely receptive to the complex, local Rajput configuration of land rights.

Tod's proclaimed 'enthusiasm' for piecing together Rajput history seems to have stemmed from an intention to prove to the world that the Rajputs were not a people without history, a category that would have relegated them to the lower, primitive end of the scale of civilization, according to the thinkers of the Scottish Enlightenment,[39] and various other French philosophers.[40] His overt ambition is to correct the false but widely circulated axiom 'that India possesses no national history'[41] and thereby 'to enlighten my native country on the subject of India'.[42] His general purpose was not, however, without any political interest, as he declared to be keen on 'throwing some light upon a people scarcely yet known in Europe and whose political connections with England seemed to me to be capable of undergoing a material change, with benefit to both parties'.[43] But Tod unambiguously describes his method as that of an anthropologist:

> For a period of ten years I was employed, with the aid of a learned Jain, in ransacking every work which could contribute any facts or incidents to the history of the Rajpoots, to diffuse any light upon their manners and character. Extracts and versions of all such passages were made by my Jain assistant into the more familiar dialects (which are formed from the Sanscrit) of these tribes, in whose language my long residence among them enabled me to converse with facility. At much expense, and during many wearisome hours, to support which required no ordinary degree of enthusiasm, I endeavoured to possess myself not merely of their history, but of their religious notions, their familiar opinions and their characteristic manners, by associating with their chiefs and bardic chroniclers, and by listening to their traditionary tales and allegorical poems.[44]

Thus, Tod had in mind the filling in of gaps in the archive of humankind, without, however, losing sight of the political and colonial nature of the presence of his British employers in India. In order to reconcile those two somewhat contradictory ambitions, he seems to have gone to considerable extremes to frame his presentation of historical information on the Rajputs with familiar references and comparisons drawn from European culture, meant to render his text comprehensible to European readers.

For example, he appears to have tried to bridge the gap between myth or legend, on the one hand, and factual history, with genealogies of flesh and blood dynasties, on the other. At the end of the second volume of the *Annals*, he includes two lengthy tables of genealogies of the divinely begotten race of the Sun (Surya Vansa) and of the Moon (Chandra Vansa, also known as Indu Vansa). The first table goes from 2200 BC to 1100 BC, beginning with the divinities Narayan, Vishnu and Brahma, descending via mythical sages like Kashyapa and Atri, and terminating with mythical characters like Ramchandra and the five Pandava brothers, from the two great Indian epics, the *Ramayana* and the *Mahabharat* – the whole with a very serious-looking date scale on the right, and a numbering of the successive generations on the left. Tod's second table spans the period from 1100 BC to AD 720, and traces the supposed descendants of the characters of the Hindu epics through several generations, to end with the solar Gehilote dynasty of Mewar. Tod's meticulousness and attempt at rationalization amidst a welter of muddling details is striking: instead of dismissing this peculiar notion of history as myth and fable, he seems to have been genuinely trying to understand the Rajputs' world-view and their explanations of their own origins – a usage of the 'table' which paradoxically renders the Other's culture more elaborate and more complex than expected.

Tod uses yet another device to make his accounts of Rajput history – both ancient and modern – palatable to a European audience. He liberally incorporates parallels with well-known figures of European culture. One such example is the tragic tale of princess Krishna Kumari, daughter of Tod's host, Rana Bheem Singh of Mewar in 1806:

> Kishna Komari (the *Virgin* Kishna) was the name of the lovely object, the rivalry for whose hand assembled under the banner of her suitors [Juggut Sing of Jaipur and Raja Maun of Marwar], not only their native chivalry, but all the predatory powers of India; and who like Helen of old, involved in destruction her own and the rival houses. . . .
>
> When the Pathan [Ameer Khan of Tonk and Rampura] revealed his design, that either the princess should wed Raja Maun [against her wishes], or by her death seal the peace of Rajwarra, whatever arguments were used to point the alternative, the Rana was made to see no choice between consigning his beloved child to the Rahtore prince, or witnessing the effects of a more extended dishonour from the vengence of the Pathan, and the storm of his palace by his licentious adherents – the fiat passed that Kishna Komari should die.[45]

Tod was a firsthand witness to this sad episode, being attached to Sindhia's court in 1806, but he saw in the tragic fate of Kishna Komari an updated, recontextualized version of several European cultural icons: Haendel's 'Jephtha's vow', Racine's 'Iphigénie', and Homer's Helen of Troy are all summoned upon the stage to depict Kishna Komari's 'barbarous immolation';[46] later on, Bukhta Singh is compared with Richard II, or Herod of the desert; Deonath, the high priest of Jodhpur, is likened to Cardinal Wolsey; and Ameer Khan, to the mad Roman emperor Caligula.[47] Through such analogies, Tod obviously seeks to make the story dramatically vivid for the reader. But in incorporating famous tragic villains and heroines into his version of the sacrifice, he also wishes to strike his reader's imagination by conjuring up visions of well-known sacrifices of innocent female victims, attaining thereby an universal register, in the spirit of the Enlightenment.

Another such episode that lends itself to parallels with ancient Greece, is General Monson's retreat from Gurrote, near Kotah, in 1817, as the Maratha Malhar Rao Holkar of Indore advanced from the south. Tod does not hesitate to compare Monson's retreat to a repeat of the 480 BC battle of Thermopylae, where the Spartan leader Leonidas I dispersed his troops to avoid them being massacred by the invading Persian hordes led by Xerxes. He draws a further parallel with Xenophon's retreat at the 401 BC Battle of Cunaxa.[48] Generally, such parallels are made with the aim of underlining the epic nature of certain military battles in the history of the Rajputs. Here, since the retreating party was made up of British troops, the parallels with heroic Greeks and Spartans pitted against barbaric Persians, confer a resoundingly positive light upon the humiliated British battalions.

Tod's deliberate attempts at situating his observations of Rajput manners and customs in a wider, comparative picture, bringing in cultural complexity and inner divisions between different Rajput groups, or using European parallels in his rendering of Rajput narratives of their past, can be interpreted as Tod's open-minded approach to all things Rajput. His vision of the Other's history certainly does not consist in forcing it into a linear, teleological model of historical development, with the more or less explicit intention of showing the Rajputs in a systematically inferior light, in contrast to their superior British colonizers. It should therefore come as no surprise that Tod's studies drew criticism and opposition both from his immediate British superiors like the British Resident in Delhi, Sir David Ochterlony,[49] and from the Bengal government. In fact, if Tod withdrew from Rajputana in June 1822,[50] it was probably because of hierarchical pressure from the British colonial authorities in Delhi and Calcutta, who disapproved of what they saw as his tendency to pander to the complaints and demands of the Rajputs. But it is certainly for those selfsame conflicting loyalties that Tod was later fondly remembered by the Rajputs themselves.[51] In his interactions with the peoples he encountered and administered, Tod can thus be said to have embodied many aspects of the unstable zones of the relationships and exchanges between colonizers and colonized natives, where no pre-established or fixed meaning existed, and where interpretation work had to be improvised – a makeshift construction erected on both sides of the colonial gulf.

13 SHIFTING PERSPECTIVES: VISUAL REPRESENTATION AND THE IMPERIAL 'I' IN ANNA JAMESON'S *WINTER STUDIES AND SUMMER RAMBLES IN CANADA* (1838)

Jennifer Scott

Born in Dublin to an Irish miniature and enamel painter (who took his family to London when his daughter was only four), an established author known for her acute observations on Shakespeare's heroines (*Characteristics of Women*, 1832), and future mentor to the Langham Place feminists, Anna Jameson was summoned to Canada in the autumn of 1836 by her husband, Robert Jameson, who had been appointed Attorney General of Upper Canada. Jameson complied as a gesture towards reconciliation with her estranged husband. When it became clear that marital reconciliation was virtually impossible, she set out to 'discover' Upper Canada on her own, and set out on a tour which took her through many Native[1] settlements. Jameson then saw much of Native life unknown to colonial travellers, before she sailed back to Britain in February 1838, having come to a separation agreement with her husband. *Winter Studies and Summer Rambles in Canada* was completed – not integrally written – and published shortly after her return. Jameson opens her travel journal with a Preface that posits that she has 'abstained generally from politics and personalities'.[2] One quickly learns, however, that her account is a highly-politicized memoir, wherein Jameson explores and criticizes the efficacy of British imperial practices and doctrines in British North America. Having travelled throughout Europe, encountering new cultures was not a new experience for Jameson, but the degree of cultural difference she encounters in Upper Canada quite obviously demands that she undergo a process of self-reflection, self-examination, and political change.

Although travel writing was a popular genre for nineteenth-century women who were looking to 'expand [their] participation in the public sphere',[3] the degree of Jameson's self-conscious and mutable politicization distinguishes *Rambles* from other examples of the genre. What even more particularly distinguishes Jameson from many of her contemporaries is the ease with which this art historian – the aspect of her work for which she was then best known (see for instance *The Poetry of Sacred and Legendary Art*, 1848) – uses her expertise with the visual realm to position herself within the colonial context. Inevitably, she reveals her connections to British imperialism in her *picturesque* 'sketches' of Upper Canada; but as she travels north and encounters the Native communities she ultimately befriends, the apolitical and nationalist self Jameson confidently displays in the Preface is overshadowed by the critique of British colonial policies.

When traced alongside her use of visual language, it appears this shift in sense of self seems to be directly linked to Jameson's sustained interaction with Native communities and individuals, whom she initially describes as 'specimens',[4] and eventually equates as her 'home ... [and her] adopted ... family'.[5] I argue that by shifting from picturesque *landscapes* or ethnic groups, to individual *portraits*, Jameson provides a lens that foregrounds a wholesale critique not only of colonial Canada, but also of the treatment of women in nineteenth-century Britain. Despite colonial efforts to establish an Upper-Canadian national identity, the shifting sense of self Jameson reveals through her changing visual referent undermines notions of nationalist 'imagined communities', and refigures them as transatlantic, feminist ones.

In her Preface to *Rambles*, Jameson adopts the trope of the humble female author, clearly glossing over her authority as an already established traveller and art historian. As such, Jameson is consciously textualizing her identity within a socially normative framework: she does not present herself as an authority figure; rather she suggests that her text is unfinished, unedited and surely presents but only one, of course modest, opinion, which she hopes will be somewhat helpful in the 'merciful construction of good women'.[6] Indeed, Jameson suggests that she employs 'the flimsy thread of sentiment' – another classic trope of femininity – to sustain the facts and observations of her text, which she insists has therefore 'little reference to the politics or statistics' of Upper Canada.[7] This authorial strategy is quite evidently intended to mask her feminist and colonial critique within familiar writing strategies of her era; in fact, Jameson was secretly following in the tradition of 'women travellers [who were] most interested in cultivating their own authority [and who] sought to compare their impressions and discoveries to those of established scholars'.[8]

As Wendy Roy explains, 'Jameson's representation of herself as 'Mrs' allowed her the freedom to travel alone and unchaperoned, and to make the kind of adventurous journey about which she wrote': Jameson's indeterminate marital status provided her with at least a minimal amount of reputability and freedom to act outside of the traditional domestic sphere of femininity, travel with the Chippewa people, and then publish an account of her adventures, all of which went against the grain of idealized British female domesticity.[9] Jameson thus cunningly uses her liminal marital status to produce herself as a fully authorized subject while establishing more permanent relationships with Native Canadians, as if she were indeed a settler, but one of the unreliable, unpredictable, subversive kind. As Karen Lawrence explains, the discourse of femininity is 'radically altered' because of Jameson's drastically-altered and geographically-shifting domestic sphere.[10] She attempts to make a 'home' for herself among diverse families, communities and geographic locales, a form of 'rambling' nomadism which creates dynamic, unfixed, fluid sites where sustained self-reflection and ideological change become possible.

As a genre, the hybridity of travel writing also allows Jameson a certain degree of freedom. The 'greater flexibility [of] this literary genre ... allowed women travellers to use it as a tool for a deliberate and explicit search for the self in contact with difference'.[11] Jameson for her part can include not only personal experience, but also political criticism and, most notably, detailed visual illustrations as well as verbal 'sketches' of her encounters. One method of 'home-making' Jameson adopts is her use of the familiar genre of the 'picturesque'. If her liminality as a female traveller, neither married nor unmarried, neither traveller nor settler, allows Jameson a method of 'rearticulating marginality or particularity',[12] her usage of the language of the picturesque enables her in fact to *permeate* the 'membrane between home and the foreign'.[13] As an art historian, Jameson would be well aware of the colonial politics surrounding specifically the picturesque genre, while also providing a recognizable discourse for her British readership. As Dianne Sachko Macleod explains, 'the picturesque aesthetic proved to be a convenient trope for British artists abroad whose training did not offer them an alternate visual vocabulary that was flexible enough to encompass what they experienced away from Great Britain's manicured shores'.[14] The recognizable language of the picturesque creates a shared imagined visual experience – and community – among Jameson's readership.

But in the colonial landscape of Upper Canada, the political implications of the act of looking are even further complicated. For in the imperial framework, visual sketches like those found in *Rambles* were 'designed to evoke visual images of their subjects and to control the gaze of their readers'.[15] Of course, it is ultimately the author or artist who determines the frame and method of visual objectivity, and as such, the reader or viewer occupies a liminal positionality akin to Jameson's. So that it may be argued that both artist and viewer, both narrator and reader, occupy a position of power *and* of subordination: both may be said to fluctuate between self-assured agency *and* indeterminacy. The framing that inevitably occurs through any discursive rendering of a colonial landscape thus serves as a reminder of the political implications of a visual occupation. As Carol Crawshaw and John Urry suggest, visual consumption does not merely provide a primer for *how* to view the landscape, but also for who is engaged in the act of looking, as the visual also produces effects of masculinity and femininity, contributing to the ongoing feminization of the land, suggesting a gendered hierarchy of power inherent in the act of looking.[16] As both recorder and viewer, Jameson thus further problematizes the notion of the feminized colonial landscape.

Through her independent representation and recording of the landscape, Jameson exerts her autonomy by taking on the typically masculine role of mastering the land through her determination of subject matter. But at the same time, if the picturesque scene 'require[s] some distinct slant of vision and some strategic measure of omission', it is also through her own 'slant of vision' and 'strategic omission' that Jameson reiterates her complex identity as art historian, cultural critic and ethnographer.[17] She can describe the discontent of Native Upper Canadian and American groups in Detroit resulting in the 'exciting', 'terrific', 'picturesque'[18] conflict of the War of Pontiac in a moment of colonial political loyalty, and in the next breath describe the fruitless destruction of Native corn fields in a moment of colonial political critique.[19] Importantly, her shifting political position is mediated by an overt visual referent: by describing the site of the war as having a 'genuine Claude Lorraine sky'[20] – an artist whose work William Gilpin's celebrated 1792 essays saw as synonymous with the picturesque[21] – Jameson reassures her readership of the recognizability of the foreign landscape, before offering a critique of the colonial treatment of Native groups.

It has been argued that in his landscape canvases, Turner, the most prominent British artist of the time, provided access to this potent colonial paradigm, making 'visual access to the land' an invitation to the British to claim foreign land as 'their national aesthetic property'.[22] Similarly, Jameson's readership can exert their claims on Upper Canada as 'their national aesthetic property' through her discursive visual sketches. Of course, the picturesque discourse also imports the ability to 'naturalize the settler subject and establish a local version of the bourgeois public sphere'.[23] Jameson's naturalization within the colonial landscape helps both to recreate a 'bourgeois sphere' among her reading public, and to restabilize Jameson's unfixed self as a British art historian in the 'new' landscape of Upper Canada. The longing for cultural recognition and stability found in *Rambles* then changes the Upper-Canadian landscape from a discrete, unique environment – marked by its utter alterity – to one where the nascent British tourist, observer, or explorer no longer looks for signs of cultural difference, but instead looks for signs of cultural recognition.

One such moment is Jameson's experience at Niagara Falls, an experience conveyed through one of her most memorable and detailed 'sketches'. Niagara Falls was, at the time Jameson was travelling, one of the few Upper-Canadian landmarks that had been previously well-visited, recorded, and made available through print culture in England. Initially disappointed in the Falls, Jameson reiterates the importance of perspective and mastery for a successful picturesque landscape; her initial approach is from above, and as a result, 'all [her] associations which in imagination [she] had gathered round the scene . . . were diminished in effect, or wholly lost'.[24] Because Jameson's perspective is dominant, she loses the sense of the picturesque – an analysis Gilpin himself would have saluted. Upon her second visit to the Falls, she is finally able to 'paint' a picturesque landscape for her readership:

> The whole scene assumed a wild and wonderful magnificence; down came the dark-green waters, hurrying with them over the edge of the precipice enormous blocks of ice brought down from Lake Eerie [*sic*]. On each side of the Falls, from the ledges and overhanging cliffs, were suspended hug icicles ... all the crags below ... had formed into immense crystals ... such as I had seen in the pictures of Staffa and the Giant's Causeway ... Wherever we stood we were on unsafe ground ... It was very fearful, and yet I could not tear myself away.[25]

Once Jameson feels sufficiently overpowered by the sublime majesty of the untamed wilderness, she can adhere to the doctrines of the picturesque, as determined by Gilpin, and exemplified in 'the pictures of Staffa' – whether these are meant to refer to reproductions of Turner's 1832 oil painting or of the then widely popular site on Niagara Falls bearing the same name, remains a matter of speculation – and the Giant's Causeway. Jameson's cultural nostalgia is here visible through her detailed efforts to recreate a recognizable sublime, but above all picturesque, landscape in the foreign land of Upper Canada.

But her positioning is still rather ambiguous: Jameson is at once disappointed and in awe; the landscape is both frightening and reassuring. What is more, 'the empty colonial surroundings fall in as backdrop, functioning metaphorically to both amplify and confirm a loss of self, a transportation through awe'.[26] The viewer-narrator is thus torn between an aesthetic response that prompts a communal identification in England, or among other British travellers who have experienced the Falls, and an individual response of disappointment, which must be fought in order to arrive at a response likely to be shared with her reading public. Ultimately, Jameson attributes her disappointment to her 'anticipation' of the Falls, suggesting that the imagined experience – as translated through print culture – can surpass the lived experience, and more specifically, that the imagined site is never wholly commensurable with the actual experience. In fact, by attributing her disappointment to her 'anticipation' rather than to her experience, Jameson can simultaneously uphold an individual response to this site of cultural recognition without an outright rejection of what was, at the time, one of the only recognizable Upper-Canadian landscapes.

This strategy emphasizes the importance of the narrative environment within which the *verbal* sketches are embedded in *Rambles*, which is to say also the importance of the question of writing *about* the Other.

The choice to *write* these landscapes, and to inscribe them within a narrative sequence, acts as a method for Jameson to convey her singular experience, while at the same time creating a material 'souvenir' to help legitimatize her observations, the written text both granting authenticity to Jameson's claims and creating a 'verifiable marker' of these experiences.[27] Jameson's choice to exclude her own *visual* renditions of Upper-Canadian scenes, and to rely instead entirely on the *verbal* sketch speaks also to a larger cultural hierarchy, one which legitimatizes the written word over other forms of communication, and legitimatizes by the same token the role of print as fundamental in creating national identities. Benedict Anderson argues for the necessity of print-capitalism 'which made it possible for rapidly growing numbers of people to think about themselves, and to relate themselves to others in profoundly new ways', as the marker of an 'imagined community'.[28] It should be remembered here that throughout her 'Winter Studies', Jameson engages in German translation, demonstrating how cultural and geographic distances might be bridged through language and by virtue of the circulation of print. Later, she turns her mind to offering translations and transpositions of Chippewa stories and songs, interspersed through her 'Summer Rambles'.

But it seems to me one should be careful to distinguish between the two kinds of occupation. For, Jameson insists, these stories and songs are not those that recount 'well-known Indian customs and repeat anecdotes to be found in all the popular books of travel'.[29] Instead, these 'very picturesque, and peculiar, and fanciful' stories are rooted within an *oral* tradition of storytelling, and as a consequence detail alternate modes of domesticity, of family, and of conflict resolution. Jameson, who has been 'working like a beaver to borrow an Indian phrase', thus chooses to align herself within the storytelling tradition of the Native Upper Canadians themselves.[30] Her easy appropriation of an 'Indian phrase' even inserts her into the Native community. This, I think, reveals the narrowness of possibility for communal identification as defined by Anderson. Jameson's own reliance on print in her attempt at transposition presumes in fact the possibility of cross-cultural success.

One can speculate that Jameson includes aspects of the Chippewa culture as a marker of respect and a willingness to share these cultural artefacts with her readers *at home*. She describes these 'picturesque' songs and stories as 'her new acquisitions', revealing a sense of ownership over the cultural artefacts of the oral Chippewa culture.[31] However, when Jameson explains the complexity of the Chippewa language, the impossibility of her task as ethnographer becomes evident:

It is not only very sweet and musical to the ear, with its soft inflections and lengthened vowels, but very complex and artificial in its construction, and subject to strict grammatical rules; this, for an unwritten language – for they have no alphabet – appears to me very curious.[32]

The ethnographer works on the assumption that oral cultures do not produce any 'complex and artificial ... construction', regulated by 'strict grammatical rules'. Jameson's sudden realization that 'primitive' culture may in fact be highly codified, and in a very complex way, is therefore perceived as raising a very serious logical difficulty: literacy being assumed to be the guarantee of a higher degree of civilization, her Native interlocutors should appear as the emblems of a lower degree of culture, on the wrong side of what Jack Goody has called the 'Great Divide' between pre-logical and logical systems of thought.[33] And yet, Jameson clearly perceives that there exists something like a higher form of Chippewa oral culture, uniting this particular group of Natives into a distinct 'imagined community'.

What Jameson's attempt to introduce the Chippewa oral culture into the print cultures of Britain and Upper Canada reveals, therefore, is a fault in Anderson's argument. Although the end result – the creation of an imagined community through language – might be the same, the establishment of this imagined Native community does not *necessarily* rely upon *print*. In fact, Jameson's transposition and subsequent publication of Chippewa songs emphasize that the tone-based structure of Chippewa music is very difficult – if not impossible – to transcribe into Western classical form, and must therefore remain *unwritten*.[34] Traditional Native music is oral, and does not conform to the European eight-note scale model.[35] Invoking the ideas of foundational ethnomusicologist Bruno Nettl, Peter Winkler explains that 'many Western musicians think of a piece of music ... not as an aural phenomenon, but as a visual representation ... This essentially 'visualist' orientation . . . easily leads to ethnocentrism'.[36]

True, Jameson's puzzled reaction, as well as her efforts at translating such songs into Western frames of meaning, also reveals her 'ethnocentrism'. Her 'visualist' and print-centric understanding of music, and of its cultural importance and role in community formation, shows how she continues to rely both on a visual referent and a written discourse. But while there is always the problem that Jameson's text continues to hierarchize the written word over other methods of communication, it is telling that her musical transposition shifts from a purely textual sketch to include a 'modular' musical staff and notes. Moreover, however impossible a 'true' transposition might be, Jameson's attempt at musical 'translation' is not entirely in vain: where her attempt proves useful is in its demonstration that print culture is one method of communicating the culture of the colony back to the imperial centre.

But throughout *Rambles*, Jameson reveals a frustration with the communicative capacity of the written word: she 'sketches', 'paints' and explains that if she were 'as a musician, [she] would *play* [her readers] Lake Ontario, rather than describe it'.[37] What she constantly suggests by doing so is that print-culture is but one way of building an imagined community. Both in primitive and civilized cultures. Indeed, if as Anderson maintains, imagined communities necessarily result in the formation of national identity, then an imagined community without national identity acting as an overarching common denominator, such as in the Native communities described by Jameson, should be impossible. Here, one should bear in mind Partha Chatterjee's important challenge to Anderson's theory: 'if nationalisms in the rest of the world have to choose their imagined community from certain 'modular' forms already made available to them by Europe and the Americas, what do they have left to imagine?'.[38] I therefore suggest extending Anderson's premise of the 'deep horizontal comradeship' of the national imaginary precipitated by the development of print capitalism, to include mass 'seeing' and 'hearing' publics as well. For example, when Jameson introduces the stories of Indian agent Henry Schoolcraft's mixed-race[39] wife, she suggests that the translation is 'surely very picturesque, and peculiar, and fanciful'.[40] Jameson's British readership, although alienated from these stories due to the impossibility of truly accurate translation from an oral language to a print language, can depend on a communal *visual* perspective to encourage a standardized experience.

What I want to study now is how Jameson then engages in individual portraits, before finally shifting her representational technique once more to encourage the juxtaposition of the Native Upper-Canadian woman and the British woman of Jameson's readership abroad. This juxtaposition encourages a critical approach to the nationalist community of British readers and through the establishment of a transatlantic imagined community linked by gender, Jameson can critique the failure of social gender roles assigned to British women in the nineteenth century.

Whereas in the first section of the text, 'Winter Studies', Jameson's use of the picturesque language is largely employed to create effective linguistic 'landscapes', in the 'Summer Rambles' section of her text similar painterly techniques are employed to 'sketch' Native communities. Initially, Jameson firmly locates herself within a colonial framework, arguing that upon her arrival in Upper Canada, she 'was thrown into scenes and regions hitherto undescribed by any traveller (for the northern shores of Lake Huron are *almost* new ground), and into relations with Indian tribes, such as few European women of *refined and civilized* habits have ever *risked* and none have recorded'.[41] By aligning herself with European women of 'refined and civilized habits', Jameson establishes the borders of her 'imagined community' with one broad stroke. Through her distinct articulation of the 'risk' of the type of exploration she has undertaken, Jameson upholds existing colonial stereotypes of the exotic 'savage'; by placing herself as the sole recorder of this landscape, Jameson re-establishes print and visual culture as being inextricable from a successful exploration.

But, once again, Jameson has also located herself within the categorical normative against which all 'Others' might be measured, thereby also naturalizing her position within the Upper-Canadian context. Here also, her identity is demonstrated as being both European and Upper-Canadian, allowing her encounter with this foreign landscape and as yet 'othered' peoples to maintain a self-identity and political position in flux. Where the consistent adherence to the picturesque tradition of assimilation breaks down is when Jameson begins to stray from its rigid confines and begins to engage in portraiture.

For example, when Jameson offers a lengthy 'portrait' of the 'famous Pottowottomie chief and conjurer called 'The Two Ears', she not only distinguishes him from his peer-group at the Grand Council of Chiefs' meeting, but her mere presence at the meeting is a method of aligning herself within the Grand Council, thus challenging all national boundaries, both imperial and indigenous. The Two Ears is described as 'hideously painted', 'squalid' and 'miserable'.[42] In contrast, Jameson then offers a portrait of another chief, whom she 'immediately distinguishe[s] from the rest ... [as her] cousin, Waub-Ojeeg',[43] who is described as 'splendid', 'tasteful' and as 'one of the finest specimens of his race [she] had yet seen'.[44] Despite Jameson's familial affiliation with the preferential Native Chief, Waub-Ojeeg, and despite what seems to be Jameson's attempt to reveal similarities between British and Native systems of government, she nevertheless slips into a colonial objectification of Two Ears and Waub-Ojeeg by referring to these individuals as 'specimens'. The perspective chosen by the narrator here is a clear indication that Jameson is struggling to refigure her social and political positioning: rather than the Grand Council being relegated to a group of shadowy, indistinguishable figures, she offers a specific, contextualized opportunity for her readership to move away from the viewerly conventions of the picturesque, and she invites her readers by the same token to identify the subjects of her portraiture as *individuals*.

There is no longer the politically safe anchor of the picturesque perspective to stabilize her British readers. On the contrary, this deviation from the principles of the picturesque forces the reader to self-politicize as the text unfolds, alongside Jameson's increasingly overt self-politicization. This is definitely the case of an explorer 'rambling' among the Natives, unfixed, in flux and her readers must now engage more closely with these portraits in context, evaluating and categorizing the 'Other' for themselves, not from stereotypes and clichés. By providing textual space for the individual portraits of Native Upper-Canadians, Jameson creates a critical site for her readership to re-evaluate their relationship between 'Self' and 'Other' previously stabilized within the frame of picturesque landscapes; by introducing highly variable individual portraits of the 'Not-Self', she also destabilizes her own position as the unnamed normative against which these 'Others' were measured.

Still, once again, Jameson's reliance on print and visual cultures to maintain a sense of self reveals a fundamental adherence to a colonial framework of exploration, documentation, and text-based culture, which vastly differs from the oral cultures of the Native Upper-Canadians. As Wendy Roy suggests in her detailed descriptions of Jameson's illustrations, the immobility of the barely visible Native in the landscapes mimics the political immobility of the Native communities in the wake of British imperialism.[45] It seems indeed that Jameson's *collective* descriptions of Native communites adhere to the same conventions of the picturesque as her landscapes. Despite the *individual* recognition provided through the verbal portraiture of Chusco,[46] Mrs Schoolcraft,[47] and the Wayish,ky (*sic*) family,[48] among others, Jameson maintains the cultural superiority of the picturesque viewer when portraying the community at large, suggesting an overall support of the imperial project. The visual colonization made possible through Jameson's picturesque narrative thus leaves in fact little room for Chippewa empowerment within the Upper-Canadian landscape. As Helsinger explains, 'to be the subject and never the viewer of these landscapes means to be fixed in a place ... circumscribed within a social position and a locality, unable to grasp the larger entity, England, which local scenes can represent for more mobile picturesque viewers'.[49] Although Jameson demonstrates empathy and a kind of respect for the Chippewa people, by rendering the community either invisible or immobile and incapable of visual reciprocity through the fixed frame of her picturesque sketches, she ultimately replicates the imperial disempowerment of the Chippewa community at large.

This disempowerment becomes more obvious in her portrait of a Chippewa man whom Jameson does not 'paint' however as an individual; instead, she collapses the cultural differences between the Ottawa and Pottowottomie groups, and marks them both as 'dandies':

> The Ottawa I soon distinguished by the decency of his dress ... the Pottowottomie by the more savage finery of his costume ... The dandyism of some of these Pottowottomie warriors is inexpressibly amusing and grotesque.[50]

Here, Jameson is not only applying a colonial stereotype – the savage as an 'amusing', comic figure, especially when engaged in mimicry – but she is also historicizing the Native masculinity within the context of nineteenth-century English 'dandyism'. The comic deviance from social heteronormativity not only allows Jameson's readership to better imagine the theatrical costuming of the Native, but also reaffirms Jameson's loyalty to normative colonial culture. Jameson's introduction of a Chippewa man in the section entitled 'Indian Dandies' makes her imperial attitude even more evident, as she explicitly aestheticizes the fierce warrior, aligning him within the framework of Englishness rather than carving a niche of individuality from within her knowledge of his own culture:

> One of these exquisites, whom I distinguished as Beau Brummel, was not indeed much indebted to a tailor, seeing as he had neither a coat nor anything else that gentlemen are accustomed to wear, but then his face was most artistically painted ... his leggings of scarlet cloth were embroidered down the sides ... his moccasins were also beautifully worked with porcupine quills; he had armlets and bracelets of silver ... and conspicuous above all, the eagle feather in his hair; showing he was a warrior, and had taken a scalp – *i.e.* killed a man.[51]

Jameson does not contextualize this warrior's dress in relation to other, perhaps relevant, cultural implications: presumably, this is not the everyday dress of the Pottowottomie, but marks ceremonial or governmental significance. She chooses rather to decontextualize his dress-code by renaming this 'exquisite' as a *beau* and nicknaming him after one of the most famous English dandies. The details with which she describes his dress also ensures her readership will receive a clear, though 'exotic' picture of this highly picturesque 'savage' – the cultural significance of Brummel's eagle feather unambiguously designating him in the end as nothing but a brutal primitive.

And yet Jameson's ambivalent positioning is conspicuous once again. For elsewhere her critique of the colonial project is explicit:

> That the poor Indians to whom reserved lands have been granted, and who, on the faith of treaties, have made their homes and gathered themselves into villages on such lands, should, whenever it is deemed expedient, be driven out of their possessions, either by purchase, or by persuasion, or by force, or by measures which include all three, and sent to seek a livelihood in distant or strange regions – as in the case of these Delawares – is horrible, and bears cruelty and injustice on the face of it.[52]

In such a passage the pathos with which the remarks are invested suggests that the narrator feels some kind of natural kinship with the poor creatures abused by the colonial system. Jameson's readership could not then ignore that the author of these lines could be no other but a *woman* explorer, sympathizing with other beings of inferior status, against the colonial order her husband stood for. The 'flimsy thread of sentiment' for which Jameson initially apologizes and which is supposed to exonerate her of any seriousness, is therefore clearly articulated on politicization. And indeed, the location of *Rambles* within the growing woman's movement of nineteenth-century Britain, together with Jameson's future participation in the 'feminist' agitation, invites the reader to draw parallels between the fate reserved to Indians in Canada and the fate allotted to women in Britain. They, too, could become the victims of broken treaties, 'driven out of their possessions, either by purchase, or by persuasion, or by force', and 'sent to seek a livelihood in distant or strange regions'.

This undoubtedly further problematizes the nationalist basis for Anderson's concept of 'imagined communities'. For, despite Jameson's condemnation that the treatment of the Natives is 'horrible' and 'bears cruelty and injustice', she suggests that although she does not 'consider the Indians as an inferior race', they do 'strike [her] as *untamable*'.[53] This is where the contradiction becomes most obvious: although she claims to value the time she has spent among Native communities, she still believes that Britain has an obligation to 'civilize' the Native population. She has found a new home among them, but she goes as far as to suggest 'the dirty, careless habits of the Indians, while sheltered only by the bark-covered wigwam, matter very little'.[54] By reducing the cultural and social practices of the Native populations to 'dirty, careless habits', Jameson reveals her own faith in the colonial project; once she spends more time amongst the different Native communities, her resolve to communicate the empowering and equalitarian aspects of these same communities strengthens. So that she eventually uses *Rambles* to undermine the nationalist agenda of the British Empire while at the same time foregrounding the importance of woman in *any* community, Upper-Canadian or British, claiming that 'the true importance and real dignity of woman is everywhere, in savage and civilized communities, regulated by her capacity of being useful'.[55] There is no easy resolution for Jameson's own political attitude; rather, what *Rambles* reveals is her growing self-awareness of the complex and interwoven fabric of a colonial, multicultural landscape. The project of *Rambles* is for Jameson to translate the Upper-Canadian experience 'as well as [she] can paint it'[56] for her readership. The impetus to continue communicating cultural difference to her readership demonstrates Jameson's willingness to acknowledge this complexity and to continue to work towards a balance between national loyalty, feminism and racial equity in Upper Canada. Jameson thus creates a gender-centric visual imagined community among Victorian British women. Despite the colonial implications of the visual consumption of the colonial landscape and the subsequent commoditization of Jameson's memoir, a political alternative does make itself available to Jameson's readership.

Benedict Anderson suggests that 'fiction seeps quietly and continuously into reality, creating that remarkable confidence of community in anonymity which is the hallmark of modern nations'.[57] I argue that Jameson's hybrid travel narrative troubles this notion of 'the Origins of National consciousness' being necessarily linked to 'the development of 'print-as-commodity'.[58] Instead, Jameson's prominent authorship, her geographically and temporally specific female readership and her creation of imagined community based upon gender rather than nation anticipates 'post-nation' theories of the twentieth century. By moving from geographic and temporal specificity to the general location of women 'everywhere', Jameson creates an imagined community that creates the potential for female political participation across the 'permeable membrane' that Jameson herself must negotiate. This community, which is neither geographical, racial, national, nor colonial, is a gendered one, and demonstrates the possibility to create imagined community that is wholly separate from Anderson's foundational, nationalist concept.

14 CHARLES DARWIN IN PATAGONIA: DESCRIPTIVE STRATEGIES IN THE *BEAGLE DIARY* (1831–1836) AND *THE VOYAGE OF THE BEAGLE* (1845)

Virginia Richter

The voyage on the *Beagle* was the defining moment in Charles Darwin's life. He was all set to become a country parson with a hobby in natural history; instead, he turned into the most eminent naturalist of his times, the author of a groundbreaking explanation of biological diversity, and a founding father of a new discipline, evolutionary biology. During his participation in the five-year circumnavigation of the globe on board HMS *Beagle* (1831–6), Darwin collected an immense amount of material concerning the animal populations, living and extinct, on different continents. In particular the very singular fauna found in South America and the Galapagos Islands would prove illuminating for his theory of the origin of species. Moreover, the publication of his travel report established his reputation as an author, not only in the field of natural history: the popular success of his *Voyage of the Beagle* was due not least to his skilful mix of serious observations and thrilling adventures, tapping into the Victorian desire for self-improvement as well as the age's machismo.

Darwin's experiences have been transmitted in different textual versions. In his diary, Darwin recorded his daily activities; he did not update the entries day to day, but rather wrote them up during the periods spent on board the *Beagle*. His prolonged sojourns on the South American mainland were described in retrospect, after his return to the ship.[1] The completed volumes of his diary were sent with his letters to his family – Darwin was writing with a particular audience in mind. Consequently, the diary, although written closer to the events, is not a raw transcription, an 'authentic', unmediated record (which remained unpublished until 1933, when it was transcribed and edited by Nora Barlow). It is a self-conscious narrative, aware of its readership, and framed by the cultural preconceptions Darwin carried with him.[2] As will be seen below, the latter inform in particular Darwin's encounters with those population groups he con-

siders uncivilized and, in his own term, savage. The diary constituted the basis
for Darwin's published travel report which appeared initially together with Captain FitzRoy's and Captain King's reports on the *Beagle's* two successive voyages.
The first expedition undertaken together with HMS *Adventure*, a hydrographic
survey of Patagonia and Tierra del Fuego (1826–30), had taken place under
the overall command of Captain Philip Parker King. When the *Beagle's* captain, Pringle Stokes, committed suicide following a severe depression, he was
replaced by Robert FitzRoy who was also in command during the second voyage
(1831–6), with Darwin on board as the captain's gentleman companion – *not*
as the expedition's official naturalist. Darwin's biographer Janet Browne emphasizes the institutional reasons that led to Darwin's appointment – his relations
to the 'Cambridge network' of natural scientists – but even more strongly the
social reasons: Darwin was chosen not because he was noticeably good at natural
history, although this was a factor in ensuring he was put forward for the voyage
by his Cambridge professor, nor because he was an aspiring 'savant', well trained
at university, but because he was an amiable man of good social standing who
looked as if he would be easy to live with.[3]

However, Darwin was eager – and encouraged by FitzRoy – to engage in
scientific observations over and above the *Beagle's* official mission, resulting
in conflicts with the ship's surgeon, traditionally in charge of this aspect of an
expedition. Darwin's private status moreover ensured that the collections of
specimens made on the voyage – the material basis for his elaboration of evolution theory – were his property, and not the Admiralty's. After his return, he
was invited to participate in the expedition's official publication, which came
out in 1838 in three volumes under the sweeping title *Narrative of the Surveying
Voyages of His Majesty's Ships Adventure and Beagle between the Years 1826 and
1836, describing their Examination of the southern Shores of South America, and
the Beagle's Circumnavigation of the Globe*. The popularity of Darwin's volume
far exceeded the demand for the other two; it was reissued separately in 1838
and 1840. But since the publication had been funded by the government, Darwin did not receive any royalties, and therefore readily accepted John Murray's
offer to publish the travel report in his popular Home and Colonial Library.
This new edition came out in 1845 with extensive revisions under the new title
*Journal of Researches into the Natural History and Geology of the Countries visited
during the Voyage of H.M.S. Beagle round the World, under the Command of Captain FitzRoy, R.N.* This version, commonly known as *The Voyage of the Beagle*,
became the basis for all further impressions.

As John Tallmadge persuasively argues, Darwin's success as an author was
due to his skilful engagement with the genre of the travel narrative; the most
popular of Victorian genres, after the novel. He achieved 'narrative integration'
– the fusion of scientific information, exciting adventures and autobiographical

elements along the lines of the *Bildungsroman* – by rearranging the chronology of his journey, highlighting certain aspects and periods, and finally, by 'creating a narrative persona that is both engaging and respectable'.[4] The result is a progressive narrative, relating the advancement of the ship's journey – presented as linear, although in fact the *Beagle* criss-crossed along the South American coast – to the protagonist-narrator's personal development, equally seen as moving forward and upward:

> Darwin's fundamental strategy for developing his text thus appears to be a recasting of his voyage from a day-to-day chronicle into an idealized circumnavigation. The new pattern conforms to an archetype of the voyage as a continuous progression from known to unknown lands, or from ignorance to knowledge on the part of the traveler; the geography of the voyage is aligned with a pattern of development in the traveler's consciousness, and the principal effect is to make the traveler the hero of his own account.[5]

In this effective repositioning of his authorial persona – at the end of which Darwin appears as a mature naturalist, 'more in control, more deliberate in his investigations, more dedicated to science, and less eager to seek adventure for its own sake'[6] – the encounters with 'savages' play a crucial role. The forward trajectory of the ship's voyage is connected to a reverse movement in time, or rather, through layers of civilization to a raw state of humanity epitomized by the inhabitants of Tierra del Fuego.

One of the most important changes between the *Diary* and the final version of the *Voyage* consists in the singling out of the South American part of the trip for the reader's attention. While the different parts of the voyage receive more or less equal treatment in the *Diary's* day-to-day log, *The Voyage of the Beagle* pays little attention to the transatlantic crossing, and already the second chapter finds us in Rio de Janeiro. Similarly, the journey home via Tahiti, New Zealand, Australia, Cape Town and a second landfall on the Brazilian coast, is condensed into about ninety pages. The *Beagle's* exploration of the South American coast and islands (including the Galapagos Archipelago), and Darwin's excursions inland, cover about three quarters of the published version, while on the actual trip, this part took up three out of the total five years. The South American sojourn clearly constitutes the heart of Darwin's finished narrative. Here, he encounters the continent's indigenous inhabitants in what appear to be their two paradigmatic states: on the brink of extinction, or almost beyond humanity, in a condition of bare life. In both cases, the encounters with these 'Others' open up, for the budding scientist, an abyss that paradoxically enhances a sense of separation while simultaneously raising the question of connections – of civilized man's connectedness to other species or to his own phylogenetic past. Darwin's journey on horseback through the Argentine pampas, where he witnessed the last phase of the systematic displacement of the Indians, in a way prepares what he saw as the most unforgettable, most challenging experience of his voyage: the encounter with the wild Fuegians in the southernmost part of the continent. While the Patagonian Indians stand for the dehumanization inflicted on indigenous populations in the colonial space, the Fuegians are a living heterochrony, a survival of humanity's prehistoric past, and thus have a double significance as reminders of modern man's humble origins and as indicators of his present superiority.

In *The Voyage of the Beagle*, Darwin describes the Indians employed by the Argentine president General Rosas as inhuman – and barely human – killers :

> They passed the night here; and it was impossible to conceive anything more wild and savage than the scene of their bivouac. Some drank till they were intoxicated; others swallowed the steaming blood of the cattle slaughtered for their suppers, and then being sick from drunkenness, they cast it up again, and were besmeared with filth and gore.[7]

These Indians, 'wild and savage', are linked both metonymically – by drinking and vomiting animal blood – and metaphorically – their behaviour during the feast and their bloodlust in the fights the next day – to animals. The Indians are thus thoroughly 'othered' as, literally, bloodthirsty brutes. But of course, their foes, the targets of Rosas's campaign, are also Indians. These mercilessly hunted and decimated groups represent the complementary image of Indians as victims, equally treated as animals – to be slaughtered:

> The Indians, men, women, and children, were about one hundred and ten in number, and they were nearly all taken or killed, for the soldiers sabre every man. The Indians are now so terrified that they offer no resistance in a body, but each flies, neglecting even his wife and children; but when overtaken, like wild animals, they fight against any number to the last moment ... My informer said, when he was pursuing an Indian, the man cried out for mercy, at the same time that he was covertly loosing the bolas from his waist, meaning to whirl it round his head and so strike his pursuer. 'I however struck him with my sabre to the ground, and then got off my horse, and cut his throat with my knife'. This is a dark picture; but how much more shocking is the unquestionable fact, that all the women who appear above twenty years old are massacred in cold blood! When I exclaimed that this appeared rather inhuman, he answered, 'Why, what can be done? They breed so!'[8]

The humanitarian traveller is shocked by these brutal biopolitics, and observes with regret that 'I think there will not, in another half century, be a wild Indian northward of the Rio Negro'.[9] Darwin describes the imperial expansion as, essentially, a failure of the self-imposed civilizing mission. The executors of Rosas's ethnic policy, the descendants of the original Spanish conquerors, are themselves rendered 'rather inhuman'. Regarding the fate of the Indians, the taking possession of their land results not only in their partial extinction, but also in the re-barbarization of the survivors. 'Not only have whole tribes been exterminated, but the remaining Indians have become more barbarous: instead of living in large villages, and being employed in the arts of fishing, as well as of the chase, they now wander about the open plains, without home or fixed occupation'.[10] The Patagonian Indians thus represent the final stage of their encounter with Western colonizers who do not bring the gift of civilization, but rather take away what little civilization the indigenous population ever possessed. These insights into the relativity of cultural encounters – 'the Christians killing every Indian, and the Indians doing the same by the Christians'[11] – however do not prepare Darwin to embrace cultural relativism when he is confronted with the Fuegians. They represent unequivocally the nadir of humanity, the antithesis of a fully human existence.

Darwin's first encounter with the Fuegians – on 17 December 1832, when the *Beagle* finally reaches the rather inappropriately named Bay of Good Success – is, in fact, not a first encounter at all. Three natives of Tierra del Fuego had been his companions on board from the moment of embarkation. These were the survivors of four Fuegians Captain FitzRoy had taken on board during the *Beagle's* first voyage with the intention of having them educated in England. For FitzRoy, it was an important purpose of the second voyage to resettle Fuegia Basket (Yorkicushlu (1821–83)), York Minster (Elleparu (1804 – before 1863)), and Jemmy Button (Orundellico (1816 – *c.* 1863)) in their native country and by this means to spread civilization and light. In both the *Beagle Diary* and *The Voyage of the Beagle,* Darwin says surprisingly little about his fellow passengers. In the *Diary*, Darwin mentions them twice in passing before the *Beagle* approaches their native country, first taking note, without further comment, of their arrival on board – 'In the evening, the Fuegians arrived by Steam Packet together with their school master Mr Jenkins. Their names are York Minster, Jemmy Button and Fuegia'[12] – and even more casually, when 'Miss Fuegia Basket, who daily increases in every direction except height',[13] appears on a sick list. It is astonishing that Darwin, ordinarily an acute and curious observer, omits any mention of his interactions with this little group; his interest is stirred only when he is confronted with the real thing, the Fuegians in a state of Nature. In the published version, the information is even more scarce. Due to Darwin's strategy of presenting a unified, well-ordered narrative, the 'civilized Fuegians', although of course present from the very beginning of the voyage, are mentioned for the first time when the *Beagle* reaches the coast of Tierra del Fuego.[14] Only when they can serve as a point of contrast to the 'savage Fuegians' do his three travel companions swim into Darwin's ken.

Darwin's description of the natives shows his implicit belief in a hierarchical stratification of human civilizations, if not of races. The savage Fuegians mark the degree zero of civilization: 'If the state in which the Fuegians live should be fixed on as zero in the scale of governments, I am afraid the New Zealand would rank but a few degrees higher',[15] or, when describing the Australian Aborigines: 'Never the less, they appear to me to stand some few degrees higher in civilization, or more correctly a few lower in barbarism, than the Fuegians'.[16] These occupants of the lowest step of human civilization are both so fascinating and so shocking because they mark the distance from Darwin's own elevated position, and the possibility of development and therefore, connection:

> It was without exception the most curious and interesting spectacle I ever beheld: I could not have believed how wide was the difference between savage and civilized man: It is greater than between a wild and domesticated animal, inasmuch as in man there is a greater power of improvement.[17]

According to Cannon Schmitt, this encounter will constitute a cornerstone in the formulation of evolution theory, but not simply as evidence of the gradation of human development. Rather, the Fuegians fulfil an almost Freudian function in Darwin's writings, ambivalently coded as uncanny or as the repressed that returns to haunt the idea of evolution. Schmitt describes this function as Darwin's 'savage mnemonics':

> The shock he evinces at the sight of them and the thought of their proximity to civilized humanity ensures that Darwin cannot forget them. That same shock, however, also demands that savages be, if not precisely forgotten, then at least displaced from their position in a theory to which they nevertheless remain ineluctably central.[18]

At key moments, but in particular in *The Descent of Man*, where he finally tackles the question of human evolution, Darwin will return to his encounter with the Fuegians, both evoking their condition of bare life 'in remembrance of the origins of the civilized' and trying 'to forget the savage's kinship with the civilized'.[19] In Darwin's diary and travel report, this sense of shock is palpable, but it is complicated by two accompanying features frequently neglected in the critical literature on Darwin's travelogues: mutual curiosity and humour. These elements are more pronounced in the *Beagle Diary* than in the published account where the descriptions of the encounters are slightly rearranged to maintain Darwin's dignity as a scientific observer and a representative of British civilization. In both texts, but in various degrees of transparency, the implications of the encounter are fairly evident: firstly, the demarcation zone separating savage and civilized man is not a given; civilization can be acquired as well as lost. In this respect, the three Fuegians returning from England, particularly Jemmy Button, play a crucial role. Secondly, through the encounter, Darwin's own superior position – as a detached observer, a scientist, an Englishman and so on – is unfixed: he recognizes not only the common humanity uniting him with these wretches, but also the fact that the observer's gaze can be reversed.

Indeed, while Darwin and his fellow-travellers are studying the Fuegians, they in turn are examined by them. The direction of the gaze is not unilateral; rather, Darwin finds himself entangled in a triangulated situation involving the Fuegians, the English crew, and the intercultural go-betweens Fuegia Basket, York Minster, and Jemmy Button. We find an arrangement that is reminiscent of Jacques Lacan's reading of Poe's *Purloined Letter*: A is looking at B looking at C.[20] A would then be in the superior position, seeing everything, B the subordinate, partial observer, C the object, the exhibit to be gazed at. However, this hierarchical triangle can be undermined in two ways: the positions can become unstable, so that A may exchange places with B or C, and vice versa; and C can consciously exhibit him- or herself, and thus become the subject and the object at the same time. In each case, the superior, detached position of the observer is undermined; he is fully involved in the reciprocity of the first encounter.

The revisions between the *Beagle Diary* and *The Voyage of the Beagle* are subtle but illuminating. In the *Diary*, the rendezvous between the ship's crew and the two groups of Fuegians occurring on 18 December 1832, one day after Darwin's shocking first confrontation with the savages, is spread out over two pages. The meetings between 'wild' and 'tame' Fuegians, which happened on two separate occasions, are accordingly described in two batches in the text, separated by general reflections on the living conditions in Tierra del Fuego. In the *Voyage*, by contrast, these meetings seem to occur in direct succession. This tightening of the narrative structure, together with certain additions and revisions, has a suggestive effect on the representation of the English visitors as well as both groups of Fuegians. In the *Beagle Diary*, Jemmy Button is the first object of the other Fuegians' interest:

> Jemmy Button came in the boat with us; it was interesting to watch their conduct to him. – They immediately perceived the difference & held much conversation between themselves on the subject. – The old man then began a long harangue to Jemmy; who said it was inviting him to stay with them: – but the language is rather different & Jemmy could not talk to them.[21]

Here, Darwin and the crew members remain securely in position A, observing the Fuegians observing Jemmy Button. Despite the language barrier, it seems to be clear that Jemmy's 'civilized' appearance causes as much astonishment in the Fuegians as their barbarous state did in Darwin the day before. They 'perceived the difference & held much conversation': this suggests that the cultural difference between the Fuegians and their returned relatives is much deeper than that between Jemmy Button and Darwin himself. This impression is corroborated by the fact that 'Jemmy could not talk to them'. In consequence, Jemmy cannot act properly as an intermediary; his translation of the old man's speech is highly dubious. All in all, the Fuegians on board the *Beagle* fail to function as connecting links bridging the shocking distance between savage Fuegians and civilized Englishmen. Rather, their cultural achievement serves to emphasize the gap, as Darwin comments elsewhere: 'It seems yet wonderful to me, when I think over all his many good qualities that he should have been of the same race, and doubtless partaken of the same character, with the miserable, degraded savages whom we first met here'.[22] Following Jemmy's first encounter with the savage Fuegians, Darwin inserts in the *Diary* a description of the latters' (lack of) dress, food, tools and weapons, (lack of) dwellings, and general living conditions. After dinner the visit is resumed, now with York Minster as the focus of attention:

> They noticed York Minster (who accompanied us) in the same manner as Jemmy, & told him he ought to shave, & yet he has not 20 hairs on his face, whilst we all wear our untrimmed beards. – They examined the color of his skin; & having done so, they looked at ours. – An arm being bared, they expressed the liveliest surprise & admiration. Their whole conduct was such an odd mixture of astonishment & imitation, that nothing could be more laughable & interesting. – The tallest man was pleased with being examined & compared with a tall sea-man, in doing this he tried his best to get on rather higher ground & to stand on tip-toes: He opened his mouth to show his teeth & turned his face en profil; for the rest of his days doubtless he will be the beau ideal of his tribe. – Two or three of the officers, who are both fairer & shorter than the others (although possessed of large beards) were, we think, taken for Ladies. – I wish they would follow our supposed example & produce their 'squaws'.[23]

In this passage most particularly, the first encounter becomes a mutual affair. Now the Fuegians act as comparative ethnologists, examining York Minster and comparing him to the crew members. Darwin emphasizes that they observe and comment upon, first York Minster's appearance, then that of the officers and crew. The discovery of the markers of ethnic difference – facial hair, different skin colour – results in wonder. When the tall Fuegian is 'examined & compared', he takes a very active part, exhibiting himself rather than submitting passively. The hierarchy of the ethnographic gaze, automatically ascribing the dominant position to the Western scientist, has been utterly subverted. Darwin comments that the Fuegians' ethnological endeavours are 'laughable', but this only underlines that the explorers-become-the-explored are no longer in a superior position. The scrutiny, the wonder and the laughter are reciprocal. This involvement in, rather than distance from, the mutual inspection is finally underpinned by Darwin's joke about the supposed ladies. Since Darwin does not understand the Fuegians at all, the gender-bending assumption springs from his own mind rather than theirs. The joke provides an insight into the precariousness of identity in the contact zone, and into the aspect of his personality that Darwin will endeavour to restrain in the published version: his desire to see the Fuegian – naked – ladies belongs to the youthful adventurer rather than the sober scientist.

In the version of the same episode printed in *The Voyage of the Beagle*, the two encounters are presented as a single continuous narrative; in addition, we find significant omissions and additions:

It was interesting to watch the conduct of the savages, when we landed, towards Jemmy Button: they immediately perceived the difference between him and ourselves, and held much conversation one with another on the subject. The old man addressed a long harangue to Jemmy, which it seems was to invite him to stay with them. But Jemmy understood very little of their language, *and was, moreover, thoroughly ashamed of his countrymen.* When York Minster afterwards came on shore, they noticed him in the same way, and told him he ought to shave; yet he had not twenty dwarf hairs on his face, whilst we all wore our untrimmed beards. They examined the colour of his skin, and compared it with ours. One of our arms being bared, they expressed the liveliest surprise and admiration *at its whiteness, just in the same way in which I have seen the ourangoutang do at the Zoological Gardens.* We thought that they mistook two or three of the officers, who were rather shorter and fairer, though adorned with large beards, for the ladies of our party. The tallest among the Fuegians was evidently much pleased at his height being noticed. When placed back to back with the tallest of the boat's crew, he tried his best to edge on higher ground, and to stand on tiptoe. He opened his mouth to show his teeth, and turned his face for a side view; and all this was done with such alacrity, that I dare say he thought himself the handsomest man in Tierra del Fuego. *After our first feeling of grave astonishment was over, nothing could be more ludicrous than the odd mixture of surprise and imitation which these savages every moment exhibited.*[24]

The revealing joke has been excised. The newly added passages (italicized by me) all serve to reduce the equality of the encounter. While in the diary entry no mention is made of Jemmy's feelings, now he is conveniently 'ashamed'. The Fuegians' curiosity no longer corresponds to that of the officers and Darwin himself; it is equated – a perfidious comparison – with the curiosity of apes in a zoo. The final sentence conclusively restores the lost balance, or rather the lost superiority: Darwin and his fellows are reconstructed as sober observers who feel 'grave astonishment', rather than rough travellers willing to fool around with the natives. The savages become, in contrast to this European gravity, odd and ludicrous.

The deeply religious Captain FitzRoy's purpose in first abducting the four Fuegians to England and then returning the three survivors, after three years, to their native country, consisted not only in giving these individuals a Christian education. These nearly or fully grown-up persons were placed at the Walthamstow Church of England infants' school, where they received training in English, 'the plainer truths of Christianity' and basic skills in husbandry, gardening etc.[25] But the second, and more important, aim was to repatriate them, improved by a shot of British civilization, and so to create a base for establishing missions in Tierra del Fuego. How foolish and ill-prepared this scheme was becomes evident when the missionary who is to accompany them begs, after a few weeks, to be taken back on board the *Beagle*; the three displaced, bewildered Fuegians are left to fend for themselves. This forced return seems particularly tragic in the case of Jemmy Button who had succeeded best in adapting to the English lifestyle. Back in the rough landscape of Tierra del Fuego, he has half-forgotten his native language, and finds himself estranged from his people. Darwin is wholly sceptical about the religious side of FitzRoy's experiment, but he is fascinated by the Fuegians' quick adaptability to English manners, by the savages' rapid ascent to a civilized state, and watches the experiment of repatriation with great curiosity. His diary entry on their parting from the *Beagle* captures all the contradictions inherent in European civilizing efforts:

> It was quite melancholy leaving our Fuegians amongst their barbarous countrymen: there was one comfort; they appeared to have no personal fears. – But, in contradiction of what has often been stated, 3 years has been sufficient to change savages, into, as far as habits go, complete & voluntary Europæans. – York, who was a full grown man & with a strong violent mind, will I am certain in every respect live as far as his means go, like an Englishman. – Poor Jemmy, looked rather disconsolate, & certainly would have liked to have returned with us; he said 'They were all very bad men, 'no sabe' nothing', – Jemmy's own brother had been stealing from him as Jemmy said, 'what fashion do you call that'. – I am afraid whatever other ends their excursion to England produces, it will not be conducive to their happiness. – They have far too much sense not to see the vast superiority of civilized over uncivilized habits; & yet I am afraid to the latter they must return.[26]

Although Darwin's belief in the superiority of his own civilization is undiminished, he is aware of the futility of their brief exposure to Englishness: the improvement of their 'habits' will not be 'conducive to their happiness'. However, it does not seem to occur to Darwin to seek for an alternative solution. The compassion and sense of frustration discernible in the diary entry are carefully watered down in the published version. Darwin presents himself as loyal to the cause of civilization and subtly distances himself from the Fuegians' plight, for instance by changing 'our Fuegians' into 'the three Fuegians':

> It was quite melancholy leaving the three Fuegians with their savage countrymen: but it was a great comfort that they had no personal fears. York, being a powerful resolute man, was pretty sure to get on well, together with his wife, Fuegia. Poor Jemmy looked rather disconsolate, and would then, I have little doubt, have been glad to have returned with us. Jemmy's own brother had stolen many things from him; and as he remarked, 'What fashion do you call that' he abused his countrymen, 'all bad men, 'no sabe' nothing', and though I never heard him swear before, 'damned fools'. Our three Fuegians, though they had been only three years with civilized men, would, I am sure, have been glad to have retained their new habits; but this was obviously impossible. I fear it is more than doubtful, whether their visit will have been of any use to them.[27]

While York Minster and Fuegia Basket are rendered more 'respectable' by the mention of their married status, Jemmy Button is represented as less 'European', less of a 'gentleman' than in the diary, mainly through the slight changes in his dialogue. Whereas the diary stresses the Fuegians' complete transformation, the concluding sentences in the published report emphasize the shortness of their contact with civilization. The word 'obviously' forecloses any questioning of the good sense of FitzRoy's proceeding. Altogether, the revised passage is less personal, less emotional, and less critical of FitzRoy's – or anybody's – civilizing mission.

Finally, Darwin's misgivings about the Fuegians' lot are realized. When the *Beagle* returns in March 1834, they come across Jemmy Button again – but now no longer the sleek dandy of former days, but 'a thin, haggard savage, with long disordered hair, and naked, except a bit of blanket round his waist'.[28] The transformation from civilized man into savage, the reversion of his former ascent, is so complete that they fail to recognize him immediately. 'We had left him plump, fat, clean, and well-dressed; – I never saw so complete and grievous a change'.[29] Again, Darwin's personal feelings, as expressed in the *Diary* – 'It was quite painful to behold him'[30] – have disappeared from the published text, and with them the questions of shirked responsibility and betrayed trust. In *The Voyage of the Beagle*, Darwin closes this episode with a pious, and unfounded, expression of hope that has no counterpart in the *Beagle Diary*:

> I do not doubt that he will be as happy as, perhaps happier than, if he had never left his own country. Every one must sincerely hope that Captain Fitz Roy's noble hope may be fulfilled, of being rewarded for the many generous sacrifices which he made for these Fuegians, by some shipwrecked sailor being protected by the descendants of Jemmy Button and his tribe![31]

In 1859, the year in which Darwin published *The Origin of Species*, eight English sailors were killed by a group of Fuegians; the one surviving eyewitness claimed that among the perpetrators was Jemmy Button.[32]

Most commentators on Darwin's five-year circumnavigation of the globe agree that he 'experiences the voyage of the *Beagle* as a journey of self-appraisal, cultural dis- and re-orientation, and negotiation between a set of pre-existing beliefs and new challenges to those beliefs'.[33] His encounter with the savage inhabitants of Tierra del Fuego forms one of the most decisive events of this journey, contributing to Darwin's growing realization that identities are unfixed and open to change, and that the seemingly stable opposition between the civilized and the uncivilized, the Self and the Other is less absolute than it seems. The *Beagle Diary* is deeply marked by the subversion of Western assumptions about the other and of the travellers' belief in their own superiority. However, the revisions in *The Voyage of the Beagle* consistently tone down the radicality of Darwin's destabilizing communicational exchange with the Fuegians. While in the *Diary*, the Fuegians appear as both the representatives of an incommensurable Other and as human beings capable of interaction, of returning the ethnographic gaze, in the *Voyage* the aspect of an evenly matched exchange is obliterated in the interest of Darwin's self-representation as a professional scientist.

15 FIELDWORK AS SELF-HARROWING: RICHARD BURTON'S CULTURAL EVOLUTION (1851–1856)

Frédéric Regard

There were many Burtons. One may find evidence of this not only in his long, motley career as 'explorer and ethnographer, polyglot and poet, consul and connoisseur of the sword, infantry officer and *enfant terrible*',[1] but also in the nature of his output: over twenty travel books, which all greatly differ from one another. Even within the short span of the first years of his writing career it may prove difficult to recognize the same author behind the little known *Sindh and the Races that Inhabit the Valley of the Indus*, published in 1851, and the celebrated *Personal Narrative of a Pilgrimage to Al-Madinah & Meccah*, published in two volumes in 1855 and 1856. Dane Kennedy's solution to the enigma consists of explaining that Burton 'moved over time from a philological to a physiological to a cultural conception of racial difference'.[2] This is certainly true, and very persuasively demonstrated. I wish to argue, however, that the shift was often more synchronic than diachronic, and that Burton's *theories* of racial difference, whatever the rationale behind them, were constantly supplanted by cultural *practices* which broke down the boundaries between Self and Other.

Burton was not the first European to venture into Sindh, where he was stationed between 1844 and 1849. The province – encompassing the lower Indus valley and annexed to the Bombay presidency in 1843 – had assumed geopolitical importance for the British in the early nineteenth century, when it had become clear that it could serve as a gateway to Afghanistan and therefore become a crucial buffer against Russian expansion. Nor was Burton the first European to cross Arabia's Empty Quarter, or even to visit Medina and Mecca, Islam's holiest cities. But being the first to encounter the not-Self was not Burton's foremost ambition, if only because first encounters had almost become a thing of the past in the 1850s. What Burton gloried in was to be the first Englishman to be able to encounter the Indians and Arabs not as a distant observer but as an *insider*, *from within*, immersed in, and so to speak 'contaminated' by the other's 'culture' (a complex word with a complex history, which, for the time being, I choose to take to mean 'a system of socially established structures of meaning')[3]. In order to grasp the full scope of Burton's challenge, one should bear in mind that Muslim culture had long been reduced to the threat posed by Barbary corsairs, and turned therefore into a 'focus of hate' for Britain's emergent national identity.[4] In Erving Goffman's terms, Muslim culture had been conveniently 'stigmatized', which is to say discredited as an emblem of humanity by the classic 'tribal stigma' – race, nation and religion.[5] It is this impurity of contact, Burton's extraordinary *internalization of encounter*, which I am interested in here.

Goffman defines 'encounter' as a social situation implying that two (or more) agents 'ratify one another as authorized cosustainers of a single, albeit moving, focus of visual and cognitive attention.'[6] Such 'face engagements', as Goffman also calls them, involve a 'preferential openness to all manner of communication', but are also constrained by 'cultural rules' which establish how individuals are to conduct themselves – a structuring of conduct which we may imagine to have been of the utmost importance in first-contact zones, where interethnic or intercultural communication must have raised a crucial difficulty, namely that 'being able to interact also implies some sharing.'[7] What makes Burton's cultural practice so fascinating is that although his writings affirm the 'face' accorded to him by various British institutions, the contextual events reported manage to queer the codified encounter. I argue that this queering of ritual encounter is achieved through the relation of a performance which dramatically redefines the classic rules of colonial interaction, as it accepts 'some sharing' and consequently entails a structuring of conduct hitherto unheard of, and more importantly still, *unwritten* of in matters of colonial attitude. It is this recalcitrance to the self's entanglement with institutionally based supports and constraints, this dialectic of identification to and distancing from the expected entity – social, racial, national and even religious – that I want to study: how Burton's 'primary adjustment' to colonial rules – that which makes him a 'normal' agent of Empire – is troubled by the explorer's 'secondary adjustments', the distancing practices which enable him to 'stand apart from the role and the self that were taken for granted for him by the institution,'[8] and how this 'underlife of an institution' is operated in Burton's writings: how contextual replacing translates into a *textual* operation of the self.

This is certainly not to deny that Burton's first books – four ethnological studies of Sindh – unmistakably bear the stamp of the East India Company officer and nineteenth-century Orientalist. His infiltration of local communities meant using mimicry and masquerade not as a tool of subversion but as a technique of surveillance, drawing up lists and 'tableaux', or tables, of the Other's culture the better to transform the unknown into the known.[9] But, following Goffman's suggestion that the self is 'a stance-taking entity', constantly gambled in interpersonal interaction,[10] I argue that imperialist discourse did not in fact precede

Burton's writing as some kind of ready-made ideological apparatus constraining his dealings with the Other; nor was it an essential, foundational, component of his identity, in the manner of an unconscious desire to domesticate the not-Self. My contention is that Burton's imperialism, or Orientalism – two terms I take to mean Burton's various manners of self-positioning in a differential system implying Self and Other –, was only a 'posture', or a linguistic stance, pragmatically produced by the very structure of some of the texts he wrote.[11] And there seems indeed to have been a variety of 'postures' in Burton's early literary career, from the scientific aloofness of the outside observer to the ambivalent intimacy procured by impersonation, as if different textual genres or sub-genres – the military report, the ethnographic description, the autobiographical sketch, the travel narrative – had been capable of operating different linguistic consciousnesses, enunciative set-ups and forms of authority. I suggest that this is the profound reason why, when confronted with alterity, Burton's self revels in refashioning itself into an unfixed, nomadic persona, a parasitic, hybrid, dialogic agency.

Again, this is not to deny the obvious imperialist dimension of Burton's ethnographic descriptions, quite evidently conceived as supporting evidence for a military report – some kind of cultural toolkit for the Westerner's domination of the Other.[12] Even in *Sindh*, 'the most ethnographically informative of his intelligence reports on the region',[13] this imperialist dimension is made explicit from the outset. Before the description of the uncharted territory has even started, the book's paratextual opening forcefully distributes roles and functions. The signatory of the report identifies himself as 'Richard F. Burton, lieutenant Bombay Army',[14] a clear reminder of the author's official status. This is immediately followed by a confirmation of the author's hierarchical relationship to a superior authority in the form of a dedication to 'the Honorable the Court of Directors of the East India Company', by 'their very obedient servant'. Burton's status is in fact marked here by a certain degree of ambiguity, due to the very structure of the scene of enunciation, which implicitly summons upon the stage the enunciator himself, but also his hierarchy, and of course the inhabitants of the valley of the Indus, alluded to in the very title of the book. From the start, the author seems therefore to be extremely reluctant to assert himself as a full, autonomous self, preferring instead to present himself as being captured at a place by this triangular relationship, which fixes him in a both statutary and subaltern position. The first lines of Burton's ethnographic description confirm this:

> The chief merits which Sindh in its present state possesses, are its capability of improvement, and its value to us as a military and commercial position. The vast heaps of ruins which cover the face of the country, the traces of great and important works, the concurrence of tradition, historians, and travellers, in describing its ancient glories, are so many proofs that the province was not always what it is now. And as its gradual decline may be attributed to internal dissensions and external wars,

with their natural result – a thinness of population caused by famine, disease, and consequent emigration – the means of restoring health and vigour to the system are always in our hands. The events of the last three years have proved the value of Sindh as a depot for the material of war, and a base for concentrating forces, establishing reserves, and executing flank movements against the unruly nations to the north and north-east.[15]

The stance adopted by the speaker clearly positions him as a spokesman for the Empire, a surrogate hegemonic centre of interpretation, conferring sense upon a reality which, were it not for the enunciator's presence, would have remained in the state of a meaningless, chaotic spatial expanse. The description of the 'present state' of Sindh is thus used by the speaker both to recall his subservience to the superior authority of the Company's Board, and to produce himself as a rational agency, lording over the Other – human and spatial – and thereby authorizing himself as a clairvoyant, towering present of enunciation. Burton's grammatical choices also draw a clear demarcation line between Self and Other, since his use of possessive pronouns and adjectives establishes a distance between 'us' and 'them', creating a radical difference between the active agencies of the Company's representatives, and the passive, muted native agencies of the annexed province. The British soldier-ethnographer thus manages to produce an image of himself that is very close to that of a monadic cell, impervious to intersubjectivity, cut off from the usual play of communication, refusing the risk of contradiction and misinterpretation.

Although as a *person* Burton is sharing the same geographical space as the native Other, as the *enunciator* of the text he produces himself not as an actant of the scene of interlocution, but as an outsider, an 'allochronic' agency, who denies himself and his potential alter ego the possibility of entering the temporal dimension of interaction, of living 'in the same Time'.[16] The lieutenant's 'presence' on the stage of encounter rests mainly on his discursive abilities, making ample usage of argumentation – there is supporting evidence of the province's 'ancient glories' – and causal analysis – the current crisis is due to 'internal dissensions and external wars'. But of course, if Burton is not fully present to the Other, it is first and foremost because he conceives of himself as representing an external, superior authority – the Company. Power is delegated to him, and this structure of authority is precisely what defines each actant's 'posture' in the text – the Board's, the officer's and the Oriental's. This explains why once the *enunciator* has transformed the reality with which his *person* is confronted into an object for the Company's gaze, roles are easily distributed, differences firmly established. This process of differentiation is achieved not only grammatically or enunciatively, but also culturally, or 'ideologically'. For Burton's text clearly 'hails' each participant into a coded existence, his report 'interpellating' each actant at a fixed place where subjectivity is accorded only insofar as it is predicated on subjection, which is how, according to Althusser, ideological apparatuses always function.[17] Sindh is 'reinscribed' from the Westerner's point of view: now a desolate landscape of 'vast heaps of ruins', it promises to recover nicely in the hands of the Westerner, whose 'means of restoring health and vigour to the system' seem to be unquestionable. The lieutenant's arrival on the scene of colonial encounter is thus presented as a promise of improvement, perhaps even, to use a concept which was starting to circulate, a promise of 'development', or 'evolution': from disorder to order, from war to peace, from ruin to wealth, from degeneration to regeneration, from barbarity to civilization.

Although the enunciator textually produces himself as a non-participant observer, his mere presence is implicitly endowed with enough power to force the province to enter into a linear, progressive – and highly Christian – logic of 'salvation'.[18] The 'ideological' dimension of the scene of enunciation is therefore inescapable: the Other's world, both spatial and temporal, is forced into a plot which stipulates not only what it ought to look like, but also how the speaker ought to take position in it to act upon it.[19] Sindh is thus summoned to meet the expectations, not to say requirements – military and commercial, but also ontological – of the British Empire. The alien territory is not here perceived as an untapped source of new knowledge (although the rest of *Sindh* constitutes a formidable ethnographic description of the province's culture); the newly-annexed territory is presented as a neutral, inert, transformable reality. This is what gives it its 'value', a term used twice in our short excerpt. What the Westerner's eye perceives is the region's potential in terms of usefulness: how the province might be used to serve the purposes of the Empire. Through the enunciator's discursive mediation, Sindh is translated, redescribed, recoded, reevaluated into a 'useful position', a 'depot', or a 'base'. It is precisely this structure of differentiation and identity-production that Burton's writing would contest immediately after the publication of the fourth and final volume of his ethnographic descriptions of the province, *Falconry in the Valley of the Indus* (1852).

It should be noted here that Burton, now a Captain, had obtained a leave from the East India Company and convinced the Royal Geographical Society to fund his exploration of the Arabian Peninsula in the summer of 1853. After three months spent in Egypt to improve his Arabic, Burton disguised himself as a Pathan – an Afghanistani Muslim – and travelled by caravan from Yanbu, a Red Sea port in western Arabia where he had arrived by boat from Suez, to Medina (25 July), then to Mecca, reached finally on 11 September 1853, an experience related in *Personal Narrative of a Pilgrimage*.

Unsurprisingly, Burton's initial intention was a caricature of imperialist bravado and virile heroism, of the type to be later derided by Conrad in *Heart of Darkness*: 'I offered my services to the Royal Geographical Society of London, for the purpose of removing that opprobrium to modern adventure, the huge white blot which in our maps still notes the Eastern and the Central regions of Arabia'.[20] Burton's purpose was highly symbolic: to assert British influence on the Peninsula by 'set[ting] foot on that mysterious spot which no vacation tourist ha[d] yet described, measured, sketched, and photographed'.[21] The secondary objectives of the expedition were various – commercial, military or ethnological – but equally imperialist in spirit. The aim was to find out if any market for horses could be opened between central Arabia and India; to obtain information for British maps of the Great Eastern wilderness; and finally, to test a theory proposed by General Sykes concerning the common origin of the Arab family.[22] Still, it appears from the rest of the narrative that, having disguised himself as a 'Darwaysh' – a 'Persian wanderer' and 'chartered vagabond'[23] – Burton did not hesitate to relinquish the comfortable, if ambiguous status of the Westerner, in order to adopt the unfixed, problematic identity of an imagined persona whose statutory authority was never fully recognized by his native interlocutors and had therefore to be permanently renegotiated. It should also be remembered that in Victorian culture, both abroad and at home, 'any sort of masquerade was regarded as socially deceitful and morally repugnant'.[24]

This time, Burton's *ethos*, the image he projects of himself through his 'rhetoric', i.e. his discursive practice, but also his demeanor and all other kinds of attitudes, including dress-code – a whole 'scenography'[25] – is that of a self caught in interaction. Identity seems to be produced exclusively 'in context', a word to be understood in the sense of a socially and linguistically interactive phenomenon.[26] For example, after having drawn a list of the various tribes of the Sinai peninsula, and reached a number of conclusions as to their racial distribution, Burton remarks that 'the Badawi race' is easily offended, and that a number of travellers have had occasion to complain of their 'insolence and extortion'.[27] But this is a European complaint to which Burton does not wish to associate. He insists that in the desert the laws of civility and hospitality as the Westerner knows them no longer apply, and that esteem and respect must be gained both through the command of the language spoken locally and through the display of physical courage – two indigenous virtues Burton himself quite evidently possesses. It is, Burton contends, the traveller's 'assumption of superiority' that the Badawi find offensive. In other words, in the desert one is not protected by 'status', an 'external social variable which does not take into account contextual dependency'; esteem and respect are rather a matter of 'local rank', a social variable whose meaning is *internal* to a particular community.[28] Respect as 'local rank' must be gained again and again, in the play of interaction, in every new specific context, as obstacles, be they linguistic or physical, present themselves. 'In the desert, man meets man', Burton concludes.[29]

It is certainly no coincidence, therefore, that Burton's account of his expedition is never purely descriptive or narrative: *Pilgrimage* often reads as a succession of scenes of dialogue, as if 'telling' were now less worth recording than 'showing'. In the course of his journey, the disguised British explorer comes across a vast array of interlocutors whose roles seem to be either to contest the authority of the 'pilgrim', or to win him over to their own sides – a far cry from the static presentation and representation of Self and Other in the introductory paragraphs to *Sindh*. At no point does a consensus emerge as to the status of the various actants of such scenes *prior* to the encounter: the 'rank' of each actant is always gambled, sometimes hotly debated, sometimes even fiercely fought over.[30] Allowing himself to be caught on a stage where roles have to be played out and identities performed, Burton's successive impersonations thus abolish the centrality and verticality of hegemonic discourse to promote instead the horizontal dialectics of verbal interaction and dialogic games. The structure of Burton's text thus produces a curious image of its author, who constantly accepts the risk, and unpredictable outcome, attached to the choice of his *fictional character*.

But if protecting, defending and maintaining social hierarchy – what Goffman calls 'face'[31] – is most of the time the central object of interpersonal rituals, this gamesmanship is also quite often at odds with what seems to be the sheer pleasure afforded by the masquerade, Burton frequently portraying himself as thoroughly caught up in the fun of the game of impersonation, joyfully gambling his identity – sometimes even his life – on the problematic outcome of the encounter. Inevitably, comic versions of such gambling may be found thoughout the narrative. For example, while still in a hotel in Suez, Burton and his Egyptian companions meet a party of married women travelling with their husbands and families, but occupying rooms adjoining theirs. Burton seems then to take a liking to one Fattuma, although the relationship never develops into a true infatuation. For what Burton particularly relishes about the conversations he and his friends have with the lady, is her talent for verbal contest. Whenever Burton proposes to Fattuma – 'Marry me, O Fattuma! O female pilgrim' – the object of his desire invariably replies that she is already married and that the match is therefore impossible ('I am mated young man'). That the proposal can be renewed and the same ambiguous answer repeatedly offered in return is in itself indicative of the playfulness of the speakers, who accept the possibility that words can be exchanged for the sake of being exchanged, with no value of truth invested in them, and no relation of superiority asserted through communicative exchange. But the challenge to status goes in fact much further. Burton and his friends, having decided that the lady, being 'a person of polyandrous propensities', could support the weight of at least three matrimonial engagements, fall into the habit of repeating their proposals to such a point that Fattuma regularly adjures Allah to cut their hearts out of their bosoms. The men then modify their initial utterance, turning it into injurious speech: 'Y'al Ago-o-oz! (Old decrepit woman). O daughter of sixty sires, and fit only to carry wood to the market'.

Whereupon the woman enters into a storm of wrath and the men rush out of one another's way 'like children'.[32]

The comedy of this almost picaresque scene is located in the sudden reversal of positions. Much of the jubilation is also due to the unexpected deconstruction of fixed identity, which incidentally invalidates the accusation sometimes levelled at Burton of being a male chauvinist constructing a myth of the Orient derived from his desire for a master–slave relationship between the sexes.[33] By enjoying the risk of interaction, the 'Orientalized' Burton accepts the possibility of losing a verbal contest, of becoming one interlocutor among many others, and most importantly of giving up the dignity of his status, thus also renouncing his masculinist assumptions of superiority. In this particular context, Burton's and the lady's utterances are simply caught in a game of exchange, in which the locutors do not defend a position or a status, but simply occupy successive, interchangeable linguistic 'postures'.[34] In this respect, the difference between Self and Other traditionally constitutive of imperialist discourse is abolished; the dramatic quality of the narrative ensures that the actants of the interlocutionary game are turned instead into 'alter egos',[35] in a transgression of hegemonic differential discourse, be it in its imperialist or in its gendering dimension.

The question that needs to be addressed now is whether there were indeed different Burtons, one caught in the classic structure of 'Orientalism'; the other immersed in interlocutionary games. What is more fundamentally at stake is to know whether the 'author' of *Personal Narrative* – a term I take to mean henceforth an intricate author-image produced not only by the *writer* of the account, but also by the *person* engaged in the expedition, by the *enunciator* of the text, as well as by the fictional *character* of the 'Persian wanderer'[36] –, consisted of successive, antagonistic agencies; or whether the conflicting selves coexisted within the same schizophrenic identity; or even whether the various agencies constituting Burton's 'authority' coincided to merge into a refashioned, dialogic self.

At the outset of his narrative, Burton, who for the occasion assumes the identity of a *writer* – an author-image produced notably by the reference made to a series of published works on a given literary market – explains in a somewhat offhand manner that the fictional identity of 'Shaykh Abdullah' was in fact one he had already adopted a few years before, under the pseudonym of 'Mirza Abdullah' – 'Mirza', Burton adds in a footnote, being a Persian variant of the Arabic 'Shaykh'.[37] My suggestion is that this reference of the writer to a former alias and borrowed identity, half Arab half Iranian, is also an implicit reference to the autobiographical sketch Burton had published in 1852 as an eighteen-page postcript to *Falconry in the Valley of the Indus*. The reason for this last-minute addition to the closing volume of the Sindh series was that the public at home had been asking themselves how Burton had contrived to acquire, within hardly five years' residence in the province, such an astounding knowledge of every aspect of society in the Indus valley. The general assumption was that the officer of the Company had mixed with the local people as one of their own, but the full extent of this potentially scandalous immersion was still a matter of speculation. The autobiographical postscript was therefore meant to provide reliable information concerning Burton's techniques of infiltration.

It appears from the extraordinary text quoted below that Burton never simply 'posed' as an Oriental in order to infiltrate the local communities, as a number of critics have tended to argue.[38] It seems rather that the process of becoming-other evinced by *Personal Narrative* had gathered momentum, before Burton's Arabian adventures, in India and that the colour with which the soldier-ethnographer was then wont to cover his white skin had started acting at a deeper level, *infiltrating* the imperial spy himself – henna working here as a metaphor of cultural adaptation. I argue that this loss of imperialist immunity is what lends the text its peculiar, in fact highly literary quality:

> With hair falling upon his shoulders, a long beard, face and hands, arms and feet, stained with a thick coat of henna, Mirza Abdullah of Bushire – your humble servant, gentle reader – set out upon many and many a trip. He was a Bazzaz, a vendor of fine linen, calicoes, and muslins; – such chapmen are sometimes admitted to display their wares, even in the sacred harem, by 'fast' and fashionable dames – and he had a little pack of *bijouterie* and *virtù* reserved for emergencies. It was only, however, when absolutely necessary that he displayed his stock-in-trade; generally he contented himself with alluding to it on all possible occasions, boasting largely of his traffic, and asking a thousand questions concerning the state of the market. Thus he could walk into most men's houses, quite without ceremony; – even if the master dreamed of kicking him out, the mistress was sure to oppose such measure with might and main. He secured numberless invitations, was proposed to by several papas, and won, or had to think he won, a few hearts; for he came as a rich man and he stayed with dignity, and he departed exacting all the honours. When wending his ways he usually urged a return of visit in the morning, but he was seldom to be found at the caravanserail he specified – was Mirza Abdullah the Bushiri.[39]

Burton is very keen not to present himself as a spy *pretending* to be someone else to obtain useful information; nor does he boast the attitude of the poseur, playing at being someone else. He describes himself as having been so caught up in the game of impersonation as to have actually *become* other, impersonation being the very origin of identity, theatricality the very essence of existence – a reversal of priorities also indexed by the grammatical inversion of subject and verb in the higly parodic formulation 'was Mirza Abdullah the Bushiri'. The text leaves no doubt as to what has taken place, i.e. a complete transmutation of identity. This is aptly conveyed by the choice of the fictional third person singular, combined with a playful use of language, as displayed for example by the eighteenth-century phrase of civility 'your humble servant', used no longer here as a marker of statutory fixity, as in *Sindh*'s paratextual opening ('their very obedient servant'), but reiterated as an ironic, almost Shandyan quotation.

As a matter of fact, the former fixed postures of the officer as agent of progress, spy and ethnographer, seem to have metamorphosed into *a fiction turned true*, or more exactly into a succession of provisional ontological truths. Burton's enunciator is very careful to write 'He was a Bazzaz' (a vendor of linen); not he 'pretended to be', or 'he passed for', or 'he dressed up as' a Bazzaz. The postscript thus inscribes a 'truth' which seems to have been deeply felt by Burton the *person* (this is after all an autobiographical sketch), and which the *writer* (who refers his readers to other good reads) transcribes into text without apparently feeling the need to take his distances from the *character* he was supposed to be only enacting. Performance has indeed turned into essence: Burton has both dramatized and fictionalized himself into a maverick Oriental, a cultural transmutation which the scene of enunciation does not choose to relegate to a past pose, preferring instead to collapse the theoretically distinct agencies of *person, writer, enunciator* and *fictional character* into a composite, dynamic identity, a transformable concretion of highly unstable, porous, overlapping identities – the hallmark of all great authors according to Maingueneau.[40]

Speaking of himself in the third person, challenging the difference between the ontological levels of fiction and reality, Burton can neither fully coincide with himself nor occupy a fixed position. His *ethos* is no longer that of a *monadic* subject, but that of an elusive, *nomadic* entity, which once captured textually cannot be clearly identified as a unitary, recognizable individual – a writer, a person, an enunciator, or a fictional character – but as a tightly interwoven fabric of all such layers. The transformation of Burton's author-image is thus remarkable: the enunciator does not produce himself as a see-all, know-all presence, towering above the reality he is describing; he portrays himself as a chameleon-like agency, engaged in contextualized linguistic games, negotiating his 'rank' in unpredictable interaction, enmeshed within local shared codes which deeply affect his status as a Westerner. This, however, does not mean that Burton now belongs to the other side, or to the side of the Other. Even when immersed in the communities he traverses, the space he comes to occupy is always, to use the Deleuzean parlance, 'deterritorialized':[41] Burton's psychic life seems to be that of a nomadic agency endlessly relocating itself in new collective arrangements which decode the reality of imperialism, freeing it of the staticity and fixity implied either by the military report or by the ethnographic description. In turn a vendor of linen and a rich stranger, a vile seducer and an ideal son-in-law, the nomadic figure is in fact a nobody, homeless and yet at home everywhere, his credibility resting mainly on the credulity of his interlocutors, which is to say on the efficacy of communicational exchange.

This 'parasitic' *ethos* is also what allows Burton's autobiographical postscript to acquire its distinct literary quality. Studying Alfred Wallace's accounts of his encounter with a baby orangutan in *The Malay Archipelago* (1894) and *My Life* (1906), David Amigoni explains that Wallace's texts, replete with 'fictional, quasi-mythic devices', illustrate to what extent the theory of evolution had managed to break down not only the species barrier, but also the boundary between natural historical and fictional writing.[42] What Amigoni's comments also suggest is that even in the case of a pre-Darwinian work – assuming that Darwin's ideas were not part of British culture before the official publication of *The Origin of Species* in 1859 – breaking down barriers can only take place fictionally, as a textual operation which may by the same token engage self-refashioning. It is certainly no coincidence if Burton's 1852 autobiographical sketch could not be integrated into the body of his dogmatically pure ethnological studies and military reports, and could find no other location but as an appendix to the very end of *Falconry*, the fourth and final volume of the Indus valley series, grafting itself onto this voluminous body to serve the dual purpose of a baffling afterthought to the serious work of ethnographic description and of a puzzling introduction to the quicksands of the Arabian deserts. It is not only that Burton's sketch reflects the uncertain conditions of its own production – the necessity of a nomadic, undercover life in cross-dressing; it is first and foremost that it produces performatively the transitional, unstable, dynamic, dialogic space of its new hybrid identity: this hybridity gives itself to *read*, as a linguistic, textual event; Burton's self-refashioning, his new style of being, is predicated on his style of speaking and, above all, his new style of *writing*.

This is illustrated, for instance, by the way the English language loses its national purity to become a linguistic mutant, contaminated by otherness, 'stained' with local colour, and thus transmuted into a mottled, 'inter-national' medium: a quick look at the *OED* would establish that 'Bazzaz' and 'caravanserail' are borrowed from the Persian; 'calicoes' and 'muslins' refer to Indian and Iraki cities; 'henna' and 'harem' are imported from the Arabic; 'papas', 'vendors', 'dames' and 'wares' come from the French, and 'virtù' from the Italian. Even when the English language seems to be cleansed of its foreign influences, it still bears symptoms of internal discordance: should we not suspect that the 'stock-in-trade' and 'bijouterie' which Burton displays before the 'fast dames' of the harems, metaphorize items the very thought of which would make the Victorian reader blush? Burton's alias, or more correctly his fictional patronym, is perhaps the most conspicuous symptom of the general law of contamination presiding over this restylization of the self: do not phrases such as 'Mirza Abdullah of Bushire' and 'Mirza Abdullah the Bushiri' – hybrids composed of Arabic ('Abdullah') and Persian ('Mirza', 'Bushir') signifiers – seem to be grafted on a deep-lying English syntactic structure surfacing through the preposition 'of' and the article 'the'? Not so much linguistic cross-dressing, therefore, as linguistic cross-pollination, of which the reader is made complicit.

I have shown elsewhere how in his first book at least – *Anahuac* (1861), an account of an exploration of Mexico in search of Toltec remains – Tylor's rhetoric hinged a serious distrust of Amerindian culture on a critique of Roman Catholicism and how, when pushed to the limits of its own rhetorical impetus, *Anahuac* proposed an implicit equation of Mexican/Indian labourers with animals, thus giving birth to the chimera of a 'Catholic mule', the repulsive emblem of an unnatural cultural offspring.[43] What makes for the fascination of Burton's early texts is that they seem on the contrary to *internalize* cultural mongrelization, raising questions concerning the coincidence of the self to itself, perceiving and accepting the inevitability of the simultaneity of being, and above all textually operating the unexpected 'dialogism' of the mottled colonial self, its very capacity to exist as a centre only insofar as what takes place is caught in a 'differential relation between a center and all that is not that center'.[44]

Burton never entirely manages to produce himself as a fully reliable institutional authority holding a statutory position and marking hierarchical differences between Self and Other. With him, the institution's programme is both implemented and undermined, as the explorer becomes aware of the linguistic postures implied by the situations of interlocution in which his adventures – and their narrativization – place him. It seems that at some point, somewhere between India and Arabia – a location which is not necessarily spatial, but may be simply 'cultural', or more accurately 'trans-cultural' – the discourse of colonial authority started to lose faith in the binary, polarizing structure of its utterances, and went through an experience of relocation and recontextualization, henceforth finding in itself traces of the language of the other, and consequently transforming mongrelization and hybridity not into a moment of monstrosity, but into 'an active moment of challenge and resistance against a dominant cultural power'.[45] Burton thus constructs a 'carnivalesque' textual image of himself which breaks down boundaries, not only between the Westerner and the Oriental, but also between real life and imagination, being and writing, the representative of the East India Company or of the Royal Geographical Society and the writer, the disguised pilgrim and the fantasized nomadic persona. Dane Kennedy remarks that Burton thus crafted 'a persona that placed him at the interstices of the great cultural divide, claiming a liminal status exempt from the codes and conventions that separeated ruler from ruled'; he also remarks that Burton's claim to ethnographic authority rests precisely on the intimacy of his association with the inhabitants of the regions explored, and on the 'unpredictable effects' such an intimate encounter between the observer and the observed could entail, concluding that Burton should therefore be considered as one of the great forerunners of fieldwork, the foundational practice of cultural anthropology.[46]

What this also suggests is that Burton should definitely be replaced at the heart of the Victorian debate on 'culture', a term which in the wake of speculative evolutionary theory would come to mean a field ('a field of symbolized bonds, restraints, but also inventive possibilities').[47] In his essay 'On the Application of Evolutionary Principles to Art and Literature', Symonds would go as far as to argue that such possibilities, whereby an individual could assert his personal capacity, could only be enacted in the new arts of Europe which he saw as creative and energetic 'hybrids' and 'mongrels'.[48] Relating Symonds's theory to the model set by Gosse's *Father and Son*, Amigoni's comment is illuminating: 'As a 'mongrel' form that incorporates many 'types' (documentary, critical essay, autobiography, the novel), it [Gosse's text] was a vehicle for asserting 'personal capacity', or the singularity of inventive self-harrowing. Hybridity is the very power that liberates 'cultural practice' from its rootedness in a 'soil' bordered by particular national boundaries'.[49] As mongrel forms that incorporated many types (the intelligence report, the ethnographic description, the autobiographical sketch, the pilgrimage narrative, the fictionalized travel narrative, etc.), Burton's first books were indeed conceived as vehicles for asserting his personal capacity as energetic hybridity, fieldwork being experienced and practised as space for cultural self-harrowing. This cultural practice of 'self-tillage', to take up another of Symonds's formulations,[50] is most palpable in the case of Burton's 'dialogic imagination', whereby a mixture of social languages are set within the limits of a single utterance to form what Robert Young calls an *intentional* hybrid.[51]

Neither here nor there, belonging to neither side and to both sides at the same time, Burton definitely chooses to relocate himself in what Bhabha calls a 'third space',[52] where culture's inevitable hybridity is inscribed and articulated, and where personal identity is restylized into a mottled, international artistic construction. But it is the written text which transmutes the British officer into a polyphonic construct, an eternally dis-placed linguistic operation. Burton should therefore be described neither as a 'poseur' nor as a simple 'spy' in the service of the Empire, two terms which would still suggest extreme polarization and the permanence of fixed landmarks – geographical, personal, linguistic, racial, national or cultural. What fundamentally distinguishes Burton from his contemporary Tylor, is that for him self-authorization is in fact concomitant with self-otherization. That is why there were many Burtons, indeed. And that is also why cultural self-harrowing could only take place in 'the underlife of the institution', beyond the expected structuring of conduct, beyond 'face-work', in a postscript which is also the reverse object of *Sindh*'s preface to ethnographic observation: literally, a 'postface'. This textual in-between space is the fantasy location where the ethnographer's cultural practice eventually manages to elude ideological interpellation; at the same time, the implicit autobiography inherent in all accounts of first encounters is allowed to sketch itself, transmuted however into a self-portrait of the explorer as artist and parasite.

16 FICTIONALIZING THE ENCOUNTER WITH THE OTHER: HENRY MORTON STANLEY AND THE AFRICAN WILDERNESS (1872–1890)

Nicoletta Brazzelli

In the second half of the nineteenth century, the exploration of Africa was marked by the hectic search for the sources of the Nile. The travellers' heroic endeavours to penetrate into the interior of the dark continent were hindered, however, by huge geographical obstacles, the harsh climate and sometimes the natives' fierce opposition. Sub-Saharan Africa was then a vast area Europeans knew very little about: white explorers had seldom ventured inland, deterred by rumours of cannibalism, tropical diseases, wild beasts, thick forests and treacherous swamps. But at the same time, the entangled vegetation of this 'terra incognita' was perceived as a primeval, virgin territory to be penetrated and conquered, notably through white male courage and physical prowess.[1] Henry Morton Stanley was probably the British archetypal hero of this colonial myth of masculinity.

Born in North Wales, Stanley expatriated to North America as a young man. He eventually became a world-famous journalist, when the *New York Herald* commissioned him to Africa to determine whether David Livingstone, the legendary Scottish missionary explorer who had been reported missing for six years, could be located. Stanley reached Zanzibar in January 1871 and proceeded to Lake Tanganyika, Livingstone's last known location, where he did find the sick explorer, a feat which greatly heightened European interest in the continent.[2] In 1874, Stanley set off on another expedition that took him across Africa from east to west, and this second 999-day epic definitely secured him a place in the popular mythology of exploration. Between 1879 and 1885, he worked in the Congo for King Leopold II, conducting expeditions and signing treaties for the Belgians; between 1887 and 1889, he commanded the 'Emin Pasha Relief Expedition', the last major European expedition into the interior of Africa, sent to the relief of the besieged governor of Equatoria, threatened by Mahdist forces.[3] What went into the records this time was the funds put at the explorer's disposal, far larger than any amount previously allocated to an African expedition, and the popular enthusiasm Stanley was able to arouse as a consequence was so great that at the end of the century his portrait was reproduced in countless advertisements, selling everything from soap to Bovril.[4] Stanley was not only an icon of imperialism; he was indeed a key figure in the European conquest of Africa, eager to use any new technology to map, classify and finally appropriate the 'uncivilized' world. His very name was inscribed on the surface of African maps (Stanley Falls, Stanley Pool); he played a crucial role in the development of British trade, and his travel accounts were filled with visions of the future European rule in Central and Eastern Africa, the slave trade routes supplanted by the British 'legitimate' commercial interests.[5]

As a matter of fact, Stanley was also severely criticized for his harsh conduct, most notably for the ruthless methods of the Emin Pasha expedition. And whereas he claimed to have contributed to eradicating slavery in the Congo, he was also held responsible for the highly controversial 1876 Bumbireh massacre on Lake Victoria. Over the past twenty years, Stanley has been accused of being a cruel imperialist, a brutal racist, and an aggressive self-made man.[6] Quite recently, however, a remarkable, yet hotly debated, reassessment of Stanley's reputation has been initiated, based on Stanley's desperate desire for recognition and self-esteem, a secret drive which may have led this poor exiled orphan to exaggerate the size and achievement of his expeditions, as well as the importance of his conflicts with the African tribes, in order to make his narratives more exciting and glamourous and thus secure him a central role in the British national imagination.[7] Indeed, there is much theatricality in his narratives: Stanley constructs Africa as a stage where he can fashion himself as a national hero, recreating the African landscape as a symbolic site of otherness to be domesticated and exploited by an ideal British Self. There is also considerable intertextuality: for Stanley should definitely be recontextualized in his Victorian cultural background, one that was haunted by the constant presence of brave white explorers travelling through unmapped regions in search of legendary treasures, a myth constructed through innumerable fictionalizations of real imperial adventures, from Henty's African stories for children to Rider Haggard's immensely popular romances (such as *King Solomon's Mines*, 1885). Stanley comes to inscribe himself within this context, while also contributing to shaping it.

'Bula Matari' ('breaker of stones'), the almost novelistic African nickname Stanley chose for himself, marches into the rainforest and fights his way down the Congo river, the shores of which are represented as a land of savage beauty and fabulous wealth, but also of fierce resistance to civilization and progress.[8] In Stanley's major exploration narratives, *How I Found Livingstone* (1872), *Through the Dark Continent* (1878) and *In Darkest Africa* (1890), the prevailing tropes of the encounter with the wilderness are indeed the 'heroic' and the 'sublime', the latter revisited and tamed in order to provide an aesthetic sanction for the values of the imperial hero.[9] Stanley's commanding gaze ranges over the surrounding scenery, bringing about spatial order and a strong sense of ownership; where chaos is first perceived, his self-representation as the 'monarch of all I survey' – the opening line of William Cowper's 'Solitude of Alexander Selkirk' (1782), supposed to have been uttered by the famous historical castaway and original of Robinson Crusoe – enables him to possess the land visually and aesthetically, envisioning the future British appropriation of the territory.[10] Employing a 'rhetoric of sovereignty',[11] fashioning himself as a larger-than-life individual penetrating a savage world, the narrator thus makes up an adventure story, where the explorer-hero encounters the unknown, where sensationalism and violence are combined to celebrate British rule, and where the conventions of the traditional quest romance are reinterpreted in the colonial context. The frontier between fact and fiction is blurred; the reader is invited to enter into an unstable zone, in which daring deeds and higher forces, good and evil, contribute to creating a sense of wonder and suscitating the expectations of a quest narrative, or treasure hunt. In order to construct a dramatic first-person narrative likely to capture the British audience's attention, the text emphasizes the alienness of the landscape and its inhabitants, whose wilderness must be exorcized, by the wonderful deeds of the prophet-like adventurer, as well as by the virtuosity of a prodigious narrator. It is these various strategies, and their cultural implications that I want to examine. What interests me, in other words, is the very *textuality* of Stanley's postures.

At the beginning of *How I Found Livingstone*, the descriptions of huge ravines, precipices and chasms, are obviously meant to remind the readers of a sublime, 'fantastic', almost Gothic environment:

> One felt better, stronger, on this breezy height, drinking in the pure air and feasting the eyes on such a varied landscape as it presented, on spreading plateaus green as lawns, on smooth rounded tops, on mountain vales containing recesses which might charm a hermit's soul, on deep and awful ravines were reigned a twilight gloom, on fractured and riven precipices, on huge fantastically-worn boulders which over-topped them, on picturesque tracts which embraced all that was wild, and all that was poetical in Nature.[12]

As the text is careful to suggest, however, Burke's 'sublime' – a source of terror and therefore of the Self's collapse – may be neutralized and even transcended by the 'picturesque', illustrated here by a succession of sketches of the African 'varied landscape' and of 'all that [is] poetical in Nature'. The narrator aestheticizes Africa's features to order them into a pattern, made perceptible through the 'picturesque tracts' the explorer follows, like lines conferring unity upon natural profusion. Although Gilpin, who strongly opposed the aristocratic prospect and its possessive assumptions in favour of the more down-to-earth experience of the 'picturesque',[13] would most probably have argued to the contrary, there is very little difference in this landscape painting between description and domestication, and such lines should be read in relation with countless other passages in Stanley's writings where the onlooker's gaze is definitely that of a man who feels at ease in an exotic but nevertheless reassuring, strangely familiar, and even controllable landscape. Surveying a scene of beautiful wildlife, the explorer conceives of himself as a new kind of Robinson Crusoe, self-appointed king of 'his' island: 'I felt proud that I owned such a vast domain'.[14] For that matter, Stanley often describes the newly-discovered land from the top of a hill, or from a promontory. From that dominant position of surveillance, he then projects his colonial fantasies onto the African land. Chaos is then magically shaped into order, as if the white man's sudden presence in the field also brought with it the perfect harmony brought about by some Biblical fiat:

> Had the first man at the time of the Creation gazed at his world and perceived it of the beauty which belongs to this part of Africa, he would have had no cause of complaint.[15]

This is strongly suggestive of another characteristic of Stanley's re-elaboration of facts: the explorer's notion of himself as a *prophet* of civilization.

In Stanley's second major narrative of exploration, *Through the Dark Continent*, mapping the course of the Congo river is described as a very dangerous enterprise. But what comes across, eventually, is the idea of a huge bulk of waters flowing from a mysterious darkness, with the white man summoned upon the stage as the Chosen One to solve the enigma:

> A secret rapture filled my soul as I gazed upon the majestic stream. The great mystery that for all these centuries Nature had kept hidden away from the world of science was waiting to be solved. For two hundred and twenty miles I had followed one of the sources of the Livingstone [the Lualaba river, the greatest headstream of the Congo River] to the confluence, and now before me lay the superb river itself. My task was to follow it to the Ocean.[16]

The Congo basin becomes the theatre of a divinely-ordered drama, with the white man as its central protagonist, playing the role of a spokesman for 'the world of science', whose sacred 'task' is to overcome the resistance of primitive Nature. Accordingly, the waterway, together with the equatorial forest, is portrayed as a dark, impenetrable wall, suggesting a universe of 'non-history',[17] which the explorer, like some prophet of superior knowledge, is expected both to reenergize and to redeem. Likewise, while mapping out the shores of Lake Victoria, Stanley tries to convey the idea of the magnitude of his 'task', comparing it to the gigantic size of the lake itself:

The lake was so large it would take years to trace its shores, and who then at the end of that time would remain alive? Therefore, as I expected, there were no volunteers for the exploration of the Great Lake. Its opposite shores, from their very vagueness of outline, and its people, from the distorting fogs of misrepresentation through which we saw them, only heightened the fears of my men as to the dangers which filled the prospect.[18]

Such extraordinary proportions call for the white man's imperial rhetoric, which classifies, labels and tames the uncharted landscapes in the name of progress and civilization. In Stanley's texts, the sublime, unruly savagery of Africa is thus gradually brought under control: light is meant to replace darkness, order to supplant disorder.[19] In this kind of scientific Morality play, the explorer's sacred role is to be the torchbearer of progress, by imposing a kind of discipline upon Central Africa, perceived initially as an infernal maze of rivers, lakes and jungles.

Like a spectral, preternatural entity, the Congo river haunts the explorer as the very image of a hell populated with vampiric figures: 'It is a murderous world, and we feel for the first time that we hate the filthy, vulturous ghouls who inhabit it'.[20] The primeval mud often obstructs the explorer's march, and the air is pestilential. The trek is made to resemble a quest narrative. As Stanley travels along, stumbling through dense weeds, crossing creeks, cataracts and falls, he domesticates the infernal sublime to turn it into an object of colonial consumption. The encounter with the sublime is thus a moment of danger for the authority of the rational Self, but it also enhances the white man's individual courage and heroism, sanctioned by Providence. Stanley frequently uses whips and guns to discipline his porters or fight the native tribes – a practice abhorrent to Livingstone – but this is also part of a general imperial rhetoric, which constantly aims to discipline the unruly nature of Africa, according to a plan for the completion of which the prophetic explorer seems to have been elected.

In his third major narrative, *In Darkest Africa*, the explorer offers a detailed classification of the different parts of the landscape, including hills, mountains, plants and flowers. Or, fighting his way through the Ituri region – one of the most impenetrable areas of the African continent – he adopts a subtler strategy, stressing instead the land's extreme monotony:

Nothing but miles and miles, endless miles of forest, in various stages of growth and various degrees of altitude, according to the ages of the trees, and varying thickness of undergrowth according to the character of the trees which afforded thicker or slighter shade.[21]

In Darkest Africa also devotes a whole chapter to the 'Great Central African Forest'. This time, the white man's physical struggle with the primeval jungle is articulated on the British writer's aestheticization of the wilderness. Stanley's sentences seem to mimic the wild creepers,[22] as the narrator urges his readers to imagine the vastness of the forest and its complexity:

> Then from tree to tree run cables from two inches to fifteeen inches in diameter, up and down in loops and festoons and W's and badly-formed M's; fold them round the trees in great tight coils, until they have run up the entire height, like endless anacondas.[23]

Still another strategy is at work in *Through the Dark Continent*, when from the summit of a hill, Stanley surveys the plateau of Uzongora, the pastoral beauty of which is gradually metamorphosed into a paean to trade:

> It is a spot from which, undisturbed, the eye may rove over one of the strangest yet fairest portions of Africa – hundreds of square miles of beautiful lake scenes – a great length of grey plateau wall, upright and steep, but indented with exquisite inlets, half surrounded by embowering plantains – hundreds of square miles of pastoral upland dotted thickly with villages and groves of banana. From my lofty eerie I can see herds of cattle, and many minute specks, white and black, which can be nothing but flocks of sheep and goats. I can also see pale blue columns of ascending smoke from the fires, and upright thin figures moving about ... What a land they possess! And what an inland sea! How steamers afloat on the lake might cause Ururi to shake hands with Uzongora, and Uganda with Usukuma, make the wild Wavuma friends with the Wazinza, and unite the Wakerewé with the Wagana! A great trading port might then spring up on the Shimeeyu, whence the coffee of Uzongora, the ivory, sheep, and goats of Ugeyeya, Usoga, Uvuma, and Uganda, the cattle of Uwya, Karagwé, Usagara, Ihangiro, and Usukuma, the myrrh, cassia, and furs and hides of Uganda and Uddu, the rice of Ukerewé, and the grain of Uzinza, might be exchanged for the fabrics brought from the coast; all the land be redeemed from wildness, the industry and energy of the natives stimulated, the havoc of the slave-trade stopped, and all the countries round about permeated with the nobler ethics of a higher humanity.[24]

This time, the gaze of the onlooker is 'undisturbed'. Like a proud monarch seated on his lofty throne, the explorer may now imagine the steamers floating on Lake Victoria, and international trade reorganizing a complex mosaic of different peoples and tribes into a coherent post-Babel network. The text thus manages to 'redeem' the land, symbolically extricating it from its original 'wildness', and subjecting it to the new principles of commerce and trade, the prelude to a 'higher humanity'. The accumulation of African names – a linguistic maze of otherwise threatening signifiers – is here reordered into a utopian vision of colonial Africa. The gaze of the explorer literally 're-presents' Africa, selecting and ordering the Other's features according to the white man's fantasy. Once again, Stanley's redescription is constructed like a painting, a visual remapping of the conquered land, in which a mythical past (a nostalgic pastoralism) and a glorious future (colonial Africa) are made to coalesce.

In Darkest Africa prefers instead to transform the wilderness into the stage of a Gothic drama.[25] Indeed, the 'Emin Pasha Relief Expedition' report includes horrific stories of floggings, mutilations and deaths. The natives themselves seem to belong to a malignant spawn, the great forest stretching from the Aruwimi to the Ituri being haunted by fiendish Pygmies. Every step discloses new obstacles and threats, and men stumble along dark corridors where 'nameless horrors' lie in wait for them:

> Ah, it was a sad night, unutterably sad, to see so many men struggling on blindly through that endless forest, following one white man who was bound whither none knew, whom most believed did not know himself. What nameless horrors awaited them further on none could conjecture? ... Therefore we pushed on and on, broke through the bush, trampled down the plants, wound along the crest of spurs zig-zagging from north-east to north-west.[26]

Stanley describes his stumbling through the dense vegetation on all fours, his skin bruised, a high fever blurring his vision. The jungle seems here to embody the very essence of evil: 'Evil hangs over this forest as a pall over the dead; it is like a region accursed for crimes; whoever enters within its circle becomes subject to Divine wrath'.[27] The ants, scorpions, lizards and boa constrictors are thus perceived as the nineteenth-century versions of the Biblical plagues inflicted upon the Egyptians. But again the context produces the British explorer as the Chosen One, the elect, the prophet of redemption and progress.

The African continent is a reminiscence of paradise lost, it is also simultaneously a promise of paradise regained. Once the white man has taken the measure of the land, wealth and prosperity may accrue, both to the uncivilized world and to the civilizing nations. In *Through the Dark Continent* also, Stanley, on sighting a large expanse of land stretching between Lakes Tanganyika and Victoria, assumes the role of a prophet predicting what great future lies in store for the as yet 'empty' landscapes he describes: 'Let us imagine a railway constructed to run from one lake to the other – what scenes unrivalled for soft beauty, luxuriance, fertility, and sublimity would be traversed!'[28] The sublime of the wilderness may be transformed into 'scenes of sublimity' for the European traveller, whose eye cannot grasp the full scope of the landscape offering itself to his gaze as long as the land has not been transfigured by capitalist ideology, sanctioned once again by an implicit but insisting Christian intertext. The explorer's eye does not see Africa as such; it deforms it, catching it in mental, highly cultural representations which systematically value maps, networks, exploitation, the sure signs of divine election – Protestant ideology re-presenting Africa.

All of Stanley's accounts evince one further major preoccupation: the invention of Africa as a figure of femininity, a feminine space in need of European exploitation, longing to be 'filled' by the white man's 'burning' desire:

> This enormous void is about to be filled up. Blank as it is, it has a singular fascination
> for me. Never has white paper possessed such a charm for me as this has, and I have
> already mentally peopled it, filled it with most wonderful pictures of towns, villages,
> rivers, countries, and tribes – all in the imagination – and I am burning to see whether
> I am correct or not.[29]

Stanley's narratives thus validate the idea that Africa is naturally open to European invasion and exploitation, paving the way for contemporary fictional re-elaborations of this sexual fantasy, whether in the form of Conrad's ironic tales of delusion and frustration, such as *Heart of Darkness* (1899), or in that of Rider Haggard's imperial romances. Suggesting also the sexual rewards awaiting the colonizers, imperial narratives construct thus one of the most potent myths of the late nineteenth century, that of the female body of the dark continent as the object of male imperial desire. Both in factual and in fictional accounts, the journey into the interior unfolds an archetypal romance. But of course, the 'dark continent' cannot then be represented as a wild, uncontrollable, absolute Other, and the text's emphasis on Africa's compliant passivity is articulated on a concomitant process of familiarization.

In *How I Found Livingstone*, the African Gothic is thus integrated into an English national scenario, whereby Stanley's narrative manages to compare the 'fantastic' landscapes of the Nullah valley with what feudal England might have looked like:

> The ground rose into grander waves – hills cropped out here and there – great castles
> of syrenite appeared, giving a strange and weird appearance to the forest. From a dis-
> tance it would almost seem as if we were approaching a bit of England as it must have
> appeared during feudalism; the rocks assumed such strange fantastic shapes.[30]

Sometimes, the comparison with other places outside Europe emphasizes the colossal, almost indescribable grandeur of the African landscapes, while still keeping them within the scope of imperialist representation and domestication:

> Beautiful, bewitching Ukawendi! By what shall I gauge the loveliness of the wild,
> free, luxuriant, spontaneous nature within its boundaries? By anything in Europe?
> No. By anything in Asia? Where? India, perhaps. Yes; or say Mingredia and Imeritia.
> For there we have foaming rivers; we have picturesque hillocks; we have bold hills,
> ambitious mountains, and broad forests, with lofty solemn rows of trees, with clean
> straight stems, through which you can see far, lengthy vistas, as you see here. Only in
> Ukawendi you can almost behold the growth of vegetation.[31]

Stanley's texts are thus also based on the celebration of a heroic *narrator*, who fashions himself as the dazzling interpreter of a formless, chaotic world, and proves even capable of writing several versions of the same archetypal adventure story.

One may well argue, therefore, that the shifting boundaries between fact and fiction are the main features of Stanley's narratives, whose textual devices amplify the explorer's experience, shape the romance of colonial conquest, and ultimately domesticate otherness. Stanley's narrator surveys the scenes of his missions in such a way as to combine the spatial arrangement with the strategic evaluation of the territory: the 'imaginative eye' of the journalist-explorer goes beyond the mere classification of visual data; the doctrine of the colonizer's 'natural', God-decreed inheritance determines in fact his manner of perceiving the landscape. Thus, Stanley's is much more an imagined than a 'real' Africa: it is a cultural invention, even if supported by the explorer's field experience. Allegories, Gothic fantasies, utopian dreams, literary topoi, archetypes, stereotypes and various other rhetorical strategies combine to convey to the reader the dizzying impression of being on the threshold of the unknown, while also being on the brink of an uncannily familiar recognition.[32] The African sublime wilderness is thus integrated into the Western discourse of knowledge and power thanks to the efficacy of a colonial rhetoric, which also by the same token turns the man of action into a popular storyteller. For such imperial romances create new heroic roles, of prophetic legitimacy, colonial masculinity and, primarily I would argue, of narrative authority.

Stanley's narratives seek therefore to textualize the dark continent, so that it can fit into the general discourse of Victorian imperial dreams and fantasies. But this act of reinscription is invested with a greater significance than that of filling a mere journalistic or military report. It also provides the explorer with an ideal opportunity to distance himself from Africa and the Africans and to reassert his own cultural identity.[33] Colonial space is represented as being both fascinating and dreadful, a marriage of heaven and hell which provides the Anglo-American reading public with a glimpse into the origins of their own evolution and civilization. The marching of the hero into the wilderness reawakens in the reader's mind an awareness of the white man's own origins, his own repressed savage impulses, as if the exploration of otherness were paralleled with a confrontation with one's secret inner self. A sort of archetypal 'Everyman', Stanley's quest thus also expresses the post-Darwinian fears of Europeans regarding Africa: his texts implicitly contemplate the possibility of the civilized man yielding to the long-repressed forces of savagery, to the 'unspeakable rites' Marlow mentions in *Heart of Darkness*, where the arch-colonialist Kurtz 'goes native'. But in the process of fictionalizing the encounter, the 'heart of darkness' is finally exorcized, silenced and transformed into an *exotic* object of consumption: Stanley portrays Africa as a land of infinite economic resources, promising invaluable opportunities for all Europeans. The explorer thus produces himself as a figure of authority, not only as an agent of civilization able to domesticate a naturally hostile environment, notably through his skilled usage of Western technological equipment,[34] but also as a master of linguistic redescription: by narrating his encounter with the African wilderness, the British explorer fictionalizes his experience, transforming and reinventing the geographical sites where his African expeditions take place, both literally and literarily.

NOTES

Introduction

1. F. Regard (ed.), *De Drake à Chatwin. Rhétoriques de la découverte* (Lyon: ENS-Éditions, 2007).
2. C. K. Zacher, *Curiosity and Pilgrimage. The Literature of Discovery in Fourteenth-Century England* (Baltimore, MD: The Johns Hopkins Press, 1976).
3. M. L. Pratt, *Imperial Eyes: Travel Writing and Transculturation* (London and New York: Routledge, 1992), p. 4.
4. See J. Goody, *The Logic of Writing and the Organization of Society* (Cambridge: Cambridge University Press, 1986), p. 182.
5. See D. Mackay, *In the Wake of Cook: Exploration, Science and Empire* (London: Croom Helm, 1985).
6. See D. Gregory, *Geographical Imaginations* (Oxford: Blackwell, 1994); D. Gregory and J. Duncan (eds), *Writes of Passage: Reading Travel Writing* (London and New York: Routledge, 1999).
7. E. Edson, *Mapping Time and Space: How Medieval Mapmakers Viewed Their World* (London: The British Library, 1997); P. Whitfield, *New Found Lands: Maps in the History of Exploration* (London: The British Library, 1998); C. Delano-Smith and R. Kain, *English Maps: A History* (London: The British Library, 1999).
8. M. Foucault, *Naissance de la clinique: une archéologie du regard médical* (Paris: Presses Universitaires de France, 1963), p. 113.
9. E. Saïd, *Orientalism* (1978; New York: Random House, 1994), p. 3.
10. R. Amossy, 'Ethos at the Crossroads of Disciplines: Rhetoric, Pragmatics, Sociology', *Poetics Today*, 22:1 (2001), pp. 1–23, p. 5.
11. See D. Amigoni, *Colonies, Cults and Evolution: Literature, Science and Culture in Nineteenth-Century Writing* (Cambridge: Cambridge University Press, 2007), p. 79.
12. Pratt, *Imperial Eyes*, p. 7.
13. E. Goffman, 'The Neglected Situation' (1964), in C. Lemert and A. Branaman (eds), *The Goffman Reader* (Oxford: Blackwell, 1997), pp. 229–33, p. 231.
14. See K. O. Kupperman, *Indians and English: Facing Off in Early America* (Ithaca, NY: Cornell University Press, 2000).
15. G. C. Spivak, *Outside in the Teaching Machine* (New York: Routledge, 1993), p. 226; I. Baucom, *Out of Place: Englishness, Empire, and the Locations of Identity* (Princeton, NJ: Princeton University Press, 1999), p. 14.

16. See E. Goffman, *Stigma: Notes on the Management of Spoiled Identity* (1963; New York: Simon and Schuster, 1986), pp. 2–6.

17. See B. Anderson, *Imagined Communities: Reflections on the Origin and Spread of Nationalism* (1983; London: Verso, 1991), p. 6.

18. J. Fabian, *Time and the Other: How Anthropology Makes Its Object* (New York: Columbia University Press, 1983), p. 148.

19. See G. Marcus, and J. Clifford (eds), *Writing Culture: The Politics and Poetics of Ethnography* (Berkeley, CA: University of California Press, 1986); M. Cronin, *Across the Lines: Travel, Language, Translation* (Cork: Cork University Press, 2000).

20. M. de Certeau, *L'Écriture de l'histoire* (1975; Paris: Gallimard, 2002), p. 16.

21. See A. Duranti and C. Goodwin (eds), *Rethinking Context: Language as an Interactive Phenomenon* (1992; Cambridge: Cambridge University Press, 1997), Introduction, pp. 2–3.

22. J. Sell, *Rhetoric and Wonder in English Travel Writing 1560–1613* (Aldershot: Ashgate, 2006), pp. 24–5.

23. L. Colley, *Britons: Forging the Nation 1707–1837* (New Haven, CT and London: Yale University Press, 1992), pp. 102–3.

24. S. Gregg, *Empire and Identity. An Eighteenth-Century Sourcebook* (Basingstoke and New York: Palgrave Macmillan, 2005), pp. 7–8, 14.

25. Sell, *Rhetoric and Wonder*, pp. 161, 188.

26. A. Burgess, *Shakespeare* (1979; London: Vintage, 1996), pp. 14–15; see P. Ackroyd, *Albion. The Origins of the English Imagination* (London: Vintage, 2004), pp. 197–207.

27. See N. Whitehead, 'The Historical Anthropology of Text: The Interpretation of Ralegh's *Discoverie of Guiana*', *Current Anthropology*, 36:1 (1995), p. 59.

28. See H. White, 'The Narrativization of Real Events', *Critical Inquiry*, 7:4 (Summer 1981), pp. 793–8, p. 795.

29. Amigoni, *Colonies, Cults and Evolution*, pp. 127–8.

30. M. Black, *Models and Metaphors: Studies in Language and Philosophy* (Ithaca, NY: Cornell University Press, 1962), pp. 24–47; A. Ortony, 'Metaphor, Language and Thought', in A. Ortony (ed.), *Metaphor and Thought* (Cambridge: Cambridge University Press, 1993), pp. 2–5.

31. See S. Greenblatt, *Marvelous Possessions: The Wonder of the New World* (Oxford: Oxford University Press, 1991), pp. 14, 147.

32. M. Park, *Travels in the Interior Districts of Africa* (1799), ed. K. M. Marsters (Durham, NC and London: Duke University Press, 2000), p. 45.

33. Shakespeare, *Othello*, I.iii.90–1.

34. J. Ross, *Exploring Baffin's Bay, and Inquiring into the Probability of a Northwest Passage* (London: John Murray, 1819), pp. 173–5.

35. D. Kennedy, *The Highly Civilized Man: Richard Burton and the Victorian World* (Cambridge, MA: Harvard University Press, 2005), p. 109.

36. J. Fabian, *Out of Our Minds: Reason and Madness in the Exploration of Central Africa* (Berkeley, CA: University of California Press, 2000), p. 8.

37. J. Cook, *The Journals of Captain James Cook on His Voyages of Discovery* (1772; abridged Harmondsworth: Penguin Classics, 2000), p. 387.

38. M. Kingsley, *Travels in West Africa* (1897; London: Phoenix Press, 2000), p. 24.

39. C. Darwin, *Journal of the Voyage of the Beagle* (1843; London: Dover Publications, 2002), pp. 210–18; see G. Beer, *Darwin's Plots. Evolutionary Narrative in Darwin, George Eliot,*

and Nineteenth-Century Fiction (1983; Cambridge: Cambridge University Press, 2000), p. 74.

40. C. Geertz, *The Interpretation of Cultures* (New York: Basic Books, 1973), p. 44.
41. M. Holquist, *Dialogism: Bakhtin and His World* (1990; New York and London: Routledge, 2002), pp. 88–9.
42. J. Derrida, *Of Grammatology* (1967), trans. G. C. Spivak (Baltimore, MD: The Johns Hopkins University Press, 1998), p. 163.

1 Campbell, Encountering Africa: Uses of the Other in The Book of John Mandeville (1357)

1. This paper, presented at the Lyon 'Unstable Zones' international conference convened by Frederic Regard in March 2007, is a revised and abridged version of part of the second chapter of my *Literature and Culture in the Black Atlantic: From Pre- to Postcolonial* (New York: Palgrave Macmillan Press, 2006; reproduced with permission of Palgrave Macmillan).
2. S. Akbari, 'The Diversity of Mankind in The Book of John Mandeville', in R. Allen (ed.), *Eastward Bound: Travel and Travellers 1050–1550* (Manchester and New York: Manchester University Press, 2004), p. 156.
3. M. C. Seymour (ed.), *Sir John Mandeville* (Aldershot: Variorum, 1993), p. 1.
4. I. M. Higgins, *Writing East: The 'Travels' of Sir John Mandeville* (Philadelphia, PA: University of Pennsylvania Press, 1997), p. 13.
5. Higgins, *Writing East*, p. 12.
6. Seymour (ed.), *Sir John Mandeville*, p. 25.
7. Edited by M. C. Seymour as *The Metrical Version of Mandeville's Travels* (London : Early English Text Society, 1973).
8. Edited by M. C. Seymour as *The Defective version of Mandeville's Travels* (London: Early English Text Society, 2002).
9. M. Letts (ed.), *Mandeville's Travels: Texts and Translations*, 2 vols (London: The Hakluyt Society, 1953), vol. 1, pp. 114–15.
10. M. C. Seymour (ed.), *The Bodley Version of Mandeville's Travels* (Oxford: Early English Text Society, O. S. 253, 1963), p. 85.
11. Ibid., p. 87.
12. Ibid., pp. 85–7.
13. Ibid., p. 87.
14. G. Heng, *Empire of Magic: Medieval Romance and the Politics of Cultural Fantasy* (New York: Columbia University Press, 2003), p. 241.
15. Seymour (ed.), *The Bodley Version of Mandeville's Travels*, p. 95.
16. J. Friedman, *The Monstrous Races in Medieval Art and Thought* (Cambridge, MA: Harvard University Press, 1981), pp. 1, 90.
17. Fabian, *Time and the Other*, p. 31.
18. Seymour (ed.), *The Bodley Version of Mandeville's Travels*, p. 97.
19. Ibid., p. 89.
20. Ibid.
21. Ibid., p. 91.
22. Fleck, 'Here, There, and In Between: Representing Difference in the Travels of Sir John Mandeville', *Studies in Philology*, 97:4 (Autumn 2000), p. 381.

23. Heng, *Empire of Magic*, p. 249.
24. Fleck, 'Here, There, and In Between', p. 385.
25. Seymour (ed.), *The Bodley Version of Mandeville's Travels*, p. 97.
26. Fleck, 'Here, There and In Between', p. 387.
27. Seymour (ed.), *The Bodley Version of Mandeville's Travels*, pp. 91–3.
28. Heng, *Empire of Magic*, p. 254.
29. Higgins, *Writing East*, p. 137.
30. Ibid., p. 114.
31. Ibid., p. 123.
32. Ibid., p. 275.
33. Heng, *Empire of Magic*, p. 275.
34. P. Strohm, 'Ripe for Conversion' (a review of Brenda Schildgen's *Pagans, Tartars, Muslims and Jews in Chaucer's 'Canterbury Tales'*), *London Review of Books*, 24:13 (2002), p. 19.
35. Akbari, 'The Diversity of Mankind', p. 157.

2 Myers and Niayesh, Naming the Other, Claiming the Other in Early Modern Accounts of First Encounters: from Mandeville to John Nicholl (1607) and Richard Jobson (1623)

1. Translated from R. Descartes, *Discours de la méthode*, 1637, in A. Bridoux (ed.), *Œuvres et lettres de René Descartes* (Paris: Gallimard, 1953), p. 129.
2. See N. R. Rennie, *Far-Fetched Facts: The Literature of Travel and the Idea of the South Seas* (Oxford: Clarendon Press, 1995), pp. 1–29.
3. R. Girard, *La Violence et le sacré* (Paris: Grasset, 1972), p. 77.
4. See for details Friedman, *The Monstrous Races in Medieval Art and Thought*, pp. 5–25.
5. Anon., 'Of the World's Wonders', in *Gesta Romanorum* (c.1472), trans. C. Swan and W. Hopper (London: George Bell and Sons, 1899), pp. 337–40.
6. J. Mandeville (attr.), *The Voyages and Trauailes of Sir John Maundeuile* (c. 1356–7; London: Thomas Este, 1582), sig. M4ᵛ.
7. W. Ralegh, *The Discovery of the Large, Rich and Beautiful Empire of Guiana* (1596), in *The English Literatures of America, 1500–1800*, ed. M. Jehlen and M. Warner (London and New York: Routledge, 1997), p. 94.
8. P. M. Anghiera, *The Decades of the Newe Worlde or West Indies,* translated and adapted by R. Eden (London: William Powell, 1555), fol. 3ʳ.
9. Ralegh, *The Discovery*, ed. Jehlen and Warner, pp. 92–3.
10. Quoted in M.-T. Jones-Davies (ed.), *Monstres et prodiges au temps de la Renaissance* (Paris: Jean Touzot, 1980), p. 27.
11. Nicholl, *An Houre Glasse of Indian Newes*, sig. B1ᵛ.
12. The expression is translated from F. Lestringant, *Une Sainte horreur, ou le voyage en Eucharistie, 16ᵉᵐᵉ-17ᵉᵐᵉ siècles* (Paris: Presses Universitaires de France, 1996), p. 36.
13. Nicholl, *An Houre Glasse of Indian Newes*, sig. B3ʳ.
14. Ibid., sig. D3ᵛ.
15. Translated from F. Lestringant, *Le Cannibale, grandeur et décadence* (Paris: Perrin, 1994), p. 19.
16. Translated from A. Rimbaud, *Œuvres complètes*, ed. R. de Renéville and J. Mouquet (Paris: Gallimard, 1946), p. 252.

17. Published in an annotated edition as *The Discovery of the River Gambra by Richard Jobson*, ed. D. P. Gamble and P. E. H. Hair (1623; London: Hakluyt Society, 1999). This is the reference edition, henceforth referred to as Jobson, *The Discovery of the River Gambra*.

18. Jobson, *The Discovery of the River Gambra*, p. 90.

19. Ibid., pp. 97 and 100.

20. Quoted in ibid., p. 97.

21. A. Pagden, *European Encounters with the New World* (New Haven, CT: Yale University Press, 1993), pp. 1–15.

22. Jobson, *The Discovery of the River Gambra*, pp. 127–8.

23. Ibid., p. 131.

3 Lemercier-Goddard, False Play and Dumb Show in *The World Encompassed by Sir Francis Drake* (1628)

1. Shakespeare, *The Tempest*, V.i.170.

2. Greenblatt, *Marvelous Possessions* (1991), p. 74.

3. F. Drake, *The World Encompassed By Sir Francis Drake, Being his next voyage to that to Nombre de Dios... Carefully collected out of the notes of Master Francis Fletcher* (1628; Ann Arbor, MI: University of Michigan Press, 1966), p. 12 (emphasis mine).

4. Ibid., p. 48.

5. Ibid., pp. 5, 7, 14.

6. Ibid., pp. 8, 62.

7. Ibid., p. 66.

8. Ibid., p. 7.

9. Ibid., pp. 54–5.

10. Ibid., pp. 59–60.

11. R. Hakluyt, *The Principall Navigations, Voiages and Discoveries of the English Nation* (London: George Bishop and Ralph Newberie, 1589), p. 643 (emphasis mine).

12. Drake, *The World Encompassed*, p. 10 (emphasis mine).

13. Ibid., p. 4.

14. Ibid., p. 108.

15. Ibid., p. 3 (emphasis mine).

16. Montrose, 'The Work of Gender in the Discourse of Discovery' (1991), in S. Greenblatt (ed.), *New World Encounters* (Berkeley, CA: University of California Press, 1993), pp. 177–217, p. 180.

17. Drake, *The World Encompassed*, p. 47.

18. Ibid., p. 36.

19. Ibid., p. 49; see also pp. 37, 50, 53, 55.

20. Ibid., p. 22.

21. Ibid., p. 28.

22. Ibid., p. 70.

23. Ibid., p. 49.

24. Ibid., p. 15.

25. Ibid., p. 53.

26. Ibid., p. 58.

27. Ibid., p. 53.

28. F. Lestringant, *Cannibals: The Discovery and Representation of the Cannibal from Columbus to Jules Verne* (Berkeley, CA: University of California Press, 1997), p. 7.
29. Drake, *The World Encompassed*, p. 23 (emphasis mine).
30. Ibid., p. 7.
31. Ibid., p. 4.
32. Ibid., p. 14.
33. Ibid., p. 19.
34. Ibid., p. 50.
35. Ibid.
36. Ibid., pp. 4–5.
37. Francis Fletcher's notes (Sloane MS.n° 61), reprinted in N. Penzer (ed.), *The World Encompassed, and Analogous Contemporary Documents Doncerning Sir Francis Drake's Circumnavigation of the World ...* (London: The Argonaut Press, 1926), p. 90.
38. Ibid.
39. Drake, *The World Encompassed*, p. 48.
40. Ibid., p. 39.
41. H. Kelsey, *Sir Francis Drake: The Queen's Pirate* (New Haven, CT: Yale University Press, 1998), pp. 184–92.
42. Drake, *The World Encompassed*, p. 67.
43. Ibid., p. 68.
44. Ibid.
45. Ibid., p. 71.
46. Ibid., p. 72.
47. Ibid.
48. Ibid.
49. S. Greenblatt, *Renaissance Self-Fashioning: From More to Shakespeare* (Chicago, IL: The University of Chicago Press, 1980), pp. 227–8.
50. Drake, *The World Encompassed*, p. 76–7.
51. Shakespeare, *The* Tempest, V.i.174–5.
52. Greenblatt, *Marvelous Possessions* (1991), p. 57; Montrose, 'The Work of Gender in the Discourse of Discovery', p. 182.
53. Drake, *The World Encompassed*, p. 80.
54. Sell, *Rhetoric and Wonder in English Travel*, pp. 149–63.
55. Kupperman, *Indians and English*, p. 16.
56. Drake, *The World Encompassed*, p. 81.

4 Cottegnies, 'Waterali' Goes Native: Describing First Encounters in Sir Walter Ralegh's The Discovery of Guiana (1596)

1. W. Ralegh (attr.), *Sir Walter Ralegh's Scepticks, or Speculation* (London, 1651), p. 80.
2. N. Whitehead, 'Introduction', in W. Ralegh, *The Discoverie of the Large, Rich, and Bewtiful Empyre of Guiana*, ed. N. Whitehead (Manchester: Manchester University Press, 1997), p. 46.
3. Ibid., p. 8.
4. A. Grafton, A. Shelford, and N. Siraisi (eds), *New Worlds, Ancient Texts: The Power of Tradition and the Shock of Discovery* (Cambridge, MA and London: Belknap Press of Harvard University Press, 1995), p. 86.

5.   Whitehead, 'Introduction', p. 107.
6.   R. J. Young, *Colonial Desire: Hybridity in Theory, Culture and Race* (London and New York: Routledge, 1995), pp. 22–3)
7.   Whitehead, 'Introduction', p. 107.
8.   Duranti, and Goodwin (eds), *Rethinking Context*, p. 27.
9.   H. K. Bhabha, *The Location of Culture* (London and New York: Routledge, 1994), pp. 121–31.
10. L. Keymis, *A Relation of the Second Voyage to Guiana. Perfourmed and Written in the Yeare 1596* (London, 1596), sig. E.
11. M. de Certeau, *L'Écriture de l'histoire* (Paris: Gallimard, 1975), p. 9.
12. S. Greenblatt, *Marvelous Possessions: The Wonder of the New World* (1991; Oxford: Clarendon Press, 2003), p. 57.
13. Whitehead, 'Introduction', p. 105.
14. Ibid., p. 30.
15. W. Ralegh, *The Discoverie of the Large, Rich, and Bewtiful Empyre of Guiana, With a relation of the great and Golden Citie of Manoa* (London, 1596), p. 6.
16. Ibid., p. 28.
17. Ibid., p. 6.
18. Ibid., p. 7.
19. Ibid.
20. T. de Bry (ed.), *Americæ pars VIII* (Frankfurt-am-Main, 1599).
21. Ralegh, *The Discoverie* (1596), pp. 61–2.
22. W. Ralegh, *Introduction*, pp. 61–2.
23. Whitehead, 'The Historical Anthropology of Text', p. 58.
24. Ralegh, *The Discoverie* (1596), p. 64.
25. Ibid., p. 77.
26. Ibid., p. 80.
27. Whitehead, 'Introduction', p. 30.
28. Ibid.
29. Ralegh, *The Discoverie* (1596), p. 51.
30. Ibid., p. 81.
31. Ibid., p. 96.
32. Ibid., p. 100.
33. Ibid., p. 99.
34. G. de la Vega, *The Royal Commentaries of Peru in Two Parts* (1607), trans. Sir P. Rycaut (London, 1688), p. 181.
35. Ibid., p. 510
36. Whitehead, 'Introduction', p. 23
37. J. Rowe, 'El Movimiento nacionál inca del siglo XVIII', *Revista Universitaria de Cuzco*, 107 (1954), pp. 17–47, p. 23; Pratt, *Imperial Eyes*, p. 144.
38. Rowe, 'El Movimiento nacionál inca', p. 27.
39. Ibid.
40. E. Bancroft, *Essay on the Natural History of Guiana in South America* (London, 1769), p. 269.
41. Bry (ed.), *Americæ pars VIII*; R. Hakluyt (ed.), *The Principal Navigations, Voiages, Traffiques and Discoueries of the English Nation, made by sea or overland*, 2nd edn (London, 1598–1600), vol. 3.
42. Whitehead, 'Introduction', p. 100.

43. J. N. Green, 'The Wreck of the Dutch East Indiaman the *Vergulde Draeck*, 1656', *International Journal of Nautical Archaeology*, 2:2 (1973), pp. 283–4; A. Oswald, 'Marked Clay Pipes from Plymouth, Devonshire', *Post-Medieval Archeology*, 3 (1969), pp. 122–42, fig. 59 number 70.
44. Whitehead, 'The Historical Anthropology of Text', p. 62.

5 Sayre, Domestication and Recognition of the Other in John Lawson's *A New Voyage to Carolina* (1709)

1. J. Lawson, *A New Voyage to Carolina*, ed. H. T. Lefler (1709; Chapel Hill, NC: University of North Carolina Press, 1967), p. 7.
2. See J. R. Randolph, *British Travelers among the Southern Indians 1660–1763* (Norman, OK: University of Oklahoma Press, 1973), p. 79.
3. The full title of the first edition was: *A New Voyage to Carolina : Containing the Exact Description and Natural History of that Country : Together with the Present State thereof. And a Journal of a Thousand Miles, Travel'd thro' several Nations of Indians. Giving a particular Account of their Customs, Manners, etc.*
4. See G. M. Sayre, *Les Sauvages Américains: Representations of Native Americans in French and English Colonial Literature* (Chapel Hill, NC and London: University of North Carolina Press, 1997), pp. 24–5.
5. Lawson, *A New Voyage to Carolina*, p. 3.
6. Ibid., pp. 51–2.
7. Ibid., p. 34.
8. Ibid., p. 10.
9. Ibid., p. 61.
10. Ibid., pp. 31, 57, 61.
11. Ibid., p. 45.
12. Ibid., p. 47.
13. Ibid., p. 40.
14. Ibid., p. 41.
15. Ibid., p. 204.
16. Ibid., p. 223.
17. Ibid., p. 221.
18. Ibid., pp. 27, 222.
19. Ibid., pp. 57–8.
20. Ibid., p. 21.
21. Ibid., pp. 13, 15, etc.
22. Ibid., pp. 18, 26, 225–6.
23. Ibid., pp. 30, 55.
24. Ibid., p. 63.
25. Ibid., p. 219.
26. Ibid., p. 45.
27. Ibid., p. 200.
28. Ibid., p. 191.
29. Ibid., p. 5.
30. Ibid., p. 240.
31. Ibid., p. 176.

32. Ibid., p. 204.
33. Ibid., p. 203.
34. Ibid., pp. 34, 38, 184–5, 220.
35. Ibid., p. 184.
36. A. L. Diket, 'The Noble Savage Convention as Epitomized in John Lawson's *A New Voyage to Carolina*', *North Carolina Historical Review*, 43:4 (1966), pp. 413–29; E. T. Shields Jr, 'Paradise Regained Again: The Literary Context of John Lawson's *A New Voyage to Carolina*', *North Carolina Literary Review*, 1:1 (1992), pp. 83–97.
37. Lawson, *A New Voyage to Carolina*, p. 243.
38. Ibid., p. 243.
39. See M. B. Campbell, *The Witness and the Other World: Exotic European Travel Writing 400–1600* (Ithaca, NY and London: Cornell University Press, 1988), pp. 2–3, 5–6, 11, 262–5.

6 Patel, The (He)art of First Encounter at Tahiti: Samuel Wallis's Conflicts of Interest (1767)

1. See E. Bohls and I. Duncan (eds), *Travel Writing 1700–1830: An Anthology* (Oxford: Oxford University Press, 2005), Introduction, p. xv.
2. T. J. Cribb, 'Writing up the Log: The Legacy of Hakluyt', in S. Clark (ed.), *Travel Writing and Empire. Postcolonial Theory in Transit* (London: Zed Books, 1999), p. 101.
3. I. S. MacLaren, 'Exploration/Travel Literature and the Evolution of the Author', *International Journal of Canadian Studies*, 5 (1992), pp. 41–3.
4. ADM 55/35, Public Records Office, London.
5. ML Safe 1/98, Mitchell Library, Sydney, Australia.
6. Cribb, 'Writing up the Log', p. 101.
7. G. Dening, *Islands and Beaches. Discourse on a Silent Land: Marquesas 1774–1880* (Oxford: Oxford University Press, 1980), p. 19.
8. Bhabha, *The Location of Culture*, p. 23.
9. Dening, *Islands and Beaches*, p. 4.
10. E. Saïd, *Orientalism* (Harmondsworth: Penguin, 1978), p. 58.
11. ADM 55/35, 8 June 1767.
12. ML Safe 1/98, 8 June 1767.
13. Ibid.
14. ADM 55/35, 8 June 1767.
15. Ibid.
16. Dening, *Islands and Beaches*, p. 4.
17. ADM 55/35, 11 June 1767.
18. ML Safe 1/98, 11 June 1767.
19. ADM 55/35, 11 June 1767.
20. Bhabha, *The Location of Culture*, pp. 64–6.
21. ADM 55/35, 11 June 1767.
22. Foucault, quoted in Bhabha, *The Location of Culture*, p. 74.
23. ADM 55/35, 18 June 1767.
24. ML Safe 1/98, 18 June 1767.
25. Bhabha, *The Location of Culture*, p. 70.
26. ADM 55/35, 18 June 1767.

27. Cribb, 'Writing up the Log', p. 104.
28. Dening, *Islands and Beaches*, p. 18.
29. ML Safe 1/98, 18 June 1767.
30. Ibid.
31. ML Safe 1/98, 19 June 1767 and ADM 55/35, 19 June 1767.
32. ML Safe 1/98, 20 June 1767 and ADM 55/35, 19 June 1767.
33. ML Safe 1/98, 20 June 1767.
34. ADM 55/35, 20 June 1767.
35. ML Safe 1/98, 20 June 1767.
36. Ibid.
37. ML Safe 1/98, 21 June 1767.
38. ADM 55/35, 21 June 1767.
39. Bhabha, *The Location of Culture*, p. 94.
40. Ibid., p. 70.
41. ML Safe 1/98, 24 June 1767.
42. ADM 55/35, 24 June 1767.
43. ML Safe 1/98, 24 June 1767.
44. ADM 55/35, 24 June 1767.
45. Ibid.
46. Saïd, *Orientalism* (1978), p. 272.
47. Dening, *Islands and Beaches*, p. 24.

7 Dromart, Distance and Proximity in James Cook's First Voyage around the World (1768–71)

1.   T. Fulford and P. J. Kitson (ed), *Travels, Explorations and Empires: Writings from the Era of Imperial Expansion 1770–1835* 8 vols (London: Pickering and Chatto, 2002), vol. 8, pp. xviii, 1.
2.   J. Cook, *The Journals of Captain James Cook: The Voyage of the Endeavour 1768–71*, ed. J. C. Beaglehole, 2nd edn (Cambridge: Cambridge University Press, 1968), p. cclxxxii.
3.   P. H. Edwards, *The Story of the Voyage: Sea Narratives in Eighteenth-Century England* (Cambridge: Cambridge University Press, 2004), p. 85.
4.   http://southseas.nla.gov.au (accessed 8 October 2008).
5.   Edwards, *The Story of the Voyage*, p. 86.
6.   Geertz, *The Interpretation of Cultures*, p. 35.
7.   13 April 1769.
8.   T. Fulford, D. Lee and P. J. Kitson, *Literature, Science and Exploration in the Romantic Era: Bodies of Knowledge* (Cambridge: Cambridge University Press, 2004), pp. 34–5; Fulford and Kitson (eds), *Travels, Explorations and Empires*, vol. 8, p. xviii.
9.   Cook, *The Voyage of the Endeavour*, p. cl; 13 April 1769.
10. 13 April 1769.
11. E. T. Hall, *The Hidden Dimension* (New York: Anchor Books, 1990), p. 7.
12. 5–8 October 1769.
13. 9 October 1769.
14. 5–8 October 1769; 18 January 1770.
15. 9 October 1769.
16. 8 October 1769.

17. 8 October 1769.
18. 8 October 1769.
19. 9 October 1769.
20. J. Gumperz, and D. Hymes (eds), *Directions in Sociolinguistics: The Ethnography of Communication* (New York and London: Holt, Rinehart and Winston, 1972), p. 39.
21. 9 October 1769.
22. 1 November 1769.
23. 13–14 April 1769.
24. 14 April 1769.
25. 14 April 1769.
26. 14 April 1769.
27. Y. Winkin, *Anthropologie de la communication* (Paris: Seuil, 2001), p. 15.
28. 14 April 1769.
29. 14 April 1769.
30. 14 May 1769.
31. 15 April 1769.
32. 15 April 1769.
33. D. Defoe, *Robinson Crusoe* (1719; Harmondsworth: Penguin Classics, 2003), p. 167; C. Rawson, *God, Gulliver, and Genocide: Barbarism and the European Imagination 1492–1945* (Oxford: Oxford University Press, 2001), p. 64.
34. 15 April 1769.
35. R. Edmond, *Representing the South Pacific* (Cambridge: Cambridge University Press, 1997), p. 57.
36. 15 April 1769.
37. 19 April 1769.
38. 25 April 1769.
39. 28 April 1769.
40. Edwards, *The Story of the Voyage*, p. 89.
41. Cook, *The Voyage of the Endeavour*, p. 399.
42. M. de Montaigne, 'Des Coches' (1588), in *Essais* (Paris: Garnier, 1948), vol. 3, p. 138.
43. 26–7 April 1769.
44. 13 May 1769.
45. Edwards, *The Story of the Voyage*, p. 89.
46. P. Watzlawick, J. H. Beavin and D. Jackson, *Pragmatics of Human Communication. A Study of Interactional Patterns, Pathologies, and Paradoxes* (New York: Norton, 1967), p. 59.

8 Moser, Walking in the Contact Zone: Georg Forster and the Peripatetic Mode of Exploration (1768–77)

1. M. Foucault, *Les Mots et les choses. Une archéologie des sciences humaines* (Paris: Gallimard, 1966), p. 229.
2. On the concept of the 'contact zone', see Pratt, *Imperial Eyes*, pp. 6–7.
3. G. Obeyesekere, *The Apotheosis of Captain Cook: European Mythmaking in the Pacific* (Princeton, NJ: Princeton University Press, 1997), p. 7.
4. C. Moser, *Kannibalische Katharsis. Literarische und filmische Inszenierungen der Anthropophagie von James Cook bis Bret Easton Ellis* (Bielefeld: Aisthesis, 2005), p. 68.

5. G. Forster, *Georg Forsters Werke. Sämtliche Schriften, Tagebücher, Briefe*, vol. 1: *A Voyage round the World*, ed. R. L. Kahn (Berlin: Akademie-Verlag, 1968), p. 171 (my italics).

6. G. Forster, *Reise um die Welt*, ed. G. Steiner (Frankfurt: Insel, 1983), p. 265.

7. J. Cook, *The Journals of Captain Cook on His Voyages of Discovery*, ed. J. C. Beaglehole, 4 vols (Cambridge: Cambridge University Press, 1955–67), vol. 1, pp. 74–118.

8. Ibid., pp. 118–39.

9. L.-A. de Bougainville, *Voyage autour du monde par la frégate du Roi* La Boudeuse *et la flûte* L'Étoile, ed. J. Proust (Paris: Gallimard, 1982), pp. 247–71.

10. R. Stockhammer, *Kartierung der Erde. Macht und Lust in Karten und Literatur* (München: Fink, 2007), p. 103.

11. Cook, *The Journal of Captain James Cook on His Voyages of Discovery*, ed. Beaglehole, vol. 1, p. 124.

12. See, for example, ibid., pp. 100–1.

13. Forster, *A Voyage round the World*, p. 295.

14. Cook, *The Journals of Captain Cook on His Voyages of Discovery*, ed. Beaglehole, vol. 2, p. 293.

15. Ibid., p. 294.

16. Moser, *Kannibalische Katharsis*, pp. 50–5.

17. Foucault, *Les Mots et les choses*, p. 144.

18. J.-J. Rousseau, *Œuvres complètes*, ed. B. Gagnebin and M. Raymond, vol. 1 (Paris: Gallimard, 1959), pp. 1062, 1066–8.

19. Cook, *The Journals of Captain Cook on His Voyages of Discovery*, ed. Beaglehole, vol. 1, p. 105.

20. M. de Certeau, *L'Invention du quotidien*, vol. 1: *Arts de faire* (Paris: Gallimard, 1990), pp. 175–80.

21. Cook, *The Journals of Captain Cook on His Voyages of Discovery*, ed. Beaglehole, vol. 1, pp. 75–6.

22. Ibid., p. 76.

23. A. D. Wallace, *Walking, Literature, and English Culture. The Origins and Uses of the Peripatetic in the Nineteenth Century* (Oxford: Oxford University Press, 1999), pp. 7–8.

24. Ibid., pp. 17–66; see also R. Jarvis, *Romantic Writing and Pedestrian Travel* (Basingstoke: Macmillan, 1997), pp. 62–88.

25. W. Gilpin, *Three Essays on Picturesque Beauty; on Picturesque Travel; and on Sketching Landscape: to which is added a Poem, on Landscape Painting* (1792; Farnborough: Gregg International, 1972), pp. 106–7.

26. R. A. Berman, *Enlightenment or Empire: Colonial Discourse in German Culture* (Lincoln, NE and London: University of Nebraska Press, 1998), p. 26.

27. Rousseau, *Œuvres complètes*, vol. 1, pp. 163–4.

28. Forster, *A Voyage round the World*, p. 175.

29. A. Appadurai, 'Putting Hierarchy in Its Place', *Cultural Anthropology*, 3 (1988), p. 37.

30. On the observer's perspective in Forster's *Voyage*, see M. Ribeiro Sanches, "Diese zarten, fast unsichtbaren Fäden der Arachne': Das wahrnehmende Subjekt und die Konstituierung von Wahrheit bei Forster', in C.-V. Klenke (ed.), *Georg Forster in interdisziplinärer Perspektive. Beiträge des Internationalen Georg-Forster-Symposions in Kassel, 1. bis 4. April 1993* (Berlin: Akademie-Verlag, 1994), pp. 133–46.

31. Forster, *A Voyage round the World*, p. 178.

32. Ibid., p. 215.

33. J. Derrida, *De la grammatologie* (Paris: Éditions de Minuit, 1967), pp. 203–34.

9 Cundell, The Disorder of Things: Empiricism and the Cartographic Enterprise, or, the Observations of Samuel Hearne (1795) and Alexander Mackenzie (1801)

1. Pratt, *Imperial Eyes*, p. 29.
2. Ibid., p. 17.
3. M. Foucault, *The Order of Things: An Archaeology of the Human Sciences* (1966), translator unknown (New York: Pantheon, 1970), p. 56.
4. Pratt, *Imperial Eyes*, p. 7.
5. Foucault, *The Order of Things*, p. 133.
6. Ibid., p. 125.
7. S. Johnson, *A Dictionary of the English Language* (1755), ed. A. McDermott (CD-ROM, Cambridge: Cambridge University Press, 1996).
8. Foucault, *The Order of Things*, p. 57.
9. Ibid.
10. Ibid., p. 56.
11. As cited in 'Observation', Def. 7b., *The Oxford English Dictionary*, online edition; http://dictionary.oed.com/.
12. Ibid.
13. Foucault, *The Order of Things*, p. 133.
14. S. Hearne, *A Journey from Prince of Wales's Fort in Hudson's Bay to the Northern Ocean. Undertaken by Order of the Hudson's Bay Company, for the Discovery of Copper Mines, a Northwest Passage, &c. In the Years 1769, 1770, 1771, & 1772* (1795; Amsterdam: Nico Israel, 1968), p. xxxvi.
15. A. Mackenzie, *Voyages from Montreal on the River St. Laurence, through the Continent of North America, to the Frozen and Pacific Oceans: In the Years 1789 and 1793. The Journals and Letters of Sir Alexander Mackenzie* (1801), ed. W. K. Lamb (Cambridge: Cambridge University Press, 1970), p. 57.
16. Mackenzie, *Voyages*, p. 60.
17. Hearne, *A Journey*, p. vi.
18. C. Chard, *Pleasure and Guilt on the Grand Tour: Travel Writing and Imaginative Geography 1600–1830* (Manchester: Manchester University Press, 1999), p. 27.
19. Hearne, *A Journey*, p. iii.
20. C. S. Houston, T. Ball and M. Houston, *Eighteenth-Century Naturalists of the Hudson's Bay* (Montreal, QC and Kingston: McGill-Queen's University Press, 2003), pp. 31–2.
21. Hearne, *A Journey*, p. iii.
22. T. Sprat, *History of the Royal Society* (1667), ed. J. I. Cope and H. W. Jones (St Louis, MO: Washington University Press, 1959), p. 113.
23. Hearne, *A Journey*, p. ix.
24. Mackenzie, *Voyages*, p. 59.
25. Ibid., p. 60.
26. H. T. Fry, 'Alexander Dalrymple and Captain Cook: The Creative Interplay of Two Careers', in R. Fisher and H. Johnston (eds), *Captain Cook and His Times* (Seattle, WA: University of Washington Press, 1979), p. 47.
27. Hearne, *A Journey*, p. v.
28. Fry, 'Alexander Dalrymple and Captain Cook', p. 41.
29. W. K. Lamb, 'Introduction', in Mackenzie, *Voyages*, p. 14.

30. Mackenzie, *Voyages*, p. 58.
31. Ibid., p. 58.
32. Ibid., pp. 58–9.
33. Ibid., p. 57.
34. Ibid., p. 256 (emphasis mine).
35. Ibid., p. 420.
36. Ibid., p. 402.
37. Ibid., p. 265.
38. Ibid., p. 366.
39. Ibid., p. 367.
40. Hearne, *A Journey*, p. xiv.
41. Ibid., p. xiii.
42. Ibid., p. 80.
43. Ibid., p. xiv.
44. Ibid., p. 104.
45. Mackenzie, *Voyages*, p. 286.
46. Hearne, *A Journey*, pp. 121–2.
47. Mackenzie, *Voyages*, p. 323.
48. Ibid.
49. Ibid.
50. Hearne, *A Journey*, p. 93.
51. Ibid.
52. Mackenzie, *Voyages*, p. 182.
53. Ibid., p. 183.
54. Ibid., p. 215.
55. Ibid., p. 196.
56. Ibid.
57. Hearne, *A Journey*, p. 55.
58. Ibid., p. 61 (emphasis mine).
59. M. Hodgson, 'The Exploration Journal as Literature', *Beaver*, 298 (Winter 1967), p. 11.
60. Ibid., p. 7.
61. Ibid., p. 11.
62. Ibid.
63. B. Greenfield, *Narrating Discovery: The Romantic Explorer in American Literature 1790–1855* (New York: Columbia University Press, 1992), p. 55.
64. Ibid., p. 55.
65. Ibid., p. 27.
66. Ibid.
67. Ibid., p. 48.
68. T. D. MacLulich, 'Canadian Exploration as Literature', *Canadian Literature*, 81 (1979), p. 73.
69. Ibid., p. 74.
70. Ibid., p. 75.
71. Greenfield, *Narrating Discovery*, p. 55.
72. Mackenzie, *Voyages*, p. 378.
73. Ibid., p. 378.
74. Ibid.
75. Hearne, *A Journey*, pp. 163–4.

76. Ibid., p. xxxix.
77. Pratt, *Imperial Eyes*, p. 30.
78. Ibid

10 Lanone, John Franklin and the Idea of North: *Narrative of a Journey to the Shores of the Polar Sea in the Years 1819–1822*

1. M. Shelley, *Frankenstein* (1818; Ware: Wordsworth Classics, 1993), p. 197.
2. This engraving is reproduced in P. Berton, *The Arctic Grail* (1988; New York: Lyons Press, 2000), p. 14.
3. Ibid., p. 15.
4. Ibid.
5. R. Davis (ed.), *Sir John Franklin's Journals and Correspondence: The First Arctic Land Expedition 1819–1922* ('Toronto, ON: Champlain Society, 1995), Frontispiece, no pagination.
6. Shelley, *Frankenstein*, p. 197.
7. G. Deleuze and F. Guattari, *A Thousand Plateaus*, trans. B. Massumi (London: The Athlone Press, 1987), p. 12.
8. J. Franklin, *Narrative of a Journey to the Shores of the Polar Sea, in the Years 1819–22* (1823; New York: Cosimo, 2005), p. 2.
9. R. Davis , 'The Travel Book's Itinerary: The Case of Sir John Franklin', in B. Olinder (ed.), *Literary Environments: Canada and the Old World* (Brussels: Peter Lang, 2006), p. 39.
10. Franklin, *Narrative of a Journey*, p. 330.
11. Ibid., pp. 324–5.
12. Ibid., p. 348.
13. Ibid., p. 169.
14. Ibid, p. 335.
15. J. Richardson, *Arctic Ordeal: The Journal of John Richardson, Surgeon-Naturalist with Franklin, 1820–2*, ed. C. S. Houston (Montréal, QC and Kingston: McGill-Queen's University Press, 1984), p. 102.
16. G. Back, *Arctic Artist: The Journal and Paintings of George Back, Midshipman with Franklin, 1819–22*, ed. C. S. Houston and I. S. MacLaren (Montréal, ON and Kingston: McGill-Queen's University Press, 1994), p. 154.
17. Franklin, *Narrative of a Journey*, p. 381.
18. Richardson, *Arctic Ordeal*, p. 146.
19. S. Grace, *Canada and the Idea of North* (Montréal, ON and Kingston: McGill-Queen's University Press, 2001), p. 43.
20. Richardson, *Arctic Ordeal*, p. xxix.
21. Richardson, in Franklin, *Narrative of a Journey*, p. 395.
22. R. Davis, 'The Travel Book's Itinerary', p. 40.
23. Franklin, *Narrative of a Journey*, pp. 395–406.
24. Ibid., p. 194.
25. Ibid.
26. Ibid., p. 139.
27. Ibid., p. 180.
28. Ibid., pp. 51–2.
29. Ibid., p. 184.

30. Ibid., p. 276.
31. R. Hood, *To the Arctic by Canoe 1819–21: The Journals and Paintings of Robert Hood, Midshipman with Franklin*, ed. C. S. Houston (1974; Montréal, ON and Kingston: McGill-Queen's University Press, 1994), p. 88.
32. See 'Keskarrah, a Copper Indian Guide, and His Daughter, Green Stockings, Mending a Snow Shoe', engraved by Edward Finden for Murray's first edition of Franklin's *Narrative*
33. 'Interior of a Cree Indian Tent, March 25 1820', engraved by Finden for Murray's first edition of Franklin's *Narrative*.
34. Back, *Arctic Artist*, p. 129.
35. Ibid., 'Figure 30', 'Figure 31', no pagination.
36. Ibid., 'Figure 34', 'Figure 35', no pagination.
37. Ibid., 'Figure 15', 'Figure 16', no pagination.
38. Richardson, *Arctic Ordeal*, p. 178. See Franklin, *Narrative of a Journey*, p. 417.
39. Richardson, *Arctic Ordeal*, p. 179.
40. Franklin, *Narrative of a Journey*, p. 419.
41. R. Barthes, *Mythologies*, trans. Annette Lavers (New York: Hill and Wang, 1972), p. 146.
42. Franklin, *Narrative of a Journey*, p. 406.
43. Richardson, *Arctic Ordeal*, p. 167.
44. R. Davis, 'The Travel Book's Itinerary', p. 42.
45. Franklin, *Narrative of a Journey*, pp. 342–3.
46. Shelley, *Frankenstein*, p. 197.

11 Bruneau, 'Cultivating that Mutual Friendship': Commerce, Diplomacy and Self-Representation in Hugh Clapperton's *Journal of a Second Expedition into the Interior of Africa from the Bight of Benin to Soccatoo* (1829)

1. J. Bruce Lockhart and P. Lovejoy (eds), *Hugh Clapperton into the Interior of Africa: Records of the Second Expedition 1825–1827* (Leiden: Brill, 2005), pp. 350–5.
2. ' Translation of 'A Letter from an African Chieftain [Bello] of Soudan, to his Majesty King George the Fourth. Brought by Mr. Clapperton'', in Bruce Lockhart and Lovejoy, *Hugh Clapperton*, p. 445.
3. 'Letter of Earl Bathurst to H. Clapperton', 30 July 1825, in Bruce Lockhart and Lovejoy, *Hugh Clapperton*, p. 355.
4. Ibid., p. 353.
5. H. Clapperton, *Journal of a Second Expedition into the Interior of Africa from the Bight of Benin to Soccatoo* (1829; London: Frank Cass, 1966, facsimile edn), pp. 93–5.
6. Ibid., pp. 140–1.
7. Ibid., pp. 139, 129.
8. Ibid., p. 13.
9. Ibid., p. 41.
10. Ibid., pp. 94–5.
11. Ibid., p. 182.
12. Ibid., p. 143.
13. See e.g. pp. 14, 62, 155–6.

14. 'Letter of Earl Bathurst to H. Clapperton', in Bruce Lockhart and Lovejoy, *Hugh Clapperton*, p. 352.
15. Clapperton, *Journal*, p. 23.
16. Ibid., p. 26.
17. Ibid., pp. 21, 80.
18. Ibid., p. 36.
19. See A.-P. Bruneau, "The King's Servant': modalités de la rencontre dans *Journal of a Second Expedition into the Interior of Africa* de Hugh Clapperton (1829)', in Regard (ed.), *De Drake à Chatwin*, pp. 147–9.
20. Clapperton, *Journal*, p. 67.
21. Ibid., p. 42.
22. Ibid., pp. 90, 134.
23. Ibid., p. 55.
24. Ibid., p. 56.
25. Ibid., p. 72.
26. Ibid., p. 78.
27. Ibid., p. 87.

12 D'Souza, Trying to Understand: James Tod among the Rajputs (1829, 1832)

1. J. Tod, *Annals and Antiquities of Rajasthan* (1829–32; Delhi: Rupa, 1997), vol. 2, p. 477.
2. Tod, *Annals and Antiquities*, vol. 2, p. 513.
3. M. Duchet, *Anthropologie et histoire au siècle des Lumières* (Paris: François Maspéro, 1971), p. 12.
4. D. Allan, *Virtue, Learning and the Scottish Enlightenment: Ideas of Scholarship in Early Modern History* (Edinburgh: Edinburgh University Press, 1993), pp.160–2.
5. Duchet, *Anthropologie et histoire*, pp. 479–80.
6. P. J. Marshall and G. Williams, *The Great Map of Mankind: British Perceptions of the World in the Age of Enlightenment* (London: Dent, 1982), p. 20.
7. E. Saïd, *Orientalism* (1978; London: Penguin Books, 1995), p. 3.
8. Tod, *Annals and Antiquities*, vol. 2, p. 521.
9. Ibid., p. 595.
10. J. Goody and I. Watt, 'The Consequences of Literacy', in J. Goody (ed.), *Literacy in Traditional Societies* (Cambridge: Cambridge University Press, 1963), pp. 44–8.
11. Tod, *Annals and Antiquities*, vol. 1, p. 251.
12. Ibid., p. 251, n. 1.
13. Ibid., vol. 2, pp. 559–60.
14. Ibid., vol. 1, p. 485.
15. Ibid., vol. 1, p. 375, n. 1.
16. Ibid., vol. 1, pp. 542–3.
17. Ibid., vol. 2, p. 539.
18. Ibid., vol. 2, p. 541.
19. N. Peabody, 'Tod's Rajasthan, and the Boundaries of Imperial Rule in Nineteenth-Century India', *Modern Asian Studies*, 30:1 (1996), pp. 185–220, pp. 201–4.
20. R. Inden, *Imagining India* (1990; London: Hurst, 2000), pp.172–80; also Peabody, 'Tod's Rajasthan'.

21. Inden, *Imagining India*, pp. 172–7.
22. Ibid., p. 180.
23. Tod, *Annals and Antiquities*, vol. 1, p.xii.
24. Ibid., pp. 132, 137.
25. H. Hallam, *A View of the State of Europe during the Middle Ages*, 2nd edn (London: John Murray, 1819), vol. 1, p. 144.
26. Ibid., pp. 200, 320.
27. Tod, *Annals and Antiquities*, vol. 1, p.132; vol. 2, pp. 90, 429.
28. Ibid., vol. 1, pp. 137, 429.
29. Ibid., vol. 1, p. 381.
30. Ibid., vol. 1, p.140; vol. 2, pp. 85, 291.
31. Ibid., vol. 1, p. 382.
32. Ibid., pp. 379, 392.
33. Peabody, 'Tod's Rajasthan', pp. 209–11.
34. Tod, *Annals and Antiquities*, vol. 1, pp. 391–2.
35. Ibid., vol. 2, p. 486.
36. Ibid., p. 503.
37. Ibid., vol. 2, p. 515.
38. Ibid., vol. 1, p. 394.
39. N. Waszek, *The Scottish Enlightenment and Hegel's Account of 'Civil Society'* (Dordrecht and London: Kluwer Academic Publishers, 1988), pp. 84–141; A. Broadie, *The Scottish Enlightenment: the Historical Age of the Historical Nation* (Edinburgh: Birlinn, 2001), pp. 75–7, 79–85; Allan, *Virtue, Learning and the Scottish Enlightenment*, pp. 147–213.
40. M. Duchet, *Le Partage des savoirs: discours historique et discours ethnologique* (Paris: La Découverte, 1985), p. 225.
41. Tod, *Annals and Antiquities*, vol. 1, p. xiii.
42. Ibid., vol. 1, p. xix.
43. Ibid., vol. 1, p.xvii.
44. Ibid., vol. 1, p.xviii.
45. Ibid., vol. 1, pp. 366, 368.
46. Ibid., vol. 1, p. 368.
47. Ibid., vol. 1, pp. 563–5.
48. Ibid., vol. 2, p. 582.
49. Tod, *Travels in Western India* (1839; Delhi: Munshiram Manoharlal, 1997), p. xxxvi.
50. Ibid., p. xlvi.
51. R. Heber, *Narrative of a Journey through the Upper Provinces of India, from Calcutta to Bombay, 1824–1825*, 4th edn, 3 vols (London: John Murray, 1829), vol. 2, p. 42.

13 Scott, Shifting Perspectives: Visual Representation and the Imperial 'I' in Anna Jameson's Winter Studies and Summer Rambles in Canada (1838)

1. While Jameson employs the now out-of-date term 'Indian' throughout her text, I have chosen to use the term Native to signify cultural and ethnic groups who may currently identify as belonging to either Metis or First Nations groups. Because Jameson is inconsistent in differentiating between mixed-race individuals, Metis individuals, and First Nations individuals, I have chosen to employ this more general term.

2. A. B. Jameson, *Winter Studies and Summer Rambles in Canada* (1838; Toronto, ON: McLelland and Stewart, 1990), p. 12.
3. M. H. Frawley, 'Borders and Boundaries, Perspectives and Place: Victorian Women's Travel Writing', in J. Pomeroy (ed.), *Intrepid Women: Victorian Artists Travel* (Aldershot: Ashgate, 2005), p. 27.
4. Jameson, *Winter Studies*, p. 28.
5. Ibid., p. 462.
6. Ibid., p. 10.
7. Ibid.
8. Frawley, 'Borders and Boundaries', p. 30
9. W. Roy, *Maps of Difference: Canada, Women, and Travel* (Montreal: McGill-Queen's UP, 2005), p. 27
10. K. Lawrence, *Penelope Voyages: Women and Travel in the British Literary Tradition* (Ithaca, NY: Cornell University Press, 1994), Introduction, p. x.
11. V. Fortunati, R. Monticelli, and M. Ascari (eds), *Travel Literature and the Female Imaginary* (Bologna: Patron, 2005), p. 11.
12. C. Kaplan, *Questions of Travel: Postmodern Discourses of Displacement* (Durham, NC: Duke University Press, 1996), pp. 143–4.
13. Lawrence, *Penelope Voyages*, p. 19.
14. D. S. Macleod, 'Women's Artistic Passages', Introduction in Pomeroy (ed), *Intrepid Women*, p. 6.
15. Frawley, 'Borders and Boundaries', p. 34.
16. C. Crawshaw and J. Urry, 'Tourism and the Photographic Eye', in C. Rojeck and J. Urry (eds), *Touring Cultures: Transformations of Travel and Theory* (London: Routledge, 1991), p. 183.
17. J. Buzzard, *The Beaten Track: European Tourism, Literature, and the Ways to Culture 1800–1918* (Oxford: Clarendon Press, 1993), p. 188.
18. Jameson, *Winter Studies*, p. 337.
19. Ibid., p. 338.
20. Ibid., p. 336.
21. C. Mulvey, 'Écriture and Writing: British Writing on Post-Revolutionary America', in M. Gildley and R. Lawson-Peeples (eds), *Views of American Landscapes* (Cambridge: Cambridge University Press, 2007), pp. 102–3.
22. E. Helsinger, 'Turner and the Representation of England', in W. J. T. Mitchell (ed.), *Landscape and Power* (Chicago, IL: The University of Chicago Press, 1994), p. 105.
23. D. Bunn, 'Our Wattled Cot: Mercantile and Domestic Space in Thomas Pringle's African Landscapes', in Mitchell (ed.), *Landscape and Power*, p. 138.
24. Jameson, *Winter Studies*, p. 59.
25. Ibid., pp. 60–1.
26. G. Whitlock, *The Intimate Empire: Reading Women's Autobiography* (London and New York: Cassell, 2000), p. 76.
27. Kaplan, *Questions of Travel*, p. 39.
28. Anderson, *Imagined Communities*, p. 36.
29. Jameson, *Winter Studies*, p. 402
30. Ibid.
31. Ibid.
32. Jameson, *Winter Studies*, p. 400.
33. Goody, *The Logic of Writing*, p. 182.

34. Jameson, *Winter Studies,* pp. 473–7.
35. R. Laubin and G. Laubin, *Indian Dances of North America: Their Importance to Indian Life* (Norman, OK: University of Oklahoma Press, 1977), p. 92.
36. P. Winkler, 'Writing Ghost Notes: The Poetics and Politics of Transcription', in D. Schwartz, A. Kassabian and L. Siegel (eds), *Keeping Score: Music, Disciplinarity Culture* (Charlottesville, VA and London: University of Virginia Press, 1997), p 171.
37. Jameson, *Winter Studies,* p. 179 (original emphasis).
38. P. Chatterjee, *The Nation and Its Fragments: Colonial and Postcolonial Histories* (Princeton, NJ: Princeton University Press, 1993), p. 5.
39. I employ the term 'mixed-race' to indicate Mrs Schoolcraft's Chippewa and British ethnicities. While 'Metis' is sometimes used to denote mixed-race individuals more generally, in the Canadian context the term has a specific political and geographical history particular to Louis Riel and the Red River Rebellion. See B. Lawrence, *Real Indians and 'Others': Mixed-Blood Urban Native People and Indigenous Nationhood* (Vancouver, BC: University of British Columbia Press, 2004).
40. Jameson, *Winter Studies,* p. 403.
41. Ibid., p. 9 (my emphasis).
42. Ibid., *Winter Studies,* p. 500.
43. Ibid.
44. Ibid., pp. 500–1.
45. W. Roy, "Here is the picture as well as I can paint it': Anna Jameson's Illustrations for *Winter Studies and Summer Rambles in Canada', Canadian Literature,* 177 (Summer 2003), pp. 97–105.
46. Jameson, *Winter Studies,* pp. 390–1.
47. Ibid., pp. 394–5.
48. Ibid., p. 456.
49. Helsinger, 'Turner and the Representation of England', p. 105.
50. Jameson, *Winter Studies,* pp. 381–2.
51. Ibid.
52. Ibid., p. 319.
53. Ibid., p. 322.
54. Ibid..
55. Ibid., p. 519.
56. Ibid., p. 371.
57. Anderson, *Imagined Communities,* p. 36.
58. Ibid., p. 37

14 Richter, Charles Darwin in Patagonia: Descriptive Strategies in the *Beagle Diary* (1831–36) and *The Voyage of the Beagle* (1845)

1. J. Tallmadge, 'From Chronicle to Quest: The Shaping of Darwin's *Voyage of the Beagle', Victorian Studies,* 23 (1980), p. 327.
2. A. Harley, 'This Reversed Order of Things: Re-Orientation aboard *HMS Beagle', Biography,* 29 (2006), p. 465.
3. J. Browne, *Charles Darwin: Voyaging* (Princeton, NJ: Princeton University Press, 1995), p. 160.
4. Tallmadge, 'From Chronicle to Quest', p. 330–1.

5. Ibid., p. 333.
6. Ibid., p. 337.
7. Darwin, *The Voyage of the Beagle*, ed. D. Quammen (1845; Washington DC: National Geographic Society, 2004), p. 89.
8. Ibid., p. 90.
9. Ibid., p. 91.
10. Ibid., p. 92.
11. Ibid., p. 91.
12. C. Darwin, *Charles Darwin's Beagle Diary*, ed. R. D. Keynes (Cambridge: Cambridge University Press, 1988), p. 7.
13. Ibid., p. 65.
14. Ibid., p. 183–4.
15. Ibid., p. 385.
16. Ibid., p. 398.
17. Darwin, *The Voyage of the Beagle*, p. 181.
18. C. Schmitt, 'Darwin's Savage Mnemonics', *Representations*, 88 (2004), p. 57.
19. Ibid., p. 57.
20. J. Lacan, 'Seminar on the 'Purloined Letter', in J. P. Muller and W. J. Richardson (eds.), *The Purloined Poe. Lacan, Derrida, and Psychoanalytic Reading* (Baltimore, MD: Johns Hopkins University Press, 1988), pp. 28–54.
21. Darwin, *Charles Darwin's Beagle Diary*, p. 124.
22. Darwin, *The Voyage of the Beagle*, p. 183.
23. Darwin, *Charles Darwin's Beagle Diary*, p. 125.
24. Darwin, *The Voyage of the Beagle*, p. 185 (emphasis added).
25. N. Hazlewood, *Savage: The Life and Times of Jemmy Button* (New York: St Martin's Press, 2001), p. 67.
26. Darwin, *Charles Darwin's Beagle Diary*, p. 141–3.
27. Darwin, *The Voyage of the Beagle*, p. 199.
28. Ibid., p. 201.
29. Ibid.
30. Darwin, *Charles Darwin's Beagle Diary*, p. 226.
31. Darwin, *The Voyage of the Beagle*, p. 202.
32. Hazlewood, *Savage*, pp. 250–65.
33. Harley, 'This Reversed Order of Things', p. 478.

15 Regard, Fieldwork as Self-Harrowing: Richard Burton's Cultural Evolution (1851–1856)

1. Kennedy, *The Highly Civilized Man*, p. 1.
2. Ibid., p. 3.
3. Geertz, *The Interpretation of Cultures*, p. 12.
4. L. Colley, *Captives: Britain, Empire and the World 1600–1850* (2002; London: Pimlico, 2003), pp. 47–8.
5. Goffman, *Stigma*, p. 4.
6. Goffman, 'The Neglected Situation', p. 231.
7. J. Gumperz, *Discourse Strategies* (Cambridge: Cambridge University Press, 1982), p. 29.

8. E. Goffman, *Asylums* (Garden City, NY: Doubleday, Anchor Books, 1961), p. 189.
9. See P. Roy, *Indian Traffic: Identities in Question in Colonial and Post-Colonial India* (Berkeley, CA: University of California Press, 1998), p. 26; also Kennedy, *The Highly Civilized Man*, p. 69.
10. Goffman, *Asylums*, p. 320,
11. See J.-J. Lecercle, *Interpretation as Pragmatics* (London: Routledge, 1999).
12. See Saïd, *Orientalism* (1994), pp. 160–1.
13. Kennedy, *The Highly Civilized Man*, p. 42.
14. R. F. Burton, *Sindh and the Races that Inhabit the Valley of the Indus* (1851; Karachi: Oxford University Press, 1973), p. xix.
15. Ibid., p. 2.
16. Fabian, *Time and the Other*, pp. 30–1.
17. L. Althusser, 'Idéologie et appareils idéologiques d'Etat' (1970), in *Positions* (Paris: Editions Sociales, 1976), pp. 115–16.
18. See Fabian, *Time and the Other*, p.17.
19. See H. White, *Metahistory: The Historical Imagination in Nineteenth-Century Europe* (1973; Baltimore, MD: The Johns Hopkins University Press, 1975), p. 22 .
20. R. F. Burton, *Personal Narrative of a Pilgrimage to Al-Madinah & Meccah* (1855–6), Memorial Edition (1893; New York: Dover, 1964), p. 1.
21. Ibid., p. 2.
22. Ibid., p. 3.
23. Ibid., p. 14.
24. Kennedy, *The Highly Civilized Man*, p. 65.
25. See Amossy, 'Ethos at the Crossroads', pp. 4–5.
26. See Duranti and C. Goodwin (eds), *Rethinking Context*, Introduction, p. 6.
27. Burton, *Personal Narrative*, p. 148.
28. J. Diamond, *Status and Power in Verbal Interaction* (Amsterdam and Philadelphia, PA: John Benjamins, 1996), pp. 9–10.
29. Burton, *Personal Narrative*, p. 148.
30. For example, ibid., pp. 191–2.
31. E. Goffman, *Encounters: Two Studies in the Sociology of Interaction* (Indianapolis, IN: Bobbs-Merrill, 1961), pp. 68, 78.
32. Burton, *Personal Narrative*, pp. 174–6.
33. See R. Kabbani, *Imperial Fictions: Europe's Myths of Orient* (London: Rivers Oram/Pandora, 1986), p. 48.
34. See Lecercle, *Interpretation as Pragmatics*, pp. 115–17.
35. Ibid.
36. See D. Maingueneau, *Le Discours littéraire: paratopie et scène d'énonciation* (Paris: Armand Colin, 2004), pp. 108–10.
37. Burton, *Personal Narrative*, p. 14.
38. Pratt, *Imperial Eyes*, p. 217; T. Richards, *The Imperial Archive: Knowledge and the Fantasy of Empire* (London: Verso, 1993), p. 24.
39. R. F. Burton, *Falconry in the Valley of the Indus* (London: John van Voorst, 1852), pp. 100–1.
40. Maingueneau, *Le Discours littéraire*, p. 108.
41. G. Deleuze and F. Guattari, *Capitalisme et schizophrénie: L'anti-Œdipe* (Paris: Minuit, 1972), pp. 309–12.

42. Amigoni, *Colonies, Cults and Evolution*, pp. 127–8.

43. F. Regard, 'The Catholic Mule: E. B. Tylor's Chimeric Perception of Otherness', *Journal of Victorian Studies*, 12:2 (Autumn 2007).

44. M. Holquist, *Dialogism: Bakhtin and His World* (London and New York: Routledge, 1990), p. 18.

45. Young, *Colonial Desire*, p. 23.

46. Kennedy, *The Highly Civilized Man*, pp. 45, 51.

47. Amigoni, *Colonies, Cults and Evolution*, p. 24.

48. J. A. Symonds, 'On the Application of Evolutionary Principles to Art and Literature', *Essays Suggestive and Speculative*, 1890, 3rd edn (London: John Murray, 1907), p. 51.

49. Amigoni, *Colonies, Cults and Evolution*, p. 188.

50. J. A. Symonds, 'Culture: Its Meaning and Its Uses', *In the Key of Blue*, 3rd edn, 1893 (London and New York: Elkin Matthews/Macmillan, 1918), p. 200.

51. Young, *Colonial Desire*, p. 20.

52. Bhabha, *The Location of Culture*, pp. 36–9.

16 Brazzelli, Fictionalizing the Encounter with the Other: Henry Morton Stanley and the African Wilderness (1872–1890)

1. F. McLynn, *Hearts of Darkness: the European Exploration of Africa* (London: Pimlico, 1993), pp. 1–2.

2. B. Riffenburgh, *The Myth of the Explorer: The Press, Sensationalism, and Geographical Discovery* (Oxford: Oxford University Press, 1993), pp. 56–65.

3. I. R. Smith, *The Emin Pasha Relief Expedition 1886–1890* (Oxford: Clarendon Press, 1972), pp. 290–300.

4. A. Ramamurthy, *Imperial Persuaders. Images of Africa and Asia in British Advertising* (Manchester: Manchester University Press, 2003), p. 45.

5. D. Bivona, *British Imperial Literature 1870–1940. Writing and the Administration of Empire* (Cambridge: Cambridge University Press, 1998), p. 48.

6. See F. McLynn, *Stanley: The Making of an African Explorer* (London: Constable, 1989); F. McLynn, *Stanley: Sorcerer's Apprentice* (London: Constable, 1991); J. Bierman, *Dark Safari: the Life Behind the Legend of Henry Morton Stanley* (London: Hodder and Stoughton, 1991).

7. See T. Jeal, *Stanley. The Impossible Life of Africa's Greatest Explorer* (London: Faber and Faber, 2007).

8. F. Driver, 'H. M. Stanley and His Critics: Geography, Exploration and Empire', *Past & Present*, 133 (1991), pp. 134–66

9. A. Libby, 'Taming the Sublime in Darkest Africa: Stanley's *How I Found Livingstone* and Burton's *Lake Regions of Central Africa*', *Nineteenth Century Prose*, 32: 2 (2005), pp. 111–15.

10. Pratt, *Imperial Eyes*, pp. 201–8.

11. D. Spurr, *The Rhetoric of Empire. Colonial Discourse in Journalism, Travel Writing and Imperial Administration* (Durham: Duke University Press, 1993), p. 17.

12. H. M. Stanley, *How I Found Livingstone: Travels, Adventures and Discoveries in Central Africa, Including Four Months' Residence with Dr. Livingstone* (1872; New York: Dover Publications, 2001), p. 136.

13. Gilpin, *Three Essays on Picturesque Beauty*, pp. 106–7.

14. Stanley, *How I Found Livingstone*, p. 262.
15. Ibid., p. 76.
16. H. M. Stanley, *Through the Dark Continent, or, The Sources of the Nile Around the Great Lakes of Equatorial Africa and Down the Livingstone River to the Atlantic Ocean* (1878; New York: Dover Publications, 1988), vol. 2, p. 72.
17. P. Halen, 'Stanley and Conrad: Founders of Alternative Discourses about Central Africa', in E. Mudimbe-Boy (ed.), *Remembering Africa* (Portsmouth, N. H.: Heinemann, 2002), p. 62.
18. Stanley, *Through the Dark Continent*, vol. 1, p. 121.
19. Bivona, *British Imperial Literature*, p. 49.
20. Stanley, *Through the Dark Continent*, vol. 2, p. 212.
21. H. M. Stanley, *In Darkest Africa, or the Quest, Rescue and Retreat of Emin Governor of Equatoria*, (London: Sampson Low, Marston, Searle and Rivington, 1890), vol. 1, p. 136.
22. P. Knox-Shaw, *The Explorer in English Fiction* (London: Macmillan, 1987), pp. 13–15.
23. Stanley, *In Darkest Africa*, vol. 2, p. 69.
24. Stanley, *Through the Dark Continent*, vol. 1, pp. 174–5.
25. T. Youngs, *Travellers in Africa: British Travelogues 1850–1900* (Manchester: Manchester University Press, 1994), p. 117.
26. Stanley, *In Darkest Africa*, vol. 1, p. 220.
27. Ibid., p. 439.
28. Stanley, *Through the Dark Continent*, vol. 1, p. 316.
29. Ibid., vol. 2, p. 152.
30. Stanley, *How I Found Livingstone*, p. 172.
31. Ibid., pp. 454–5.
32. D. Carroll, 'African Landscape and Imperial Vertigo', in S. Gatrell (ed.), *English Literature and the Wider World* (London and Atlantic Highlands, N. J.: The Ashfield Press, 1992), vol. 4, pp. 157–65.
33. T. Youngs, "My Footsteps on These Pages': The Inscription of Self and 'Race' in H. M. Stanley's *How I Found Livingstone*', *Prose Studies*, 13: 2 (1990), p. 236.
34. M. Torgovnick, *Gone Primitive. Savage Intellects, Modern Lives* (Chicago: The University of Chicago Press, 1990), p. 33.

WORKS CITED

Ackroyd, P., *Albion. The Origins of the English Imagination* (London: Vintage, 2004).

Akbari, S., 'The Diversity of Mankind in *The Book of John Mandeville*', in R. Allen (ed.), *Eastward Bound: Travel and Travellers 1050–1550* (Manchester and New York: Manchester University Press, 2004), pp. 156–76.

Allan, D., *Virtue, Learning and the Scottish Enlightenment: Ideas of Scholarship in Early Modern History* (Edinburgh: Edinburgh University Press, 1993).

Allen, B. (ed.), *The Faber Book of Exploration. An Anthology of Worlds Revealed by Explorers through the Ages* (London: Faber and Faber, 2002).

Althusser, L., 'Idéologie et appareils idéologiques d'Etat' (1970), in *Positions* (Paris: Editions Sociales, 1976), pp. 79–137.

Amigoni, D., *Colonies, Cults and Evolution: Literature, Science and Culture in Nineteenth-Century Writing* (Cambridge: Cambridge University Press, 2007).

Amossy, R., 'Ethos at the Crossroads of Disciplines: Rhetoric, Pragmatics, Sociology', *Poetics Today*, 22:1 (2001), pp. 1–23.

Anderson, B., *Imagined Communities: Reflections on the Origin and Spread of Nationalism* (1983; London: Verso, 1991).

Anghiera, P. M., *The Decades of the Newe Worlde or West Indies,* translated and adapted by R. Eden (London: William Powell, 1555).

Anon., *Gesta Romanorum* (*c.* 1472), trans. C. Swan and W. Hopper (London: George Bell and Sons, 1899).

Appadurai, A., 'Putting Hierarchy in Its Place', *Cultural Anthropology*, 3 (1988), pp. 36–50.

Back, G., *Arctic Artist: The Journal and Paintings of George Back, Midshipman with Franklin, 1819–22*, ed. C. S. Houston and I. S. MacLaren (Montréal, ON and Kingston: McGill-Queen's University Press, 1994).

Bancroft, E., *Essay on the Natural History of Guiana in South America* (London, 1769).

Baucom, I., *Out of Place: Englishness, Empire, and the Locations of Identity* (Princeton, NJ: Princeton University Press, 1999).

Beer, G., *Darwin's Plots. Evolutionary Narrative in Darwin, George Eliot, and Nineteenth-Century Fiction* (1983; Cambridge: Cambridge University Press, 2000).

Berman, R. A., *Enlightenment or Empire: Colonial Discourse in German Culture* (Lincoln, NE and London: University of Nebraska Press, 1998).

Berton, P., *The Arctic Grail* (1988; New York: Lyons Press, 2000).

Bhabha, H. K., *The Location of Culture* (London and New York: Routledge, 1994).

Bierman, J., *Dark Safari: The Life Behind the Legend of Henry Morton Stanley* (London: Hodder and Stoughton, 1991).

Bivona, D., *British Imperial Literature 1870–1940: Writing and the Administration of Empire* (Cambridge: Cambridge University Press, 1998).

Black, M., *Models and Metaphors: Studies in Language and Philosophy* (Ithaca, NY: Cornell University Press, 1962).

Bohls, E., A. Duncan, and I. Duncan (eds), *Travel Writing 1700–1830: An Anthology* (Oxford: Oxford University Press, 2005).

Bougainville, L.-A. de, *Voyage autour du monde par la frégate du Roi La Boudeuse et la flûte L'Étoile*, ed. J. Proust (Paris: Gallimard, 1982).

Broadie, A., *The Scottish Enlightenment: the Historical Age of the Historical Nation* (Edinburgh: Birlinn, 2001).

Browne, J., *Charles Darwin: Voyaging* (Princeton, NJ: Princeton University Press, 1995).

Bruce Lockhart, J., and P. Lovejoy (eds), *Hugh Clapperton into the Interior of Africa: Records of the Second Expedition, 1825–1827* (Leiden: Brill, 2005).

Bry, T. de (ed.), *Americæ pars VIII* (Frankfurt-am-Main, 1599).

Bunn, D., 'Our Wattled Cot: Mercantile and Domestic Space in Thomas Pringle's African Landscapes', in W. J. T. Mitchell (ed.), *Landscape and Power* (Chicago, IL: The University of Chicago Press, 1994), pp.127–73.

Burgess, A., *Shakespeare* (1979; London: Vintage, 1996).

Burton, R. F., *Sindh and the Races that Inhabit the Valley of the Indus* (1851; Karachi: Oxford University Press, 1973).

—, *Falconry in the Valley of the Indus* (London: John van Voorst, 1852).

—, *Personal Narrative of a Pilgrimage to Al-Madinah & Meccah, 1855–56*, Memorial edn (1893; New York: Dover, 1964).

Buzzard, J., *The Beaten Track: European Tourism, Literature, and the Ways to Culture 1800–1918* (Oxford: Clarendon Press, 1993).

Campbell, K., *Literature and Culture in the Black Atlantic: From Pre- to Postcolonial* (New York: Palgrave Macmillan, 2006).

Carroll, D., 'African Landscape and Imperial Vertigo', in S. Gatrell (ed.), *English Literature and the Wider World*, vol. 4 (London and Atlantic Highlands, NJ: The Ashfield Press, 1992), pp. 157–72.

Certeau, M. de, *L'Écriture de l'histoire* (1975; Paris: Gallimard, 2002).

—, *L'Invention du quotidien*, vol. 1: *Arts de faire* (Paris: Gallimard, 1990).

Chard, C., *Pleasure and Guilt on the Grand Tour: Travel Writing and Imaginative Geography 1600–1830* (Manchester: Manchester University Press, 1999).

Chatterjee, P., *The Nation and Its Fragments: Colonial and Postcolonial Histories* (Princeton, NJ: Princeton University Press, 1993).

Clapperton, H., *Journal of a Second Expedition into the Interior of Africa from the Bight of Benin to Soccatoo* (1829; London: Frank Cass, 1966, facsimile edn).

Colley, L., *Britons: Forging the Nation 1707–1837* (New Haven, CT and London: Yale University Press, 1992).

—, *Captives: Britain, Empire and the World 1600–1850* (2002; London: Pimlico, 2003).

Cook, J., *The Journals of Captain Cook on His Voyages of Discovery*, ed. J. C. Beaglehole, 4 vols (Cambridge: Cambridge University Press, 1955–67).

—, *The Journals of Captain James Cook on His Voyages of Discovery* (1772; abridged Harmondsworth: Penguin Classics, 2000).

—, *The Journals of Captain James Cook: The Voyage of the Endeavour 1768–1771*, ed. J. C. Beaglehole, 2nd edn (Cambridge: Cambridge University Press, 1968).

Crawshaw, C., and Urry, J., 'Tourism and the Photographic Eye', in C. Rojeck and J. Urry (eds), *Touring Cultures: Transformations of Travel and Theory* (London: Routledge, 1991), pp. 176–95.

Cribb, T. J., 'Writing up the Log: The Legacy of Hakluyt', S. Clark (ed.), *Travel Writing and Empire. Postcolonial Theory in Transit* (London: Zed Books, 1999), pp. 100–12.

Cronin, M., *Across the Lines: Travel, Language, Translation* (Cork: Cork University Press, 2000).

Darwin, C., *Journal of the Voyage of the Beagle* (1843; London: Dover Publications, 2002).

—, *Charles Darwin's Beagle Diary*, ed. R. D. Keynes (Cambridge: Cambridge University Press, 1988).

—, *The Voyage of the Beagle*, ed. D. Quammen (1845; Washington DC: National Geographic Society, 2004).

—, *The Origin of Species*, ed. G. Beer (1859; Oxford: Oxford University Press, 1996).

—, *The Descent of Man*, ed. J. H. Birx (1871; Amherst: Prometheus Books, 1998).

Davis, R. (ed.), *Sir John Franklin's Journals and Correspondence: The First Arctic Land Expedition 1819–1922* (Toronto, ON: The Champlain Society, 1995).

—, 'The Travel Book's Itinerary: The Case of Sir John Franklin', in B. Olinder (ed.), *Literary Environments: Canada and the Old World* (Brussels: Peter Lang, 2006), pp. 39–50.

Defoe, D., *Robinson Crusoe* (1719; Harmondsworth: Penguin Classics, 2003).

Delano-Smith, C., and R. J. P. Kain, *English Maps: A History* (London: The British Library, 1999).

Deleuze, G., and Guattari, F., *Capitalisme et schizophrénie: L'anti-Œdipe* (Paris: Minuit, 1972).

—, *Mille Plateaux* (1980), trans. B. Massumi, *A Thousand Plateaus* (London: The Athlone Press, 1987).

Dening, G., *Islands and Beaches. Discourse on a Silent Land: Marquesas 1774–1880* (Oxford: Oxford University Press, 1980).

Derrida, J., *De la grammatologie* (Paris: Éditions de Minuit, 1967).

—, *Of Grammatology* (1967), trans. G. C. Spivak (Baltimore, MD: The Johns Hopkins University Press, 1998).

Descartes, R., *Discours de la méthode*, 1637, in A. Bridoux (ed.), *Œuvres et lettres de René Descartes* (Paris: Gallimard, 1953).

Diamond, J., *Status and Power in Verbal Interaction* (Amsterdam and Philadelphia, PA: John Benjamins, 1996).

Diket, A. L., 'The Noble Savage Convention as Epitomized in John Lawson's *A New Voyage to Carolina*', *North Carolina Historical Review*, 43:4 (1966), pp. 413–29.

Drake, F., *The World Encompassed By Sir Francis Drake, Being his next voyage to that to Nombre de Dios ... Carefully collected out of the notes of Master Francis Fletcher* (1628; Ann Arbor, MI: University of Michigan Press, 1966).

Driver, F., 'H.M. Stanley and His Critics: Geography, Exploration and Empire', *Past & Present*, 133 (1991), pp. 134–66.

Duchet, M., *Anthropologie et histoire au siècle des Lumières* (Paris: François Maspéro, 1971).

—, *Le Partage des savoirs : discours historique et discours ethnologique* (Paris: La Découverte, 1985).

Duranti, A., and C. Goodwin (eds), *Rethinking Context: Language as an Interactive Phenomenon* (1992; Cambridge: Cambridge University Press, 1997).

Edmond, R., *Representing the South Pacific* (Cambridge: Cambridge University Press, 1997).

Edson, E., *Mapping Time and Space: How Medieval Mapmakers Viewed Their World* (London: The British Library, 1997).

Edwards, P. H., *The Story of the Voyage: Sea Narratives in Eighteenth-Century England* (Cambridge: Cambridge University Press, 2004).

Fabian, J., *Time and the Other: How Anthropology Makes Its Object* (New York: Columbia University Press, 1983).

—, *Out of Our Minds: Reason and Madness in the Exploration of Central Africa* (Berkeley, CA: University of California Press, 2000).

Fleck, A., 'Here, There, and In Between: Representing Difference in the Travels of Sir John Mandeville', *Studies in Philology* 97:4 (2000), pp. 379–400.

Forster, G., *Georg Forsters Werke. Sämtliche Schriften, Tagebücher, Briefe*, vol. 1: *A Voyage round the World*, ed. R. L. Kahn (Berlin: Akademie-Verlag, 1968).

—, *Reise um die Welt*, ed. G. Steiner (Frankfurt: Insel, 1983).

Fortunati, V., Monticelli, R., and Ascari, M. (eds), *Travel Literature and the Female Imaginary* (Bologna: Patron, 2005).

Foucault, M., *Naissance de la clinique: une archéologie du regard médical* (Paris: Presses Universitaires de France, 1963).

—, *Les Mots et les choses. Une archéologie des sciences humaines* (Paris: Gallimard, 1966).

—, *The Order of Things: An Archaeology of the Human Sciences* (1966), translator unknown (New York: Pantheon, 1970).

Franklin, J., *Narrative of a Journey to the Shores of the Polar Sea, in the Years 1819–1822* (1823; New York: Cosimo, 2005).

Frawley, M. H., 'Borders and Boundaries, Perspectives and Place: Victorian Women's Travel Writing', in J. Pomeroy (ed.), *Intrepid Women Victorian Artists Travel* (Aldershot: Ashgate, 2005), pp. 27–38.

Friedman, J. B., *The Monstrous Races in Medieval Art and Thought* (Cambridge, MA: Harvard University Press, 1981).

Fry, H. T. 'Alexander Dalrymple and Captain Cook: The Creative Interplay of Two Careers', in R. Fisher and H. Johnston (eds), *Captain Cook and His Times* (Seattle, WA: University of Washington Press, 1979), pp. 41–57.

Fulford, T., D. Lee, and P. J. Kitson, *Literature, Science and Exploration in the Romantic Era: Bodies of Knowledge* (Cambridge: Cambridge University Press, 2004).

Fulford, T., and P. J. Kitson, (eds), *Travels, Explorations and Empires 1770–1835*, 8 vols (London: Pickering and Chatto, 2002).

Geertz, C., *The Interpretation of Cultures* (New York: Basic Books, 1973).

Gilpin, W., *Three Essays on Picturesque Beauty; on Picturesque Travel; and on Sketching Landscape: to which is added a Poem, on Landscape Painting* (1792; Farnborough: Gregg International, 1972).

Girard, R., *La Violence et le sacré* (Paris: Grasset, 1972).

Goffman, E., 'The Neglected Situation' (1964), in C. Lemert and A. Branaman (eds), *The Goffman Reader* (Oxford: Blackwell, 1997), pp. 229–33.

—, *Stigma: Notes on the Management of Spoiled Identity* (Englewood Cliffs, NJ: Prentice Hall, 1963; New York: Simon and Schuster, 1986).

—, *Asylums* (Garden City, NY: Doubleday, Anchor Books, 1961).

—, *Encounters: Two Studies in the Sociology of Interaction* (Indianapolis, IN: Bobbs-Merrill, 1961).

Goody, J., *The Logic of Writing and the Organization of Society* (Cambridge: Cambridge University Press, 1986).

—, and Watt, I., 'The Consequences of Literacy', in J. Goody (ed.), *Literacy in Traditional Societies* (Cambridge: Cambridge University Press, 1963), pp. 27–68.

Grace, S. E., *Canada and the Idea of North* (Montréal, ON and Kingston: McGill-Queen's University Press, 2001).

Grafton, A., Shelford, A. and Siraisi, N. (eds), *New Worlds, Ancient Texts: The Power of Tradition and the Shock of Discovery* (Cambridge, Mass. and London: Belknap Press of Harvard University Press, 1995).

Green, J. N., 'The Wreck of the Dutch East Indiaman the *Vergulde Draeck*, 1656', *International Journal of Nautical Archaeology*, 2:2 (1973), pp. 267–89.

Greenblatt, S., *Renaissance Self-Fashioning: From More to Shakespeare* (Chicago, IL: The University of Chicago Press, 1980).

—, *Marvelous Possessions: The Wonder of the New World* (1991; Oxford: Clarendon Press, 2003).

— (ed.), *New World Encounters* (Berkeley, CA: University of California Press, 1993), pp. 177–217.

—, *et al.* (eds), *The Norton Shakespeare* (London and New York: Norton, 1997).

Greenfield, B., *Narrating Discovery: The Romantic Explorer in American Literature 1790–1855* (New York: Columbia University Press, 1992).

Gregg, S., *Empire and Identity. An Eighteenth-Century Sourcebook* (Basingstoke and New York: Palgrave Macmillan, 2005).

Gregory, D., *Geographical Imaginations* (Oxford: Blackwell, 1994).

—, and Duncan, J. (eds), *Writes of Passage: Reading Travel Writing* (London and New York: Routledge, 1999).

Gumpertz, J., and D. Hymes (eds), *Directions in Sociolinguistics: The Ethnography of Communication* (New York and London: Holt, Rinehart and Winston, 1972).

—, *Discourse Strategies* (Cambridge: Cambridge University Press, 1982).

Hakluyt, R., *The Principall Navigations, Voiages and Discoveries of the English Nation* (London: George Bishop and Ralph Newberie, 1589).

—, *The Principal Navigations, Voiages, Traffiques and Discoueries of the English Nation, made by sea or overland*, 2nd edn (London, 1598–1600).

Halen, P., 'Stanley and Conrad: Founders of Alternative Discourses about Central Africa', in E. Mudimbe-Boy (ed.), *Remembering Africa* (Portsmouth, NH: Heinemann, 2002), pp. 56–73.

Hall, E. T., *The Hidden Dimension* (New York: Anchor Books, 1990).

Hallam, H., *A View of the State of Europe during the Middle Ages*, 2nd edn, 3 vols (London: John Murray, 1819).

Harley, A., 'This Reversed Order of Things: Re-Orientation aboard *HMS Beagle*', *Biography*, 29 (2006), pp. 462–80.

Hawkesworth, J. (ed.), *An Account of the Voyages Undertaken … in the Southern Hemisphere … by Commodore Byron, Captain Carteret, Captain Wallis and Captain Cook … Drawn up from the Journals which were kept by the several Commanders And from the Papers of Joseph Banks Esq.*, 3 vols (London : W. Strahan and T. Cadell, 1773).

Hazlewood, N., *Savage: The Life and Times of Jemmy Button* (New York: St Martin's Press, 2001).

Hearne, S., *A Journey from Prince of Wales's Fort in Hudson's Bay to the Northern Ocean. Undertaken by Order of the Hudson's Bay Company, for the Discovery of Copper Mines, a Northwest Passage, &c. In the Years 1769, 1770, 1771, & 1772* (1795; Amsterdam: Nico Israel, 1968).

Heber, R., *Narrative of a Journey through the Upper Provinces of India, from Calcutta to Bombay, 1824–1825*, 4th edn, 3 vols (London: John Murray, 1829).

Helsinger, E., 'Turner and the Representation of England', in W. J. T. Mitchell (ed.), *Landscape and Power* (Chicago, IL: The University of Chicago Press, 1994), pp. 102–25.

Heng, G., *Empire of Magic: Medieval Romance and the Politics of Cultural Fantasy* (New York: Columbia University Press, 2003).

Higgins, I. M., *Writing East: The 'Travels' of Sir John Mandeville* (Philadelphia, PA: University of Pennsylvania Press, 1997).

Hodgson, M., 'The Exploration Journal as Literature', *Beaver*, 298 (Winter 1967), pp. 4–12.

Holquist, M., *Dialogism: Bakhtin and His World* (1990; London and New York: Routledge, 1990).

Hood, R., *To the Arctic by Canoe 1819–1821: The Journals and Paintings of Robert Hood, Midshipman with Franklin*, ed. C. S. Houston (1974; Montréal, ON and Kingston: McGill-Queen's University Press, 1994).

Houston, C. S., T. Ball, and Houston, M., *Eighteenth-Century Naturalists of the Hudson's Bay* (Montreal, QC and Kingston: McGill-Queen's University Press, 2003).

Inden, R., *Imagining India* (1990; London: Hurst, 2000).

Jameson, A. B., *Winter Studies and Summer Rambles in Canada* (1838; Toronto, ON: McLelland and Stewart, 1990).

Jarvis, R., *Romantic Writing and Pedestrian Travel* (Basingstoke: Macmillan, 1997).

Jeal, T., *Stanley. The Impossible Life of Africa's Greatest Explorer* (London: Faber and Faber, 2007).

Jones-Davies, M.-T. (ed.), *Monstres et prodiges au temps de la Renaissance* (Paris: Jean Touzot, 1980).

Jobson, R., *The Discovery of River Gambra*, ed. D. P. Gamble and P. Hair (1623; London: Hakluyt Society, 1999).

Johnson, S., *A Dictionary of the English Language* (1755), ed. A. McDermott (CD-ROM, Cambridge: Cambridge University Press, 1996).

Kabbani, R., *Imperial Fictions: Europe's Myths of Orient* (London: Macmillan, 1986).

Kaplan, C., *Questions of Travel: Postmodern Discourses of Displacement* (Durham, NC: Duke University Press, 1996).

Kelsey, H, *Sir Francis Drake: The Queen's Pirate* (New Haven, CT: Yale University Press, 1998).

Kennedy, D., *The Highly Civilized Man: Richard Burton and the Victorian World* (Cambridge, MA: Harvard University Press, 2005).

Keymis, L., *A Relation of the Second Voyage to Guiana. Perfourmed and Written in the Yeare 1596* (London, 1596).

Kingsley, M., *Travels in West Africa* (1897; London: Phoenix Press, 2000).

Knox-Shaw, P., *The Explorer in English Fiction* (London: Macmillan, 1987).

Kupperman, K. O., *Indians and English: Facing Off in Early America* (Ithaca, NY: Cornell University Press, 2000).

Lacan, J., 'Seminar on the 'Purloined Letter', in J. P. Muller and W. J. Richardson (eds.), *The Purloined Poe. Lacan, Derrida, and Psychoanalytic Reading* (Baltimore, MD: Johns Hopkins University Press, 1988), pp. 28–54.

Laubin, R., and Laubin, G., *Indian Dances of North America: Their Importance to Indian Life* (Norman, OK: University of Oklahoma Press, 1977).

Lawrence, B., *Real Indians and 'Others': Mixed-Blood Urban Native People and Indigenous Nationhood* (Vancouver, BC: University of British Columbia Press, 2004).

Lawrence, K., *Penelope Voyages: Women and Travel in the British Literary Tradition* (Ithaca, NY: Cornell University Press, 1994).

Lawson, J., *A New Voyage to Carolina*, ed. H. T. Lefler (1709; Chapel Hill, NC: University of North Carolina Press, 1967).

Lecercle, J.-J., *Interpretation as Pragmatics* (London: Routledge, 1999).

Lestringant, F., *Le Cannibale, grandeur et décadence* (Paris: Perrin, 1994).

—, *Une Sainte horreur, ou le voyage en Eucharistie, 16ème–17ème siècles* (Paris: Presses Universitaires de France, 1996).

—, *Cannibals: The Discovery and Representation of the Cannibal from Columbus to Jules Verne* (Berkeley, CA: University of California Press, 1997).

Letts, M. (ed.), *Mandeville's Travels: Texts and Translations*, 2 vols (London: Hakluyt Society, 1953).

Libby, A., 'Taming the Sublime in Darkest Africa: Stanley's *How I Found Livingstone* and Burton's *Lake Regions of Central Africa*', *Nineteenth Century Prose*, 32:2 (2005), pp. 108–26.

Mackay, D., *In the Wake of Cook: Exploration, Science and Empire* (London: Croom Helm, 1985).

Mackenzie, A., *Voyages from Montreal on the River St. Laurence, through the Continent of North America, to the Frozen and Pacific Oceans: In the Years 1789 and 1793. The Journals and Letters of Sir Alexander Mackenzie*, ed. W. K. Lamb (Cambridge: Cambridge University Press, 1970).

MacLaren, I. S., 'Exploration/Travel Literature and the Evolution of the Author', *International Journal of Canadian Studies*, 5 (1992), pp. 39–68.

Macleod, D. S., 'Women's Artistic Passages', Introduction in J. Pomeroy (ed.), *Intrepid Women: Victorian Artists Travel* (Aldershot: Ashgate, 2005).pp. 1–9.

MacLulich, T. D., 'Canadian Exploration as Literature', *Canadian Literature*, 81 (1979), pp. 72–85.

Maingueneau, D., *Le Discours littéraire: paratopie et scène d'énonciation* (Paris: Armand Colin, 2004).

Mandeville, J. (attr.), *The Voyages and Trauailes of Sir John Maundeuile* (c. 1356–7; London: Thomas Este, 1582).

Marcus, G., and Clifford, J. (eds), *Writing Culture: The Politics and Poetics of Ethnography* (Berkeley, CA: University of California Press, 1986).

Marshall, P. J., and Williams, G., *The Great Map of Mankind: British Perceptions of the World in the Age of Enlightenment* (London: Dent, 1982).

McLynn, F., *Stanley: The Making of an African Explorer* (London: Constable, 1989).

—, *Stanley: Sorcerer's Apprentice* (London: Constable, 1991).

—, *Hearts of Darkness: the European Exploration of Africa* (London: Pimlico, 1993).

Montaigne, M. de, 'Des Coches' (1588), in *Essais*, vol. 3 (Paris: Garnier, 1948).

Montrose, L., 'The Work of Gender in the Discourse of Discovery' (1991), in S. Greenblatt (ed.), *New World Encounters* (Berkeley, CA: University of California Press, 1993), pp. 177–217.

Moser, C., *Kannibalische Katharsis. Literarische und filmische Inszenierungen der Anthropophagie von James Cook bis Bret Easton Ellis* (Bielefeld: Aisthesis, 2005).

Mulvey, C. 'Écriture and Writing: British Writing on Post-Revolutionary America', in M. Gildley and R. Lawson-Peeples (eds), *Views of American Landscapes* (Cambridge: Cambridge University Press, 2007), pp. 100–10.

Nicholl, J., *An Houre Glasse of Indian Newes* (London: E. Allde for N. Butter, 1607).

Obeyesekere, G., *The Apotheosis of Captain Cook: European Mythmaking in the Pacific* (Princeton, NJ: Princeton University Press, 1997).

Ortony, A., 'Metaphor, Language and Thought', in A. Ortony (ed.), *Metaphor and Thought* (Cambridge: Cambridge University Press, 1993), pp. 1–18.

Oswald, A., 'Marked Clay Pipes from Plymouth, Devonshire', *Post-Medieval Archeology*, 3 (1969), pp. 122–42.

Pagden, A., *European Encounters with the New World* (New Haven, CT: Yale University Press, 1993).

Park, M., *Travels in the Interior Districts of Africa* (1799), ed. K. M. Marsters (Durham, NC and London: Duke University Press, 2000).

Peabody, N., 'Tod's Rajasthan and the Boundaries of Imperial Rule in Nineteenth-Century India', *Modern Asian Studies*, 30:1 (1996), pp. 185–220.

Pearson, W. H., 'Hawkesworth's Alterations', *Journal of Pacific History*, 7 (1971), pp. 45–72.

Penzer, N. M. (ed.), *The World Encompassed, and Analogous Contemporary Documents Concerning Sir Francis Drake's Circumnavigation of the World* (London: The Argonaut Press, 1926).

Pratt, M. L., *Imperial Eyes: Travel Writing and Transculturation* (London and New York: Routledge, 1992).

Ralegh, W., *The Discoverie of the Large, Rich, and Bewtiful Empyre of Guiana, With a relation of the great and Golden Citie of Manoa* (London, 1596).

— (attr.), *Sir Walter Ralegh's Scepticks, or Speculation* (London, 1651).

—, *The Discovery of the Large, Rich and Beautiful Empire of Guiana* (1596), in *The English Literatures of America, 1500–1800*, ed. M. Jehlen and M. Warner (London and New York: Routledge, 1997).

—, *The Discoverie of the Large, Rich, and Bewtiful Empyre of Guiana*, ed. N. Whitehead (Manchester: Manchester University Press, 1997), pp. 1–116.

Ramamurthy, A., *Imperial Persuaders. Images of Africa and Asia in British Advertising* (Manchester: Manchester University Press, 2003).

Randolph, J. R., *British Travelers among the Southern Indians 1660–1763* (Norman, OK: University of Oklahoma Press, 1973).

Rawson, C., *God, Gulliver, and Genocide: Barbarism and the European Imagination 1492–1945* (Oxford: Oxford University Press, 2001).

Regard, F. (ed.), *De Drake à Chatwin. Rhétoriques de la découverte* (Lyon: ENS-Éditions, 2007).

—, 'The Catholic Mule: E. B. Tylor's Chimeric Perception of Otherness', *Journal of Victorian Studies,* 12:2 (Autumn 2007), pp. 225–37.

Rennie, N. R., *Far-Fetched Facts: The Literature of Travel and the Idea of the South Seas* (Oxford: Clarendon Press, 1995).

Richards, T., *The Imperial Archive: Knowledge and the Fantasy of Empire* (London: Verso, 1993).

Riffenburgh, B., *The Myth of the Explorer: the Press, Sensationalism, and Geographical Discovery* (Oxford: Oxford University Press, 1993).

Rimbaud, A., *Œuvres complètes*, ed. R. de Renéville and J. Mouquet (Paris: Gallimard, 1946).

Robertson, G., *The Discovery of Tahiti. A Journal of the Second Voyage of H.M.S. Dolphin round the World under the Command of Captain Wallis, R. N., in the Years 1766,1767 and 1768 written by her Master George Roberston*, ed. H. Carrington (London: Hakluyt Society, 1948).

Ross, J., *Exploring Baffin's Bay, and Inquiring into the Probability of a Northwest Passage* (London: John Murray, 1819).

Rousseau, J.-J., *Œuvres complètes*, ed. B. Gagnebin and M. Raymond, vol. 1 (Paris: Gallimard, 1959).

Roy, P., *Indian Traffic: Identities in Question in Colonial and Post-Colonial India* (Berkeley, CA: University of California Press, 1998).

Roy, W., "Here is the picture as well as I can paint it': Anna Jameson's Illustrations for *Winter Studies and Summer Rambles in Canada*', *Canadian Literature,* 177 (Summer 2003), pp. 97–119.

—, *Maps of Difference: Canada, Women, and Travel* (Montreal, QC: McGill-Queen's University Press, 2005).

Saïd, E., *Orientalism* (Harmondsworth: Penguin, 1978),

—, *Orientalism* (1978; New York: Random House, 1994).

—, *Orientalism* (1978; London: Penguin Books, 1995).

Sayre, G. M., *Les Sauvages Américains: Representations of Native Americans in French and English Colonial Literature* (Chapel Hill, NC and London: University of North Carolina Press, 1997).

Schmitt, C., 'Darwin's Savage Mnemonics', *Representations,* 88 (2004), pp. 55–80.

Sell, J., *Rhetoric and Wonder in English Travel Writing 1560–1613* (Aldershot: Ashgate, 2006).

Seymour, M. C. (ed.), *The Bodley Version of Mandeville's Travels* (Oxford: Early English Text Society, O. S. 253, 1963).

—, *The Metrical Version of Mandeville's Travels* (Oxford: Early English Text Society, O. S. 269, 1973).

—, *Sir John Mandeville* (Aldershot: Variorum, 1993).

—, *The Defective Version of Mandeville's Travels* (Oxford: Early English Text Society, O.S. 319, 2000).

Shelley, M., *Frankenstein* (1818; Ware: Wordsworth Classics, 1993).

Shields Jr, E. T., 'Paradise Regained Again: The Literary Context of John Lawson's *A New Voyage to Carolina*', *North Carolina Literary Review*, 1:1 (1992), pp. 83–97.

Smith, I. R., *The Emin Pasha Relief Expedition 1886–1890* (Oxford: Clarendon Press, 1972).

Spivak, G. C., *Outside in the Teaching Machine* (New York: Routledge, 1993).

Sprat, T., *History of the Royal Society* (1667), ed. J. I. Cope and H. W. Jones (St Louis, MO: Washington University Press, 1959).

Spurr, D., *The Rhetoric of Empire. Colonial Discourse in Journalism, Travel Writing and Imperial Administration* (Durham, NC: Duke University Press, 1993).

Stanley, H. M., *Through the Dark Continent, or, The Sources of the Nile Around the Great Lakes of Equatorial Africa and Down the Livingstone River to the Atlantic Ocean*, 2 vols (1878; New York: Dover Publications, 1988).

—, *How I Found Livingstone: Travels, Adventures and Discoveries in Central Africa, Including Four Months' Residence with Dr. Livingstone* (1872; New York: Dover Publications, 2001).

—, *In Darkest Africa, or the Quest, Rescue and Retreat of Emin Governor of Equatoria*, 2 vols (London: Sampson Low, Marston, Searle and Rivington, 1890).

Stockhammer, R., *Kartierung der Erde. Macht und Lust in Karten und Literatur* (München: Fink, 2007).

Strohm, P., 'Ripe for Conversion' (a review of Brenda Schildgen's *Pagans, Tartars, Muslims and Jews in Chaucer's 'Canterbury Tales'*), *London Review of Books*, 24:13 (2002), pp. 18–20.

Symonds, J. A., 'On the Application of Evolutionary Principles to Art and Literature', *Essays Suggestive and Speculative*, 1890, 3rd edn (London: John Murray, 1907), pp. 27–53.

—, 'Culture: Its Meaning and Its Uses', *In the Key of Blue*, 3rd edn, 1893 (London and New York: Elkin Matthews/Macmillan, 1918), pp. 195–216.

Tallmadge, J., 'From Chronicle to Quest: The Shaping of Darwin's *Voyage of the Beagle*', *Victorian Studies*, 23 (1980), pp. 325–45.

Tod, J., *Annals and Antiquities of Rajasthan*, 2 vols (1829–32; Delhi: Rupa, 1997).

—, *Travels in Western India* (1839; Delhi: Munshiram Manoharlal, 1997).

Torgovnick, M., *Gone Primitive. Savage Intellects, Modern Lives* (Chicago, IL: The University of Chicago Press, 1990).

Vega, G. de la, *The Royal Commentaries of Peru in Two Parts* (1607), trans. Sir P. Rycaut (London, 1688).

Wallace, A. D., *Walking, Literature, and English Culture. The Origins and Uses of the Peripatetic in the Nineteenth Century* (Oxford: Oxford University Press, 1999).

Waszek, N., The Scottish Enlightenment and Hegel's Account of 'Civil Society' (Dordrecht and London: Kluwer Academic Publishers, 1988).

Watzlawick, P., Beavin, J. H., and Jackson, D. D., *Pragmatics of Human Communication. A Study of Interactional Patterns, Pathologies, and Paradoxes* (New York: Norton, 1967).

Whitehead, N., 'The Historical Anthropology of Text: The Interpretation of Ralegh's *Discoverie of Guiana*', *Current Anthropology*, 36:1 (1995), pp. 53–74.

White, H., *Metahistory: The Historical Imagination in Nineteenth-Century Europe* (1973; Baltimore, MD: The Johns Hopkins University Press, 1975).

—, 'The Narrativization of Real Events', *Critical Inquiry*, 7:4 (Summer 1981), pp. 793–8.

Whitfield, P., *New Found Lands: Maps in the History of Exploration* (London: The British Library, 1998).

Whitlock, G., *The Intimate Empire: Reading Women's Autobiography* (London and New York: Cassell, 2000).

Winkin, Y., *Anthropologie de la communication* (Paris: Seuil, 2001).

Winkler, P., 'Writing Ghost Notes: The Poetics and Politics of Transcription', in D. Schwartz, A. Kassabian and L. Siegel (eds), *Keeping Score: Music, Disciplinarity, Culture* (Charlottesville, VA and London: University of Virginia Press, 1997), pp. 169–204.

Young, R. J., *Colonial Desire: Hybridity in Theory, Culture and Race* (London and New York: Routledge, 1995).

Youngs, T., '"My Footsteps on These Pages": The Inscription of Self and "Race" in H. M. Stanley's *How I Found Livingstone*', *Prose Studies*, 13: 2 (1990), pp. 230–49.

—, *Travellers in Africa: British Travelogues 1850-1900* (Manchester: Manchester University Press, 1994).

Zacher, C. K., *Curiosity and Pilgrimage. The Literature of Discovery in Fourteenth-Century England* (Baltimore, MD: The Johns Hopkins Press, 1976).

INDEX